Your Newborn

Head to Toe

Your Newborn

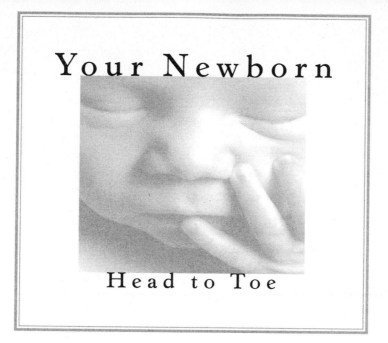

Head to Toe

Everything You Want to Know About
Your Baby's Health Through the First Year

CARA FAMILIAN NATTERSON, M.D.

LITTLE, BROWN AND COMPANY
New York   Boston

Little, Brown and Company
Time Warner Book Group
1271 Avenue of the Americas, New York, NY 10020
Visit our Web site at www.twbookmark.com

First Edition

The information in this book is not intended to replace the services of trained health
professionals. You are advised to consult with your child's health care professional re-
garding your child's health on a regular basis, and in particular with regard to matters
that may require diagnosis, a specialist referral, or medical attention. Anytime there is
particular concern about a medical problem, you should call your doctor, or, if it is an
emergency, call 911. The medications and medical advice described in this book are
generally in accordance with the standards of care set forth by the American Academy
of Pediatrics.

Library of Congress Cataloging-in-Publication Data

Natterson, Cara Familian.
    Your newborn : head to toe : everything you want to know about your baby's
health through the first year / Cara Familian Natterson. — 1st ed.
    p. cm.
Includes bibliographical references and index.
ISBN 0-316-73913-8
    1. Infants (Newborn) — Care. 2. Infants (Newborn) — Health and hygiene.
I. Title.

RJ253.N37 2004
649'.122 — dc22

                                                          2003058801

10 9 8 7 6 5 4 3 2 1

Q-MART

Book design by JoAnne Metsch

Printed in the United States of America

For Paul and Talia

Contents

Contents

Acknowledgments

This book could not have been written without the support of my partners at Tenth Street Pediatrics. You have been the ultimate mentors, teachers, and friends.

A number of physicians spent precious time editing the book for content. Many thanks to Dan Delgado, Richard Ehrlich, Andy Fine, Catherine Fuller, Heather Fullerton, William Hohl, Robert Kleinman, David Krasne, Terry Krekorian, Ved Lhonde, Jennifer Lightdale, Dixie Richards, Shannon Thyne, and Kenneth Wright.

What would I have done without the help of the hospital and office nurses? Your daily pearls of wisdom continue to teach me more than many texts ever could. I am especially indebted to the nurses at Tenth Street and at St. John's Hospital.

Parents also served as invaluable readers and contributors to this text. Many thanks especially to Jane and John Mass and Amy Schulhof and Lee Helman.

To each of my brothers, three completely different sources of inspiration, and to my mom, who knew how to do everything without any handbooks — thank you for your love and support. And finally, to my husband, Paul: my editor, my colleague, my best friend, my muse. Thank you.

Introduction

No matter how many times I witness the birth of a child, the event seems a miracle. The baby's adjustment to the world is in itself amazing, a miraculous transition from living upside down in a cramped, warm pool to feeding, crying, and breathing. But a baby's first weeks and months are not always seamless, and parents often worry that there is something wrong with their child. What is that funny rash? Why do her eyes look that way? Are his feet supposed to do that?

As a pediatrician, I have the privilege of sharing in the lives of thousands of parents and their newborn babies. My job is to help parents cope with common — and not so common — issues that arise from the earliest hours of life through adolescence, from vaccinations to sore throats to ear infections. This book is written to address the most frequently asked health questions surrounding the first hours, weeks, and months of a baby's life. For each body part, the book catalogs why a baby's body works the way it does, distinguishes between normal issues and ailments, and offers suggestions as to what you can do to prevent and treat the most common baby illnesses. I will not only suggest when you should call a doctor but also clarify why a health care provider's hands-on help is needed.

The range of questions asked of me is broad and endlessly varied. One parent may ask questions about her child's development, another about how to discipline effectively, and still another about how to get his baby to sleep through the night. *All* parents, however, ask pediatricians about their child's health. There are many sources of information on parenting skills and developmental milestones, but when your child is unwell, the only place to turn is your baby's pediatrician. I wrote this book because parents constantly ask me to recommend a good resource to keep on the shelf in case a health question comes up. Until now, I have not been able to find a book written for parents exclusively about their baby's health.

In my years as a pediatrician, I have found that parents want, above all else, clear explanations and supportive suggestions. I have also found that it is easy to become overwhelmed in a doctor's office or hospital — parents tell me they typically forget half (or all!) of what a doctor has said during a visit. They are up generating lists of questions the night before they come into the office but then forget the questions they want to ask until the visit is over. This text is meant to fill in the gaps, explaining things in a clear and logical way so that parents can understand why a doctor may have given a particular piece of advice. It will answer many of your questions, whatever time of day or night they come to you. It is certainly not meant to replace a doctor's advice but rather to be used in conjunction with it.

Parents also tell me of their frustration with the Internet. Because there is so much information out there, one may find it an overwhelming challenge to separate the good from the bad, the accurate from the absurd. I have included Web sites at the end of each section, with links to topics covered in the text. I have identified sites that are written for parents and operated by well-established educational institutions or foundations.

Throughout the text, there are some guideposts to help you. Several medical terms are written in bold italics in an effort to help you become familiar with the phrases you may hear in the hospital or doctor's office. Also, underneath the title of each section in part two, an age range is provided to give a sense of when in the first year of life a specific issue typically arises. Some of the topics included are applicable well past a baby's first birthday, but since this book concentrates on the first year, the stated age range only goes up to twelve months.

Your Newborn: Head to Toe was born out of thousands of visits with families across the country. On the phone, in the office, in the hospital, these families taught me how to care for their children. It is with great pleasure that I have written this book. It is for all parents, whether their health concerns involve the top of their baby's head, the bottom of her feet, or anywhere in between.

Part One

The Hospital

Types of Delivery:
Vaginal Versus Cesarean Section

◆

Babies are delivered one of two ways: vaginally or by cesarean section. In vaginal deliveries, most babies are pushed through the birth canal. But sometimes, despite vigorous pushing by the mother, the baby just can't get out on his own. In these cases, aids such as forceps or vacuums can be used.

In a cesarean section (also called a C-section), the uterus is cut open so the doctor can pull the baby out of the womb. Some C-sections are planned in advance, but other times they happen emergently.

Depending on the type of delivery, a baby may be faced with a variety of challenges. This chapter covers the delivery experience from the baby's point of view, explaining how your baby may be affected by different delivery techniques.

VAGINAL DELIVERY

Vaginal deliveries aren't always just about pushing the baby out. If the baby is stuck in the birth canal, then obstetricians have a variety of tools to help deliver the baby without requiring a cesarean section. The two most common are the vacuum and the forceps.

Vacuum. A vacuum is a plastic cup about the size of an apple. It is dome shaped, with a balloon-inflated rim. If the baby's head is visible in the vaginal canal but the baby is not coming out, then your obstetrician may choose to place the vacuum on the baby's head. A pump connected to the vacuum cup generates suction so that the cup attaches firmly. Once the vacuum is in place, the obstetrician waits for a contraction. When this happens, the mother pushes and the obstetrician pulls at the same time. The vacuum often helps to ease the baby out of the birth canal.

Because the vacuum generates so much suction, it can cause swelling on the baby's head. This swelling is usually only superficial — involving the scalp or skull but not the brain below. This can cause a prominent, boggy bump on the head for a day or two. Rarely a vein in the scalp will break, causing a large bruise in the area where the vacuum was placed. While the swelling and bruising can appear dramatic, they almost always go away by the time the baby leaves the hospital.

In rare cases, the vacuum can cause a tear in specific veins, resulting in a **subgaleal hematoma**. This injury can be dangerous because the broken vessels can bleed into a large space around the skull. Over several days (or sometimes hours), the blood loss can be significant, stealing blood supply away from the rest of the baby's body. While this is exceedingly rare, a baby with a large subgaleal bleed can develop jaundice or even shock. In most cases, however, the prognosis is good.

Forceps. Forceps are metal tongs used by the obstetrician to grip the sides of a baby's head and help pull the baby out of the vaginal canal. Like vacuums, forceps are used when the head is visible but the baby does not continue to descend through the birth canal. The obstetrician uses the forceps to grab the head gently and then pull when there is a contraction. The combination of the mother pushing and the doctor pulling helps guide the baby out of the vaginal canal.

The forceps can scrape or bruise the sides of the head where they grip the baby. Usually this is along the temples. The bruises and scrapes almost always heal in the first few days of life. If the forceps hit a particular spot on the side of the face, they can irritate a nerve that travels to the eye and the mouth. If the nerve is stunned, the eyelid on that side of the face may be unable to close and the mouth may droop. This is called a *Bell's palsy*. In almost all cases, the nerve returns to normal within a few days and the Bell's palsy goes away.

Additional Resources
http://www.medem.com (Go to "search medical library" in upper right-hand corner and type in "forceps" or "vacuum.")

◇   ◇   ◇

CESAREAN SECTION

A cesarean section is the surgical way of delivering a baby. A C-section will be performed for a number of reasons — sometimes the baby is in the wrong position for vaginal delivery (a baby whose feet are pointed toward the vaginal canal is called *breech*), sometimes the baby is too big to get out through the vaginal canal, and sometimes the mother has a medical condition that makes a C-section necessary. Sometimes the C-section must be performed emergently because the delivery is not progressing or because the health of either the mother or the baby is in danger. Regardless of the cause for the C-section, life for the first few hours or days is generally not much different for a baby born by C-section than for one delivered vaginally, with only a couple of exceptions.

First, a baby born by C-section is slightly more likely than a baby born vaginally to have fluid in her lungs. When water is present in the lungs, the baby must work harder to breathe air, so she may make grunting sounds or breathe very fast. When a baby is living in the womb, the lungs are filled with amniotic fluid. Because a developing baby doesn't breathe air, the water doesn't cause a problem. But once the baby is born, the water needs to leave the lungs quickly so that the lungs can work effectively. Doctors once thought that when babies traveled through the small vaginal canal, the extra water was literally squeezed out of their lungs. Now we know that probably isn't true. Instead, the act of labor stimulates *endorphins* — chemicals that make labor pains feel a little less intense — in both mom and baby. Endorphins help mop up water from the lungs. So, when a baby is delivered by C-section without much (or any) active labor beforehand — as in the case of a scheduled C-section — the baby is more likely to be born with some extra fluid in her lungs. A baby who is forced to work hard to breathe because of extra fluid has *transient tachypnea of the newborn (TTN)*.

Second, a baby born by C-section is more likely to be sleepy during the first hours (or even days) of life. This is a direct result of the anesthesia that the mom received during the delivery. This is described in more detail in chapter 8.

Additional Resources
http://www.medem.com (Go to "search medical library" in upper right-hand corner and type in "cesarean section.")
http://www.nlm.nih.gov/medlineplus/encyclopedia.html (Click on "C–Cg," then scroll down to "C-section.")

Apgar Score

As soon as a baby is born, a doctor, nurse, or midwife present for the delivery will assign a numerical score. Five minutes later, a second score is given. A pediatrician named Virginia Apgar created the scoring system in 1952. She determined that five characteristics in a newborn — heart rate, breathing (or respiratory effort), muscle tone, skin color, and response to stimulation — could predict a child's health status. Each characteristic may earn up to two points (and as few as zero), for a maximum score of ten.

	0	1	2
Heart rate	absent	slow (<100 beats/min.)	normal (>100 beats/min.)
Respiratory effort	absent	weak cry	strong cry
Muscle tone	limp	some extremity flexion	good flexion
Color	all blue	body pink, extremities blue	all pink
Response to stimulation	none	grimace	cough, sneeze, cry

(From www.medem.com)

In general, babies who score above seven are considered healthy. Sometimes the baby is a little stunned after delivery, having passed through a tight vaginal canal or having been rapidly pulled from the uterus in a C-section, so the initial (one minute) score may be low. The American Academy of Pediatrics (AAP) has written the following about Apgar scores:

A low 1-minute Apgar score does not correlate with the infant's future outcome. The 5-minute Apgar score, and particularly the change in the score between 1 and 5 minutes, is a useful index of the effectiveness of resuscitation efforts. However, even a 5-minute score of 0 to 3 . . . is limited as an indicator of the severity of the problem and correlates poorly with future neurologic outcome. An Apgar score of 0 to 3 at 5 minutes is associated with an increased risk of cerebral palsy in full-term infants, but this increase is only from 0.3% to 1%. A 5-minute Apgar score of 7 to 10 is considered normal. Scores of 4 through 6 are intermediate and are not markers of high levels of risk of later neurologic dysfunction. . . . Such scores are affected by physiologic immaturity, medication, the presence of congenital malformations, and other factors.

Therefore, while Apgar scores may reflect a baby's condition at that moment, the doctors and nurses examining your baby just after delivery should determine his health status. A head-to-toe exam tells a lot more than a numerical score.

Do not expect your baby to get a perfect score of ten! A ten is nearly impossible because the hands and feet of a newborn almost always remain bluish until the baby is a day or two old. Therefore, the maximum score for color is usually one, and the maximum Apgar score is usually nine.

Additional Resources
http://www.nlm.nih.gov/medlineplus/encyclopedia.html (Click on "Ah–Ap," then scroll down to "APGAR.")
http://www.aap.org/policy/01457.html
http://www.medem.com (Go to "search medical library" in upper right-hand corner and type in "Apgar.")

3

Big Baby

Babies are meant to grow rapidly in the third trimester. But sometimes they can get too big. When a baby is too big, he is called *large for gestational age,* or *LGA.* LGA babies weigh more than 90 percent of all babies of the same gestational age.

Most pregnant moms know they are carrying big babies because of ultrasound measurements that are taken throughout the pregnancy. Your obstetrician will prepare you for this if it is a possibility.

Some LGA babies can be delivered vaginally, but the greatest risk here is *shoulder dystocia.* With shoulder dystocia, the baby's head comes through the birth canal but the shoulders are too broad, so the baby gets stuck halfway. This can be life threatening. In some cases the baby's collarbone (called the *clavicle*) will break, allowing him to fit through the vaginal canal. Other times the obstetrician may purposefully break the clavicle to help the baby out. Otherwise the obstetrician must perform an emergency C-section, pushing the head back up through the vaginal canal and pulling the baby out through the opened uterus.

A broken clavicle generally heals with ease. However, a group of nerves called the *brachial plexus* runs underneath the clavicle. If these nerves are damaged when the clavicle is fractured, then the baby may have difficulty moving his arm or hand on the same side of the fracture. Even if there is a brachial plexus injury, most of the time it heals on its own. But occasionally a baby will need physical therapy to help heal the nerves, and in extremely rare cases, the nerves suffer permanent damage.

Some LGA babies are so huge that they are unable to fit through the birth canal at all and instead must be delivered by C-section. This is purely a matter of size: if the baby cannot fit through the canal, then a C-section must be done.

Many LGA babies are big because of genetics: big parents have big babies. There are other reasons, however, for a baby to be LGA. By far the most common is maternal *gestational diabetes.* Diabetes is a condition in which the blood sugar is too high. Some women will develop diabetes only during their pregnancy, with their high blood sugars resolving when they are no longer pregnant. A woman with maternal diabetes has high sugar levels in her blood, and she passes these on to her growing fetus. In response to the high sugar levels, the baby produces extra *insulin.* Insulin helps sugar get into cells, and as a result, the extra sugar and the extra insulin together cause excessive fetal growth and fat deposition. Obstetricians follow women with gestational diabetes closely throughout their pregnancies. Gestational diabetes is most often diagnosed in the second trimester. After it is diagnosed, a pregnant woman will be counseled about how to modify her diet to minimize the risks of diabetes. Some women require medicine to manage their diabetes.

Right after delivery, when the blood supply from the placenta is cut off, the baby's sugar level drops. This drop is exaggerated in babies with high insulin levels. Therefore a baby born to a mother with gestational diabetes can experience a rapid and dramatic decline in blood sugar. If the level sinks too low, then the baby will be jittery and fussy. Despite his desperation for food, he may be unable to feed well.

Breast-fed babies get especially frustrated because the breast milk does not come in for two or three days, and feeding at the breast takes work. Therefore, in the first few days of life, they get few calories from feeding and spend many calories trying to get them. Because LGA babies may experience rapid blood-sugar drops (called *hypoglycemia*), they often need to be supplemented with formula or sugar water. Once the blood-sugar levels have stabilized, they can breast-feed exclusively. Rarely a baby's blood sugar will drop so low that he needs sugar directly in the vein. Through an IV (intravenous line) a solution of saline and sugar is infused into the bloodstream. Once the blood sugar level rises, the baby can try feeding by mouth, and once he can do this successfully, the IV can be discontinued.

If a baby is showing signs of hypoglycemia, then a blood test should be done to check the actual blood sugar level. This can be performed as a heel stick (see chapter 29). If the level is extremely low, or if it fails to increase despite giving the baby sugar water or formula, then more comprehensive tests must be done to look for the cause of the low sugar level. These include a check of the electrolytes or serum glucose, a complete blood count, and sometimes a blood culture. These tests require drawing blood from a vein, not a poke of the heel. For more information about these tests, see chapter 29.

Opinions differ as to the actual numeric value of blood glucose that should qualify as hypoglycemia. Currently the standard of care is that if the blood glucose concentration is lower than 40 mg/dl, then the child is considered hypoglycemic. If the baby has absolutely no symptoms, then some doctors will allow the level to go down to 30 mg/dl for full-term infants (and even lower for premature or small-for-gestational-age babies) before intervening. These values can be measured using a finger-prick machine or blood that is drawn from a vein and sent to the hospital laboratory.

Additional Resources
http://www.nlm.nih.gov/medlineplus/encyclopedia.html (Click on "F," then scroll down to "fractured clavicle in the newborn.")
http://www.southeastmissourihospital.com/HEALTH/PEDS/hrnewborn/lga.htm
http://www.packardchildrenshospital.org (Go to "search" in upper right-hand corner and type in "LGA.")

Small Baby

◊

A baby born smaller than usual for the number of gestational weeks is called *small for gestational age,* or *SGA.* By definition, an SGA baby is smaller than 90 percent of all babies born at the same number of weeks' gestation. Usually SGA babies are simply petite, with small heads, shortened length, and low weight. However, an SGA baby can be disproportionately small, with low weight but a normal head size and length.

The most common cause of SGA is genetics. Small parents have small babies. Babies can also be SGA, however, because they did not get the nutrition they needed while in the womb. When poor nutrition is the cause, the baby has *intrauterine growth retardation,* or *IUGR.* The causes of IUGR are varied. Chromosomal abnormalities can be associated with IUGR, as can maternal illness or placental abnormalities. Poor maternal nutrition, cigarette use, or drug use can also contribute to IUGR. Twins will often be small because two are sharing the blood supply. In fact, the more babies a mother carries, the greater risk for those babies to be small.

Small babies (unlike large ones) tend to be very easy to deliver. However, they have some increased risks just after birth. They can have low oxygen levels or low sugar levels. They can have low body temperatures, and they may be unable to get their temperature up to normal without the help of a heater. SGA babies can also have low Apgar scores. If an SGA baby experiences any of these complications, then he will likely be observed in the hospital nursery or Neonatal Intensive Care Unit (NICU). Sometimes an SGA baby cannot breast-feed or bottle-feed immediately because he gets too cold when not in an incubator or under a heater. Other times he will have trouble breathing effectively and need supplemental oxygen. In the hospital, an SGA baby will be supplemented with everything he needs — oxygen, sugar water, heat — until he can manage on his own. This is a matter of time and depends on how small the baby is at birth and how fast he gains weight.

Additional Resources

http://www.southeastmissourihospital.com/HEALTH/PEDS/hrnewborn/sga.htm

http://www.packardchildrenshospital.org (Go to "search" in upper right-hand corner and type in "SGA.")

Nuchal Cord

---◆---

The umbilical cord is long and mobile, moving within the uterus throughout fetal life. One end is firmly attached to the placenta and the other end to the baby, so as the baby flips and turns during the pregnancy, the cord can coil, double back on itself, and even form a knot! Usually the cord will wind and unwind itself. However, if it wraps around the baby just before delivery, then as the baby travels through the vaginal canal (or even as she is being pulled out of the uterus during a C-section), the cord can get caught. Most often the cord wraps around the neck, creating a noose called a *nuchal cord.*

It is amazing that a baby is usually fine despite having the cord wrapped around her neck. This makes sense because a baby doesn't use her lungs to breathe until after birth, so as long as blood flow through the cord is not interrupted, the nuchal cord doesn't limit her oxygen supply while in the womb. The trouble comes as the baby is descending through the birth canal. With one end attached to the placenta, the cord is pulled taut as the baby is delivered. The noose can become tight, and it can push on the baby's neck. The cord can also become kinked, unable to maintain its normal blood flow to the baby. If either of these is happening, then the baby's distress is usually picked up on monitors that have been placed on the mother's belly during delivery.

In extreme cases, an emergency C-section may be done. More often, though, the cord is long enough that even after the baby passes through the entire vaginal canal, the cord never becomes too tight and the baby does fine.

If a nuchal cord is present, then as soon as the baby's head comes out, the obstetrician will slide the cord over the head before the rest of the baby is delivered. Many babies born with nuchal cords look blue in the face right after delivery. Usually within minutes, the color becomes normal.

Additional Resources
http://www.evidence.com/animation/bp-9.html

6

Meconium in the Womb

◆

When the intestines form inside a growing fetus, waste collects. This waste is a mixture of old cells, swallowed liquids, and other products made by the developing intestines. Therefore the first poops a baby passes are made of this nine-month-old waste collection, and they come out in the form of a thick, sticky greenish-black paste called *meconium.*

Most babies poop within twenty-four hours of being born. But some babies will poop *before* they are delivered. This is especially common in babies who experience stress in the womb, for instance when there is a decrease in oxygen flow to the baby. It can also happen in overdue babies, because their intestines are meant to have been working already. However, any baby more than 34 weeks' gestation has the ability to pass meconium in the womb.

A baby who has pooped in the womb is surrounded by the meconium — it is on his skin and in his mouth. When he is delivered, in the first breath of life he can inhale some of the meconium that has collected in his mouth. With a big enough breath and thick enough meconium, this sticky substance can get sucked into the lungs, making it difficult for the baby to breathe. Sometimes, since babies' lungs do expand and contract slightly in utero, meconium can get into the lungs even before birth.

Therefore, if the amniotic fluid is stained green (a sign that the baby has pooped in the womb), then as soon as the baby is delivered, the obstetrician will suck out the fluid in the nose and mouth with a handheld syringe. The baby is quickly handed to the pediatrician or nurse in the delivery room. If the meconium is thin and watery, then the pediatrician will allow the baby to take a breath, watching closely for difficulty with breathing. But if the meconium is thick, then the pediatrician will take a look deep into the baby's mouth, sometimes placing a tube through the mouth and down into the lungs to suck out any meconium sitting at the entrance to the lungs. The baby is then allowed to breathe and the suction is repeated, this time clearing the contents of the stomach.

The process of checking for meconium may prevent *meconium aspiration syndrome*. When meconium is aspirated deep into the lungs, it can plug the airways, preventing the flow of oxygen into the body. It can also cause thick puddles in the lungs — breeding grounds for infection. A baby known to have had thick meconium in the womb will be watched carefully. If he has difficulty breathing, an X ray will usually be done. The baby's oxygen level will be measured using a pulse oximeter (see chapter 29). If the oxygen level is low or if the baby is having significant difficulty breathing, then he will be observed in the hospital nursery or the Neonatal Intensive Care Unit (NICU). Some babies need supplemental oxygen delivered by a nasal cannula or breathing tube. These techniques are described in detail in the section on blueness in chapter 28. When a baby has symptoms of meconium aspiration, he may be given antibiotics to prevent the development of pneumonia.

Additional Resources

http://www.nlm.nih.gov/medlineplus/encyclopedia.html (Click on "M–Mf," then scroll down to "meconium" or "meconium aspiration syndrome.")

7

Mom Has a Fever Around
Time of Delivery

◆

Women often have elevated body temperature around the time of delivery. A normal body temperature is 98.6°F, but it can vary a degree or two. Therefore a laboring or postpartum woman is not considered febrile unless her temperature is above 100.4°F.

Fever has many causes. The epidural meant to relieve the pain of childbirth can actually cause fever. In some women, the fever may be a result of the drugs used in the epidural. In others, the epidural itself may be linked to the rise in temperature. Studies show that epidurals left in for more than four to six hours are associated with a much higher risk of fever during delivery. Though the fevers due to epidurals are typically low, they can be high in some cases.

Another cause of fever is infection. Like anyone else, a laboring woman can have an infection — she may be fighting off a regular cold or she may have a urinary tract infection (UTI) or sinusitis. The infection can also be in the womb itself. Infection of the placenta or amniotic fluid is called *chorioamnionitis.* This particular type of infection is worrisome because it can easily spread to the baby.

Finally, fever can be caused by the stress of delivery itself. The body releases chemicals during stressful events, and these chemicals may cause the body temperature to rise.

Because the causes of fever vary, both the mom and the baby must be protected from any potential dangers. Chorioamnionitis presents the greatest risk to both mother and child. While the infection starts in the womb, it can spread to the mother's bloodstream or to the baby's body. Chorioamnionitis can be the cause of preterm labor and premature delivery.

A baby born to a mother with chorioamnionitis can become seriously ill, with infection in the blood (bacteremia), in the lungs (pneumonia), and even in the fluid surrounding the brain (meningitis). Therefore, whenever a mother has a high fever just before, during, or after delivery, she will be given strong antibiotics until the source of the infection can be determined. These antibiotics are almost always given intravenously. If the antibiotics are started at least four hours before delivery, then they get into the baby's bloodstream and the baby will generally be well protected against a spreading infection. However, if the antibiotics are not started within four hours of delivery or if the mother's fever does not begin until after delivery, then the baby may need treatment of her own. When this happens, the baby will typically get a complete blood count and a blood culture to determine whether or not there is any evidence of infection. If the tests look suspicious for infection, then the baby will be started on antibiotics until confirmatory tests are done. These tests are covered in chapter 29.

While this may seem excessive — especially if the cause of the fever turns out to be the epidural or normal delivery stress — it is always better to be safe than sorry. Remember, even though babies don't often have obvious symptoms, they can get very sick very fast, and it is always best to catch an infection earlier rather than later. When a newborn has an overwhelming infection, she may develop fever, lethargy, irritability, poor feeding, or just low oxygen level. The body changes that accompany overwhelming infection are called *sepsis*. Sepsis can occur at any age and can be the result of many different infections. Fever and sepsis in young babies are covered in detail in chapter 28.

Additional Resources
http://www.cincinnatichildrens.org/health/info/pregnancy/diagnose/
chorioamnionitis.htm

8

Mom Has Anesthesia
During Delivery

Many women choose to have anesthesia during delivery. By far the most common way for drugs to be delivered is through low-dose IV narcotics or an *epidural,* where drugs are injected into the lower back, into spaces around the spinal cord. The drugs numb the nerves to the uterus and birth canal, making labor and delivery significantly more comfortable for many women. But the drugs also affect the nerves to the muscles of the pelvis and the legs, so in some instances a laboring woman can find it difficult to move her legs or to push the baby effectively. According to some studies, the use of epidurals has been associated with an increased need for vacuum or forceps assistance or for C-section (from www.acog.org). In order to minimize the leg and pelvic floor effects, combinations of drugs are now used. The net result is that less of each medicine is given, and the muscles are more likely to retain their strength through labor.

Mothers who have C-sections will often have epidurals as well. The epidural is dosed so that the mother does not feel the incision. Epidural anesthesia creates a "level" of numbness: the more medicine that is used in the epidural, the higher up the body the numbing travels. Therefore women having a C-section can be numb below the waist but awake and alert (and sensitive) above. In rare circumstances, a C-section must be done emergently and the mother requires rapid sedation. In these cases, the anesthesia is given using a spinal, intravenous, or inhaled route (or a combination), and the mother may be asleep for the delivery.

The drugs given during delivery do enter the mother's bloodstream; therefore they do get into the baby's blood via the placenta. While the mom feels most of the side effects of anesthetic drugs, the baby can experience a few. The most common side effects for the mom include numbing of the muscles needed for walking or urinating, as well as itching, nausea, vomiting, fever, or chills.

In babies, the side effects are far less well understood. Some babies will be very sleepy after a delivery in which large amounts of anesthesia are used. As the medicine wears off, the baby wakes up without difficulty. But during the sleepy period — which can last between six and twenty-four hours — the baby may not be very interested in feeding. Some babies need to be monitored more closely when anesthesia is used during the delivery, so a *scalp electrode* may be put onto the baby's head. The electrode is hooked up to a machine monitoring the baby's vital signs. This process is generally benign, but after delivery the site on the baby's scalp where the electrode was placed may look scabbed and in rare cases may become infected. There are reports that babies can have trouble breathing after epidural anesthesia is used, presumably because these drugs can suppress breathing when given in high doses. This is exceedingly rare and resolves when the drugs leave the baby's system.

Finally, as mentioned in the previous section on maternal fever during delivery, the presence of an epidural increases the risk of fever just before, during, or after delivery. If the mother has a fever in this time window, then there is a chance that she has an infection of the placenta or the amniotic fluid. If she does not receive antibiotics at least four hours prior to delivery, then the baby may end up having blood tests or receiving antibiotics in the first few days of life to ensure that he is not infected. This series of events is important because an infected baby can become very sick very fast, so it is better to err on the side of caution.

Additional Resources
http://www.medem.com (Go to "search medical library" in upper right-hand corner and type in "epidural.")

9

Premature Baby

The age of a growing fetus is *not* counted from the actual time of conception, when the egg fuses with the sperm. Rather, it is calculated from the beginning of the *last menstrual period (LMP)*, about two weeks *before* conception. The number of weeks that pass since the LMP is called the *gestational age*. A baby's due date occurs at 40 weeks of gestation. But a baby is considered *full term* if she is born anytime after 37 gestational weeks. Babies born before 37 weeks are called *premature*.

Amazingly a fetus follows a very specific calendar of development. We know — almost to the day — what's happening inside her growing body. Because of this rigid schedule of development, a doctor can predict what a premature baby will and will not be able to do based on her gestational age. Each of the baby's organs, from the lungs to the skin to the gastrointestinal tract, may run into trouble if a baby is born prematurely.

Some premature babies need to spend time in the Neonatal Intensive Care Unit (NICU) because they have complications associated with their prematurity. The NICU provides one nurse for every one to two babies; nursery units for healthier babies that simply need some extra observation or minimal medical care provide one nurse for every three to six babies (on average). The nurses in the NICU are really the primary sources of health information for parents. These nurses know every little detail about the babies they care for. Most parents rely heavily upon these nurses to explain what is happening to their baby and why. Sometimes a nurse will refer a question to the doctor involved, but more often the nurses provide the majority of information to the parents.

The following is a general guide to how each organ system develops and what happens in each part of the body when a baby is born prematurely. These are general concepts and do not necessarily apply to all babies. In fact two babies born at the same gestational age often have entirely different courses in the hospital.

SKIN

Full-term babies have thick, often wrinkled skin. But premature babies have thin skin. In fact the more premature the baby, the thinner her skin will be. In very premature babies, the skin is translucent, with veins and arteries visible beneath.

The skin is a very important barrier. It keeps a baby warm and holds fluids inside the body. Without mature skin, a baby cannot maintain a normal body temperature. She also risks becoming dehydrated because water evaporates easily through the immature skin layer. Therefore the more premature the baby, the more important it is to help keep fluids and heat inside her body.

Some premature babies are fine as long as they are kept in an *isolette,* a warm plastic incubator with removable walls and top. However, some babies have such thin skin that even the warmth and humidity of the isolette is not enough. These babies must be covered with a thin layer of — believe it or not — plastic wrap. The plastic sits on top of the skin, preventing the escape of moisture and heat. Because babies who are this premature always have breathing tubes (see the lung section that follows), there is no risk of suffocation.

The skin can become infected quite easily in the NICU. While the nurses take extra care to clean the skin and minimize irritants coming in contact with it, many of the monitors and tape products that are used to secure tubes are extremely irritating. The thinner the skin, the more likely it is to become irritated. Babies in the NICU often require IVs or blood draws, and the sites of the needle pokes can bruise or even become infected. Nurses watch closely for signs of skin infection. If they see any, then the irritant will be removed and moisturizers or antibiotics will be used.

◆   ◆   ◆

LUNGS

The lungs mature around 34 weeks of gestation. Before they are mature, they are small and filled with fluid. Their walls are stiff. They are not ready to breathe air and therefore cannot exchange oxygen for carbon dioxide. Once the lungs mature, a baby will generally be able to breathe on his own. But if he is born before his lungs have matured to this stage, then the baby will need help with breathing.

Premature babies with immature lungs will often be *intubated* shortly after delivery. Intubation is the process of placing a breathing tube through the mouth and into the lungs. The tube, called an *endotracheal tube (ETT),* is connected to a breathing machine called a *ventilator.* The machine simulates breaths, pushing oxygenated air into the lungs and helping carbon dioxide to move out.

The closer a baby is to being full term, the less likely he will need to be intubated. Some very premature babies are able to breathe largely on their own, with the help of a little supplemental oxygen. If an ETT is not necessary, then a baby can receive oxygen through a *face mask* or *nasal cannula,* or through *nasal CPAP.* The cannula is a plastic tube about one to two millimeters in diameter that wraps around the baby's head, resting below his nose just above the upper lip. It has two prongs at the nostrils that direct oxygen up the nose. CPAP (which stands for "continuous positive airway pressure") is a mask that fits over the nose. It generates pressure so that the oxygen is forced into the baby's nose and lungs with each breath. CPAP provides a little more breathing support than a nasal cannula.

Because many premature babies have stiff lungs, they are given a medicine called *surfactant* to help the lungs become more compliant. This medicine is a synthetic compound of the proteins and lipids that line the lungs of newborns. Natural surfactant is produced around the 34th week of gestation, when the lungs become mature. Synthetic surfactant is given directly into the lungs through an ETT. Surfactant is sometimes administered immediately after delivery — even in the delivery room — but other times a baby is observed for several hours before it is used. Some babies who can breathe marginally well without an ETT will have one only when receiving the medicine. The tube can be removed minutes after it is put in, or if necessary it can be left in place for weeks at a time.

Premature babies often require some help with breathing, and the first step is usually to use a handheld *bag-mask* to blow air into the baby's lungs. The mask is held over the baby's nose and mouth, and the bag is squeezed to push air into his chest. Because the lungs can be stiff, the force of air from the bag can occasionally pop a small hole in the lungs. This hole is called a *pneumothorax.* When this happens, air collects not just inside the lung with the hole but around it too. The lung cannot inflate fully, and despite efforts to aid breathing, the body's oxygen levels will often drop. If the pneumothorax is big, then the air will need to be drained. This is done by sticking a needle into the pocket of air. The needle is inserted through the skin of the chest wall. Sometimes a syringe can be attached to the needle to slowly suck out the air manually; other times a special catheter called a *chest tube* must be placed through the chest wall to continuously suck out the air. A small pneumothorax can often be watched over time. If it is small enough, then the air will dissolve on its own. Supplemental oxygen is given to any baby with a pneumothorax.

Another complication of premature lungs is *pneumonia,* or infection of the lungs. Pneumonia can occur when there are pockets of fluid that facilitate the growth of bacteria. Because premature babies often have extra fluid in their lungs, they are at risk for pneumonia. If a premature baby has a fever or if his oxygen levels begin to drop, then pneumonia may be suspected. An X ray can be done to look for the infection. Sometimes blood tests such as a complete blood count or a blood culture will be helpful (see chapter 29). Most of the time, antibiotics will be started even without positive proof of the pneumonia. This conservative approach is used because a premature baby has a very immature immune system, so an infection in one part of the body can spread quickly to other parts of the body. Starting antibiotics early can minimize the risk for spreading infection. If the tests turn out to be normal, then the antibiotics will be stopped.

◆   ◆   ◆

HEART

The heart forms early during fetal development — it is one of the first structures visible on a prenatal ultrasound. But in order for it to work optimally outside the womb, the heart relies on a dramatic shift in blood flow during the first few hours and days of life.

The heart is divided into two halves: the right side receives oxygen-depleted blood from the body and pumps it to the lungs, where it gets oxygenated; the left side receives the oxygenated blood from the lungs and pumps it out to the body. In the womb, a baby does not get oxygen by breathing through the lungs. Rather, his oxygen comes from his mother's blood via the placenta and the umbilical cord. Instead of going through the right side of the heart and out to the lungs (as is the case in the normal baby after birth), the blood in the fetus goes through the right side of the heart and then joins the blood being pumped through the left side out to the body. One piece of tissue responsible for redirecting the fetal blood flow is called the ***ductus arteriosus.*** This connection closes within the first two to three days after birth so that blood can flow through the lungs effectively. A ductus arteriosus that stays open too long after birth is called a ***patent ductus arteriosus (PDA).***

Premature babies have a much higher risk of PDA than do full-term babies. The problems associated with PDA range from a heart murmur to low oxygen levels. Often signs of a PDA are visible on chest X rays. A premature baby will be watched closely for a PDA, and if he has one, it can be closed using medicine or surgery. The medicine is called ***indomethacin.*** It is effective some of the time, but it cannot be used in a baby with poorly functioning kidneys. Because some premature babies are slow to gain normal kidney function, indomethacin is not always an option. The surgical procedure is called a *ligation*. The tissue is tied off or closed with a staple. As soon as either of these measures works, the blood no longer flows through the PDA and normal circulation begins.

◇   ◇   ◇

GASTROINTESTINAL TRACT

The gastrointestinal (GI) tract becomes fairly functional around 34 weeks of gestation. Before then, a baby will likely have some difficulty coordinating a suck and swallow, digesting normally, and moving her bowels. Therefore a premature baby often needs help receiving nutrition.

A very premature baby will be unable to tolerate any food by mouth. Instead she will need to have fluids given through an IV. When the fluids are continued for an extended period of time (longer than a couple of days), they are mixed with minerals and vitamins to maximize nutrition. This formulation is called *TPN*, or *total parenteral nutrition.*

Eventually a premature baby will begin to take formula or pumped breast milk. The point at which this will happen depends on the circumstances of each child. The feedings are typically started using not a bottle but rather a small feeding tube (called a *nasogastric tube*, or *NG tube*) that is inserted through the nose and passed into the stomach. The tube is kept in place until bottle feedings are started; otherwise trauma would be incurred every time a baby needed to be fed (the tube would have to be passed eight to twelve times a day). The feedings initially may be given continuously, with very small amounts of formula or breast milk dripping around-the-clock into the stomach. Once the baby can tolerate this, the feeding schedule will be changed to *bolus* feeds, whereby the baby gets larger amounts of formula or breast milk every two to three hours. Once she can handle this, bottle- or breast-feeding will be tried. The process of slowly shifting a baby's feeding pattern is called *advancing feeds*.

Some premature babies require more calories than breast milk or standard formula provide. Breast milk and formula contain 20 calories per ounce. There are also fortified formulas with 22 or 24 calories per ounce. Though these formulas help with weight gain, they are not always well tolerated by babies.

Sometimes a baby must be formula-fed (for instance, when there is no pumped breast milk available), but the GI tract is too immature to break down or absorb certain components of formula. For these babies, there are formulas that have predigested fatty acids or additives that provide extra amounts of what the baby needs.

A premature baby is at increased risk of infection of her GI tract. The infection is different from the GI infections of older babies and children — those that typically cause vomiting and diarrhea. Rather, these infections occur because the blood flow to a premature GI tract can be irregular. When a segment of bowel does not receive enough blood flow, that area can be injured from lack of oxygen. When the bowel is injured, bacteria living in that area can multiply. This is called *necrotizing enterocolitis,* or *NEC.* It is a serious infection, requiring antibiotics and sometimes surgery. If left untreated, NEC can cause sepsis. Feedings by NG tube or by mouth must be stopped until the NEC has resolved.

◆   ◆   ◆

URINE AND STOOL

Babies urinate all the way through their fetal development, so it is no surprise that a premature baby, like a full-term baby, urinates soon after he is born. But babies typically do not stool until about 34 weeks of gestation, so it is surprising that a premature baby begins stooling very shortly after he is born. He usually will not stool in large amounts or very frequently, but he is able to move his bowels even before he begins eating.

The nurses in the NICU will take extra care to measure how much urine and stool a baby produces within each 24-hour period. Diapers are typically weighed in order to calculate the daily amount. If a baby has a catheter in the bladder, then the urine will be collected in a bag so that the volume can be easily measured.

It is important to keep track of how much urine and stool a baby is putting out so that it can be compared with how much fluid the baby is taking in. These numbers — often called the *ins and outs* — should be relatively well balanced. If they are not, then the baby may be getting too much or too little fluid, which can lead to other problems.

The color and quality of the urine and stool are also important. Bloody stool can be an indicator of infection, as can dark or foul-smelling urine.

◇   ◇   ◇

MONITORS, IVS, AND OTHER TUBES

A baby in the NICU will usually be hooked up to several monitors. The tubes and wires attached to a baby can look overwhelming.

All babies in isolettes have temperature probes placed on the middle of their chest or abdomen. This probe is a sticker attached to the baby's skin and connected by a long skinny wire to a monitor outside the isolette. The probe allows the nurses to constantly monitor a baby's temperature without having to use a traditional thermometer.

Many premature babies need intravenous lines (IVs). These are catheters that are inserted into veins to help deliver medicines and draw blood. Sometimes catheters are placed in arteries to monitor vital signs. Only in newborns can catheters be put into the belly button to monitor the baby. The belly button contains two umbilical arteries and one umbilical vein. Shortly after birth, these vessels begin to shrink down. But in the first several hours of life, they are open, and a catheter can be inserted into one (or more) of them. *Umbilical artery catheters (UACs)* and *umbilical vein catheters (UVCs)* are very helpful because they allow for continual monitoring of the blood pressure and other vital signs. Typical IVs can also be used in babies. These catheters are placed in the arm or leg or sometimes the scalp. They provide access to deliver medication or fluids to the baby.

The various breathing tubes are reviewed in detail in the section on lungs earlier in this chapter and also in chapters 18 and 28. The most common mechanisms for oxygen delivery include the endotracheal tube — which is inserted all the way into the lungs — the face mask, the nasal cannula, and the nasal CPAP.

If there is concern about the urine or urinary tract, then a catheter may be placed through the urethra into the bladder. This tube drains the bladder, collecting urine as it is produced.

Most babies in the NICU wear eye shields at some point during their hospitalization. This may be done because the isolette is too bright or because there are treatments being given that can be toxic to the eyes. One example of this is phototherapy for jaundice (see chapter 11). Babies placed under bright phototherapy lights will often have their eyes covered. The eye shields look like cloth sunglasses. They are soft and strapped around the baby's head.

Additional Resources
http://www.medem.com (Go to "search medical library" in upper right-hand corner and type in "premature birth.")
http://www.packardchildrenshospital.org (Go to "search" in upper right-hand corner and type in "prematurity.")

10

Postmature Baby

———————◇———————

A baby's due date is 40 weeks after the mother's last menstrual period began. A baby that has not been delivered by the due date is described as being *postdates*. A baby that is more than two weeks overdue is called *postterm.*

Overdue babies are generally quite healthy. They have long fingernails and toenails, and their skin is often dry and peeling. Many have grown excess downy hair (called *lanugo*) on their shoulders and down their backs. They are almost always bigger than average, sometimes nine pounds or more. Because these babies can be big, they can have complications such as *shoulder dystocia* during delivery. This is covered in chapter 3.

Overdue babies can also have *meconium* in the womb. Because these infants are chronologically ready to be born days earlier, their intestines are ready to go to work. Therefore these babies are more likely to poop while still in the womb. Postterm babies can also experience stress when the placenta stops working as well as it has been for the past several months. Stressed babies are more likely to pass meconium in the womb. The complications of meconium are described in chapter 6.

The most worrisome problem for postterm babies is that after 42 weeks, the placenta may stop functioning altogether. The uterus may shrink and the fetus may move less. Because of this risk, overdue babies are closely monitored. Every few days an ultra-sound is performed to look at fetal movement and measure the fetus.

Therefore a mother who is past her due date will be evaluated frequently by her obstetrician, and often, labor will be induced. These moms are brought to the hospital and given a medicine — *oxytocin* (also known as *pitocin*) — to stimulate labor. Occasionally the baby *still* doesn't seem to want to come out, so a C-section must be performed.

Additional Resources
http://www.emedicine.com/med/topic3248.htm
http://www.packardchildrenshospital.org (Go to "search" in upper right-hand corner and type in "postmaturity.")

Part Two

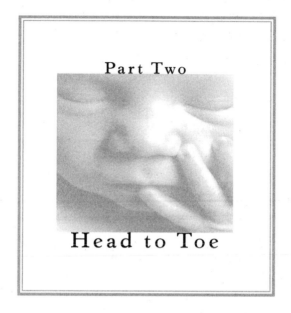

Head to Toe

11

Skin Color and Texture

◇

The womb is filled with amniotic fluid. The fetus grows and develops in this liquid bath. The fetus actually produces this fluid — it is made largely from his urine. Therefore the fluid inside the baby's body is similar to the liquid surrounding it, and this is why a baby in the womb does not get wrinkled like you would if you stayed in the bath too long.

During delivery, the baby travels through the birth canal or is pulled through an incision in the uterus in a cesarean section. During either of these journeys, a baby's skin can become scraped or bruised.

Once a baby is born, he has left the warm, moist environment of the womb and entered the cool, dry air. The change in his surroundings dramatically affects his skin. Sometimes the skin becomes dry and peels; other times it breaks out in a rash. From the minute the baby is born, he is exposed to multiple skin irritants in the form of soaps, perfumes, lotions, and detergents. The change in environment makes pristine baby skin not so pristine after all.

The skin can turn a variety of colors — from yellow to red to blue — in different circumstances. As pigment appears over the first few hours and days of life, the skin can become dark or olive or remain pale.

The skin is the largest organ in the body, and it acts as a remarkable barometer of what's going on both inside and outside.

RASHES: ERYTHEMA TOXICUM, BABY ACNE, AND MILIA
(Birth–3 Months)

What is happening inside my baby's body?
There are a variety of normal rashes that pop up over the first few hours, days, and weeks of a baby's life. Rashes can be caused by a variety of things. Some are the result of irritants to the skin such as detergents, perfumes, or chemicals. Other rashes come from hormonal changes in the baby's blood, caused by maternal hormones slowly leaving the baby's system in the days and weeks after birth. And the drying effects of air cause still other rashes — remember, a newborn has been in a pool for nine months! This section covers the three most common infant rashes: erythema toxicum, baby acne, and milia.

Erythema toxicum is a terrible name for a totally normal newborn rash. It looks like pea-size red splotches with yellow "heads" (that can seem like they are filled with pus) in the middle. It usually appears on the face, chest, or back in the first day or two of a baby's life and lasts up to a week. In its most extreme form, erythema toxicum can cover the baby from head-to-toe. In this case it is called *neonatal pustulosis.* The two rashes are the same — pustulosis is simply more plentiful than erythema toxicum. Neither is painful nor itchy for the baby.

Baby acne doesn't show up until a baby is three or four weeks old and can last days or weeks. The pimples are small and often cover the face, neck, chest, and back. Baby acne is caused by the slow decline in maternal hormones that traveled across the placenta while the fetus was developing. As a baby gets older, mom's estrogen slowly leaves his body. It is thought that when the estrogen level drops, the skin breaks out with acne. Think of it like backward puberty: just as with a teenager, when hormone levels change, the skin becomes pimply.

Milia are tiny white spots across a newborn's nose, chin, or forehead. They are present at birth and gradually disappear over the first few months of a baby's life. Milia are hard and sometimes look like pinpoint pimples. They come from the oil glands underneath the skin.

What can I do?
Nothing. There are no soaps, lotions, or medications that make these rashes go away faster. In fact most lotions and creams make the skin more irritated and can cause new rashes to crop up on top. And because none of these rashes are painful, you don't need to worry about soothing your baby's skin.

When does my doctor need to be involved?
Your doctor need only be involved when the rashes look infected. The signs of skin infection are warmth, extreme redness, pus, or fever.

What tests need to be done, and what do the results mean?
These are normal newborn rashes, so no tests are necessary. If the rash becomes infected — which is rare — then tests are still probably not necessary. Rather, your doctor will likely suggest an antibiotic.

What are the treatments?
There are no treatments for these rashes — only time. Again, remember that the rashes will typically become more irritated when lotions are applied.

What are the possible complications?
There are almost never complications with normal newborn rashes. They go away on their own with time, and your baby's beautiful skin will be restored.

Additional Resources
http://www.nlm.nih.gov/medlineplus/encyclopedia.html (Click on "Si–Sp," then scroll down to "skin characteristics in newborns.")

◆   ◆   ◆

STORK BITES AND ANGEL KISSES
(Birth–12 Months)

What is happening inside my baby's body?
Stork bites and **angel kisses** refer to the pink or red patches on a baby's scalp, along the neck, down the back, or across the eyelids — anywhere, actually, in the midline of the body. The first gets its name from the mythical stork that carries newborns (the tale goes that the stork grips the baby on the back of the neck); the second is from stories of angels who supposedly plant kisses on the eyelids of infants. In reality, they are simply areas of skin with extra blood vessels close to the surface. When a baby cries or has a fever, the blood vessels fill and the patches become redder.

About one in three babies is born with a stork bite or angel kiss. As a baby ages, the patches usually disappear. Most stork bites are gone by 18 months, except those on the nape of the neck, which often last a lifetime.

What can I do?
You do not need to do anything for stork bites and angel kisses. These normal areas of discoloration will usually fade over time.

When does my doctor need to be involved?
Because stork bites and angel kisses are normal, your doctor does not need to see the child or prescribe anything.

What tests need to be done, and what do the results mean?
Both stork bites and angel kisses are normal, so they require no tests.

What are the treatments?
There are no treatments. These patches usually fade with time.

What are the possible complications?
There are no complications from stork bites and angel kisses. Most of these fade with time, but classically the stork bites at the nape of the neck will remain for life.

Additional Resources
http://www.nlm.nih.gov/medlineplus/encyclopedia.html (Click on "Sq–Sz,"
then scroll down to "stork bite.")

◆   ◆   ◆

MONGOLIAN SPOTS
(Birth–12 Months)

What is happening inside my baby's body?
Mongolian spot is the name of an area of bluish discoloration on
a baby's skin. Because of its blue or purple color, the patch can
sometimes look like a bruise. Mongolian spots are usually on the
lower back or buttocks but can extend all the way down the legs
or up to the shoulders. They are extremely common in dark-
skinned babies.

Mongolian spots are caused by *pigmented cells,* or a collection
of the cells that carry skin color. Though some remain for a lifetime, most Mongolian spots fade over the first three to four years
of life.

What can I do?
Mongolian spots are normal. There is nothing you need to do.

When does my doctor need to be involved?
Your doctor does not need to be involved with the care of Mongolian spots.

What tests need to be done, and what do the results mean?
Because Mongolian spots are normal, tests do not need to be
done.

What are the treatments?
There are no treatments. Mongolian spots usually fade in the first
few years of life.

What are the possible complications?
There are no complications associated with Mongolian spots. The
muscles and bones underneath them are normal.

Additional Resources
http://www.nlm.nih.gov/medlineplus/encyclopedia.html (Click on "Mg–Mz,"
then scroll down to "Mongolian blue spots.")

HEMANGIOMAS
(Birth–12 Months)

What is happening inside my baby's body?

A *hemangioma* is a collection of blood vessels underneath the skin. The area can look flat or raised; round or irregularly shaped; and bright red, blue, or dark purple. Some hemangiomas are as small as a pencil eraser; others are as big as a dollar bill. Some are called strawberry patches because they have the color and texture of the fruit. These marks are incredibly common among infants — up to 10 percent of all babies have one by the time they are a year old.

There are three types of hemangiomas: the typical *strawberry hemangioma* that is flat or slightly raised and bright red; the *deep hemangioma* that lives further beneath the skin surface and can look purple or blue; and a combination type (called *mixed hemangioma*) that has elements of both the strawberry and the deep types.

While some hemangiomas are present at birth, most appear during the first two or three months of life. At first all three types of hemangiomas may look white, blue-gray, or pink. Over a few weeks, though, the strawberry hemangiomas become quite red (like the color of a fire engine) whereas the deep hemangiomas remain bluish. The blood vessels of a hemangioma grow rapidly — faster, even, than the rest of the baby. This is why a hemangioma often triples or quadruples in size over the first year of life.

Eventually the hemangiomas stop growing, usually around the first birthday but sometimes not until the second birthday. With a strawberry hemangioma, the first sign that the hemangioma is no longer growing is typically the appearance of a surrounding white patch, resembling a halo. Next the hemangioma will develop white spots within it that make it look like it has been sprinkled with salt. These are signs that the blood vessels of the hemangioma are beginning to shrink away (the medical term is *involute*). Over the next few years, the hemangioma will look pinkish-gray and then will fade and — if it was ever raised — flatten. Fifty percent of all hemangiomas are invisible by age five, 75 percent by age seven, and 90 percent by age nine. Many times all that is left is a light pink or white patch on the skin where the hemangioma once grew. Even more often there is no physical reminder.

What can I do?

You do not need to do anything to care for a hemangioma, unless it bleeds. In this case, hold a damp cloth or gauze against the bleeding hemangioma with gentle pressure. If the area does not stop bleeding after five to ten minutes, then call your doctor.

When does my doctor need to be involved?

When you first notice a hemangioma, let your doctor know. This is nonurgent, so you can wait until your next scheduled appointment.

Call your doctor if the hemangioma bleeds excessively. A hemangioma that bleeds once and stops on its own does not need to be seen by the doctor. However, if the hemangioma bleeds for more than ten minutes despite the application of pressure, or if it bleeds regularly because it sits in a spot where the baby can rub it against a car seat, mattress, or other object, then your doctor should be informed.

If the hemangioma causes a *mass effect* — whereby it pushes on neighboring organs — then ongoing medical attention is warranted. Mass effect is discussed in more detail in the following passages.

What tests need to be done, and what do the results mean?

Because hemangiomas are made of blood vessels, and because blood vessels provide the transit system for blood throughout the body, organs underneath the skin can grow hemangiomas too. Therefore, when a hemangioma is deep or mixed, a CT scan or MRI can help to show whether or not internal organs are involved. This is a rare condition. When a hemangioma is massive, a complete blood count is required.

What are the treatments?

Hemangiomas that bleed excessively need to be either treated with medication or removed. This also applies to hemangiomas that become physically disfiguring — such as rapidly growing masses on the face.

There are two types of treatment: medical and surgical. Medical treatment uses steroids — drugs that help stop the further growth of blood vessels. Steroids must be given for several weeks or even months at relatively high doses, and therefore a child may experience some side effects such as change in appetite, moodiness or irritability, temporarily slowed growth, swelling (especially in the face), stomach ulcers, and inability to receive routine childhood vaccines while on the medicine. All of these side effects go away once the medicine is stopped.

The second treatment is surgery, either with a laser or with a scalpel (traditional surgery). Lasers can target the vessels that are growing rapidly within the hemangioma. This stops their growth and allows the area to shrink down. With traditional surgery, the hemangioma is removed entirely using a scalpel.

The approach to treating a hemangioma — that is, whether it is with drugs or a laser or a scalpel — depends on the size, shape, location, and type of hemangioma. Consult a dermatologist or surgeon to help you determine the most appropriate treatment approach.

What are the possible complications?

The hemangioma can grow so rapidly that the skin above it splits open, causing an *ulceration.* This area often bleeds and can become infected. Also, depending on where a hemangioma is located, it can cause problems with normal functions such as breathing (if it is in the neck) or urinating (in the groin). This is the previously mentioned mass effect. When a hemangioma occupies space in the body, it can push on or into structures that normally occupy that particular space.

The most serious complication seen with a hemangioma is *Kasabach-Merritt syndrome.* This is very rare. It occurs when platelets, the components of the blood that help form clots, are destroyed as the blood flows through a hemangioma. The blood then circulates through the rest of the body with a limited ability to clot. This can lead to dangerous internal bleeding. Kasabach-Merritt is virtually only present in association with extremely large hemangiomas.

Additional Resources
http://www.birthmarks.org/parents/book/heman_life.shtml
http://www.nlm.nih.gov/medlineplus/encyclopedia.html (Click on "H–Hf," then scroll down to "hemangioma.")

◆　◆　◆

PORT-WINE STAINS
(Birth–12 Months)

What is happening inside my baby's body?
A port-wine stain is a type of birthmark found in one out of every two hundred babies. Also called *nevus flammeus,* it can look pink, dark red, or purple (like wine, hence its name). It is typically flat with irregular borders. Port-wine stains are created by small blood vessels that lie close to the skin's surface. They are usually on the face or neck but can be found just about anywhere on the body. Port-wine stains are permanent birthmarks.

What can I do?
You cannot and need not do anything.

When does my doctor need to be involved?
Your pediatrician will talk with you about the port-wine stain. In most cases, there is nothing to do, no medicine to take, and no cream that needs to be put on. But if the port-wine stain involves one or both eyes, then an ophthalmologist (eye doctor) should check the eye regularly.

What tests need to be done, and what do the results mean?
When the eye is involved, a measurement of pressure inside the eye should be taken to check for glaucoma. An ophthalmologist usually takes this measurement. Sometimes an X ray or CT scan of the head will be done as well to look at the skull or the brain.

What are the treatments?

There is a wide range of possible treatments for a port-wine stain, depending on its size and location. Among the most common is laser treatment, which can destroy the tiny vessels under the skin but leaves the overlying skin intact. There are a variety of types of lasers that can be used. Unless the port-wine stain involves other organs in the body, most of these treatments are strictly cosmetic and are not done until the teen or adult years.

What are the possible complications?

When one or both eyes are involved in the port-wine stain, a child can develop *glaucoma,* or increased pressure inside the eye. If glaucoma remains untreated, then it can eventually cause blindness.

Another possible complication of a port-wine stain is *hypertro-phy,* or noticeable overgrowth of the tissue underneath the port wine. Hypertrophy is more difficult to treat and often causes disfigurement if allowed to grow unchecked.

When a child has a port-wine stain in addition to nervous-system problems, the combination is called *Sturge-Weber syndrome.* There is a risk of blood-vessel growth in other parts of the body, especially on the brain (called *angiomas*). Therefore children with Sturge-Weber syndrome may have seizures or slowed development. Neurologists and dermatologists often work together to help these children.

A port-wine stain located on a limb can cause the veins of that limb to become enlarged (called *varicose veins*). The surrounding skin, tissue, and bones can also grow excessively so that one arm (or leg) can become quite a bit larger than the other. This rare condition is called *Klippel-Trenaunay syndrome.*

Additional Resources
http://www.nlm.nih.gov/medlineplus/encyclopedia.html (Click on "Pm–Pz," then scroll down to "port-wine stain.")

◆   ◆   ◆

MOLES AND BIRTHMARKS
(Birth–12 Months)

What is happening inside my baby's body?
A mole is also known as a *nevus*. It is made from a collection of pigmented skin cells. Almost all adults have moles, and almost all moles appear after birth. Moles can be located anywhere on the skin, with wide ranges in shape and size. They are made up of pigment-producing skin cells called *melanocytes.*

Congenital means a feature present at or before birth, so a mole present at the time of birth is called a *congenital nevus.* While most of these are benign, they do have a slightly increased risk of turning into skin cancer over time. The bigger the mole, the greater the risk. There is one especially large mole called a *giant congenital nevus* that ranges from about two to eight inches in size. This can cover an entire arm, leg, or a large portion of the trunk, back, or face.

A health-care provider should examine any congenital nevus and then follow it over time, looking for changes in the size, color, or appearance. Often a dermatologist will also be involved.

What can I do?
There is nothing you need to do about birthmarks or moles, except to point them out to your doctor. If a mark is changing, then it may help to take a picture every few weeks or months to document these changes.

When does my doctor need to be involved?
When there is a significant change in the size, shape, or color of a mole, inform your doctor. Sudden changes — such as bleeding, itching, or ulceration — should be evaluated. This is usually when a dermatologist will become involved.

What tests need to be done, and what do the results mean?
Tests almost never need to be done on birthmarks or moles on an infant. Very rarely, a dermatologist may want to take a small

biopsy — a sample of the tissue in the mole — to determine whether the mark is *benign* (not worrisome) or *malignant* (cancerous).

What are the treatments?

If a mole is determined to be worrisome by a pediatrician or dermatologist, then it may need to be removed.

What are the possible complications?

The birthmark or mole can become malignant over time. It is estimated that about 1 percent of infants have congenital nevi, most of these being small. In a small nevus, the risk of malignant change is minimal and really only exists during and after puberty.

If the nevus is bigger than 1.5 cm, however, then there is a higher chance that *melanoma* (a type of skin cancer) will develop in the mole — about 5 percent. It is estimated that three quarters of these transformations to a malignancy occur before a child reaches seven years of age. Remember, though, that despite these statistics, the overall risk of developing melanoma is still estimated to be no different for people with congenital nevi than for those without.

For some people with giant moles, nevus cells spread to the brain or the spinal cord. This is called *neurocutaneous melanosis (NCM)*. MRI studies estimate that about one in three people with giant nevi have NCM. These people may have absolutely no symptoms at all, or they may have symptoms associated with the central nervous system such as headaches, vomiting, or seizures. It is difficult to predict which people will have the symptoms. Dermatologists and neurologists should be involved in the care of anyone with NCM.

Additional Resources
http://www.nlm.nih.gov/medlineplus/encyclopedia.html (Click on "B–Bk," then scroll down to "birthmarks — pigmented.")
http://www.kidsplastsurg.com/pigmentedlestreat.html

◈   ◈   ◈

DRY SKIN (ECZEMA)
(1–12 Months)

What is happening inside my baby's body?
Most babies have dry skin — or at least patches of it — at some
point in time. When your baby is born, skin that has been bathed
in water for nine months suddenly gets a rude awakening . . . air!
The baby's skin dries out quickly and easily. Then, each time you
bathe her, the skin is air-dried a little more. Eventually parts of the
skin become scaly.

Air is not the only source of dry, flaky skin. If your baby is sensitive to the perfumes in detergents, to the colors in lotions, to
clothing material (such as wool), or to some component of the
breast milk or formula she is drinking, then her skin will often
react by drying out even more.

The medical term for dry skin is *eczema* or *atopic dermatitis.*
Depending on the cause, eczema can have many forms. Classic
eczema first appears on the cheeks as two perfectly round,
slightly red circles. It also shows up as dry patches behind the
ears and sometimes as crusting on the scalp (called *cradle cap*).
Over the first few weeks, it moves to the wrists and ankles, and
sometimes to the arms, thighs, or abdomen. Eczema can look like
white flakes on the baby's skin, colorless pinpoint bumps, or fire-
engine-red patches.

When dry skin is caused by an allergy, it is called *irritant dermatitis.* This can be confused with eczema. The rash of irritant
dermatitis typically appears wherever the irritant contacts the skin.
If the irritant is detergent, then the rash will appear only where
clothes washed in that detergent touch the baby's skin. If it is a
lotion or soap, then the rash will appear only where the lotion or
soap is applied. If it is a food, however — including a component
of formula or something a breast-feeding mom has eaten — then
the rash may be around the mouth and anus, or it may spread
from head to toe.

What can I do?
When something irritates the skin, remove the irritant. You should use only color-free, perfume-free detergents, soaps, and lotions. Hypoallergenic moisturizers will help return water to the dry skin. Minimizing bath frequency cuts down on the drying effect of constant washing.

When does my doctor need to be involved?
Skin that bleeds because it is so dry needs to be treated by a doctor. If the skin breaks open, then it can become infected. If eczema continues to spread despite attempts to reduce it, then your doctor should be involved. A baby who is clearly uncomfortable because of eczema should be evaluated.

What tests need to be done, and what do the results mean?
Eczema rarely requires any sort of testing, unless it is so severe that an underlying allergy is suspected. Unfortunately allergy testing is not very accurate in children younger than two years of age. In fact, even when testing is done, the source of the eczema is not always identified. Therefore it is often easiest to use trial and error, removing suspected allergens and then reintroducing them one at a time to see what happens. In the case of suspected food allergy, the trial-and-error method is called a *food challenge.* The food that is thought to be the cause of the allergy can be stopped for several weeks; a rash or diarrhea upon reintroduction usually suggests food allergy. In the case of breast-feeding, the mother must stop eating the food that is thought to be causing the problem and then, when she begins again, assess her baby for signs of allergy. In the case of formula-feeding, you can change the type of formula (i.e., cow's milk versus soy) to see if the skin improves. Again, if the rash returns when the original formula is reintroduced, then that type of formula is the cause.

The two main types of allergy testing are skin testing and RAST (blood) testing. Neither test is perfectly reliable in children younger than two years, but both deserve a brief mention because they may be considered for infants and young children with severe allergies.

Skin testing involves pricking a baby's skin with tiny needles, each coated with a specific allergen — cat dander, mold, egg, etc.

FOODS FOR BREAST-FEEDING WOMEN TO AVOID
◆

If you are breast-feeding, then the foods (and drinks) you consume will make their way — in some form — into the breast milk. Some babies are fine no matter what their moms eat. Others are very sensitive, becoming gassy or rashy or fussy with certain foods. Below is a list of the biggest offenders, the foods most commonly associated with reactions in babies. If you think your baby is reacting to something in your milk, then try removing each of the following items (listed below) from your diet, one at a time. It may take several days to see results, but if the baby improves, then you've found the likely culprit. Some moms prefer to remove many of these things at once and then add them back one at a time to identify the source of the problem. Either approach will work.

> *Citrus: orange, lemon, lime, grapefruit*
> *Berries: strawberries, raspberries, blueberries, cherries*
>   *(this includes flavorings such as those found in yogurt)*
> *Nuts*
> *Shellfish*
> *Wheat*
> *Dairy*
> *Tomato*
> *Broccoli*
> *Onions*
> *Corn*

If the area around a specific needle prick becomes red and irritated, then the test is positive. This test works well on children older than two years, as long as someone can convince them to participate. In children younger than two years, negative results do not mean much — only a positive test proves an allergy. For example, if the skin in the area around the cat-dander needle does not react, the child may still have an allergy to cat dander and the test can appear falsely normal.

RAST testing is the most common blood test used to check for allergies. Blood testing is helpful if the skin is so severely irritated that skin testing cannot be done or if there is concern that a skin test will cause a severe reaction. Blood tests are also sometimes used in small babies when skin tests do not yield any results. Like skin tests, RAST tests are not always definitive in babies.

It is important to remember that antihistamines — such as Benadryl, Claritin, and Zyrtec — can interfere with allergy test results. If your child is taking any medicines, then discuss this with your doctor several days before allergy testing. The medicine may need to be stopped prior to the testing.

What are the treatments?

The best treatments for eczema are (1) moisturizing and (2) removing the irritant. Skin that is simply dry responds well to thick moisturizers. Remember, these need to be color-free and perfume-free or they may worsen the problem. If an allergy is suspected, then remove the irritant. Sometimes this is a matter of trial and error — when the cause of the allergy is not obvious, each potential irritant should be removed one at a time to look for improvement. (The opposite is also true: all potential irritants can be removed at once and then they can be added back, one at a time, to determine the cause.)

Severe cases of eczema may be treated with a steroid cream or a nonsteroid anti-inflammatory cream. These are used in addition to moisturizers. Steroid creams come in many strengths. Some are over the counter and some require a prescription. These creams may have side effects if they are used too often or over too big an area. Over time they can cause the skin to thin, changing the pigmentation. The body absorbs steroid creams, so when they are applied over a large area of skin or when they are used too often, the body may absorb a high dose of steroid, causing mood or appetite changes. Nonsteroid anti-inflammatory creams are now available. These work well to calm inflamed skin and have fewer side effects than steroids.

What are the possible complications?

The most common complication of eczema is skin infection. This occurs when the skin becomes so dry that it cracks, or when a baby pulls and scratches at the irritated area. Skin infection can require antibiotic treatment.

There are also many conditions associated with eczema, each of which may cause problems of its own or may complicate eczema flares. These include *anaphylaxis* (shock), asthma, rashes other than eczema (such as hives), and infection of the ears, sinuses, and even bloodstream. All these conditions tend to be associated with eczema because they share the common problem of inflammation. In each of these scenarios, inflammation exists somewhere in the body — the skin, sinuses, lungs, and so on — and the inflammation makes it difficult for that part of the body to work effectively. In the case of the lungs, inflammation makes breathing difficult because it clogs the airways. In the case of the skin, inflammation causes swelling, irritation, and itchiness. In the sinuses, it causes congestion, creating an environment ripe for bacterial infection. The coexistence of the triad of eczema, asthma, and allergy is so common that it has a name: *atopy.*

Additional Resources
http://www.kidshealth.org/parent/medical/allergies/eczema_atopic_
dermatitis.html
http://www.nationaljewish.org/medfacts/testing.html

◇　◇　◇

DIAPER RASHES
(Birth–12 Months)

What is happening inside my baby's body?

Diaper rashes are rashes limited to the skin underneath the diaper. They most commonly affect the buttocks but can be located just about anywhere a diaper can reach. Diaper rashes come in four varieties: simple irritation, chafing rashes, yeast infections, and bacterial skin infections. There are other rashes that appear on other parts of the body — such as eczema, psoriasis, impetigo, and scabies — that may emerge in the diaper area as well. These are not exclusively "diaper rashes" and therefore are not covered in this section.

Irritation rashes are the most common. Disposable diapers with strong absorbent chemicals or flowery perfumes can easily irritate pristine baby skin. Cloth diapers that are washed in perfumed detergents or dried with a fabric softener can do the same thing. Urine or stool that sits next to the skin for a long time can cause rashes. Just the simple act of covering the diaper area with a diaper can be enough to cause a rash. All of these irritants create a similar picture: splotchy or pinkish-red skin and unhappy babies — sometimes crying with each diaper change or even with a simple cleaning of the area.

Chafing rashes are also extremely common. When the diaper rubs against the skin, or when skin folds rub against one another in the groin, the area can become red. Chafing is made worse when babies have healthy fat folds because these folds trap moisture, adding another source of irritation. Chafing rashes usually look redder than simple irritant rashes. Extreme rubbing can cause bleeding or blistering. The worst part of the rash is usually tucked deeply underneath folded skin, where air does not circulate.

Yeast infections (typically caused by *candida*) in the diaper area are also common. This is because yeast is a normal inhabitant of the human body, and it grows best in areas that are warm, moist, and dark. The heavily diapered groin is an ideal breeding ground for yeast. Most people expect yeast to look white, as it does in the mouth (in the form of *thrush*), but this is not so in the diaper area. Rather, it looks leathery or shiny and appears on a base of red, irritated skin. Yeast diaper rashes sting with diaper changes, and they often last longer than many other types of diaper rash. Yeast diaper rashes can occur on their own or on top of another diaper rash — irritated skin breeds yeast easily. Therefore the signs of yeast may appear all over the diaper area or isolated in small patches, alone or on top of a preexisting rash.

Bacterial infections in the diaper area are a consequence of irritated skin that has become infected by bacteria that are normally not a problem. Like yeast, bacteria are normal inhabitants of the human body. But when the bacteria creep into breaks in the skin, they can grow rapidly. The result is fiery red skin, some-

DISPOSABLE VERSUS CLOTH DIAPERS

◆

Disposable diapers were first invented in 1949. Since then, there has been an ongoing controversy over which is better: disposable or cloth. Diaper type is a matter of personal choice — one is not clearly better than the other. Disposable diapers, however, are extremely convenient. Over the years, they have become increasingly absorbent, wicking urine away from a baby's skin almost as soon as it collects in the diaper. Unfortunately, along with the benefits of superabsorbency come some downfalls. Sensitive baby skin can react to some of the chemicals in the diaper. Even non-superabsorbent diapers can be perfumed and irritating to the skin. Cloth diapers do not have any chemicals or perfumes (unless they are washed in fragranced detergents or dried with fabric softeners), so they tend to be less irritating. Sometimes the cloth is used directly against the baby's skin while other times a small towel is placed inside it to collect urine and stool, requiring fewer laundry cycles and prolonging the life of the diaper itself. While cloth diapers were once fastened with safety pins, many are now fashioned with Velcro tabs to make them easier to use.

times oozing with yellow liquid or white pus. Some bacterial infections will scab over. Most are warm to the touch and cause intense pain with diaper changes. They can appear as distinct spots all over the area or as a continuous swath of infected skin.

What can I do?

The best way to treat or prevent a diaper rash is to keep a baby's bottom as clean and dry as possible. The longer a child sits in a wet or dirty diaper, the more the skin comes into contact with urine and stool.

When a rash begins, keep your baby out of diapers as much as possible. Leave your baby naked on the bottom for several minutes between diaper changes, or put her on a towel and leave her naked for a longer time. Air will actually help heal most rashes.

Rashy diaper areas should be wiped with water and cotton instead of perfumed baby wipes. The prepackaged wipes can sting irritated skin and can make a rash worse, so if they must be used, rinse them with water first. Alcohol-free, perfume-free wipes are another alternative.

Many rashes respond well to a small amount of cornstarch applied to the diaper area between changes. The cornstarch wicks away moisture, reducing the likelihood of yeast growth. A little bit of air, followed by the cornstarch, may be all that is necessary to nip an early diaper rash in the bud. However, if a rash is progressing, then a diaper cream containing zinc — which helps heal broken-down skin — may be more effective. Antifungal creams can also be used if yeast has begun to grow. These and other creams are reviewed in the following passages.

When does my doctor need to be involved?

You should call your doctor if the rash persists despite your best efforts. Most rashes will improve within three or four days. After a week of no improvement, call your doctor.

If a rash continues to worsen, with signs of bacterial infection — very red skin, pus or yellow liquid oozing, warm to the touch — then your doctor should definitely take a look. If the rash becomes so severely infected that it causes a baby to have a fever, then a visit to the doctor is necessary. Your doctor should also be involved immediately if the skin on the diaper area peels off in sheets.

What tests need to be done, and what do the results mean?

Tests are rarely, if ever, needed in the case of diaper rash. There are, however, two exceptions. First, a severe bacterial infection sometimes requires a culture to determine the precise cause. It is only necessary if the rash is extremely severe and has not responded to any treatments.

The other exception is the case of a persistent diaper rash that is not severe but rather just doesn't go away. There are some causes of diaper rash — eczema and psoriasis among them — that also result in rashes on other parts of the body. When the diaper area is the first to be involved, it can seem like a run-of-the-mill diaper rash that just won't go away. Sometimes a visit to the dermatologist or a small skin biopsy can help make the diagnosis. Other times the rash will move to other parts of the body and the cause will become obvious without any tests.

What are the treatments?

Air, air, and more air. Air is always the best initial treatment for a diaper rash. Even if this doesn't solve the problem entirely, a rash will almost always improve with airing out.

Chafing rashes do well with simple cornstarch, which helps to dry the area and minimizes potential yeast growth. (Cornstarch is generally recommended in lieu of baby powder made from talc because the baby powder can be inhaled deep into the lungs, causing irritation.) When cornstarch fails to work, creams containing zinc often help. Zinc heals skin and provides a strong barrier against the irritants in urine and stool. There are literally hundreds of diaper creams on the market that promise ingredients that will heal the skin. The only ingredients proven to improve irritant rashes and heal skin are allantoin, calamine, cod-liver oil, dimethicone, kaolin, lanolin, mineral oil, petroleum, white petrolatum, and, of course, zinc.

Other additives often advertised in creams but not proven to be effective include cholecalciferol, peruvian balsam, bismuth subnitrate, and vitamin E.

Finally, *avoid* creams that have the following ingredients because they may make the condition worse: boric acid, camphor, phenol, methyl salicylate, or compound of benzoin tincture.

If an irritant rash becomes infected with yeast, then antifungal creams may be necessary. These creams help to slow the growth of the yeast. It is important to remember that yeast thrives in warm, dark, moist environments. Therefore the antifungal creams will help, but they work much better if they are used sparingly and in conjunction with airing out the diaper area. The most common antifungal creams include nystatin, terbinafine, or "-azole" (clotrimazole, ketoconazole, econazole, miconazole) in the ingredients.

What are the possible complications?
The most common type of diaper rash — irritant diaper rash —
may evolve into a yeast or bacterial rash over time. Therefore the
biggest complication of a diaper rash is . . . another diaper rash!
Other, less common complications include scarring, bleeding, and
pain with urination and stooling. The latter occur because the irritated skin stings when it comes into contact with urine or stool.

Additional Resources
http://www.uspharmacist.com (Go to "search" in upper right-hand corner
and type in "diaper rash.")
http://www.nlm.nih.gov/medlineplus/encyclopedia.html (Click on "D–Di,"
then scroll down to "diaper dermatitis — candida-associated" or "diaper
dermatitis — irritant-induced.")

◆   ◆   ◆

YELLOWNESS (JAUNDICE)
(Birth–2 Weeks)

What is happening inside my baby's body?
Jaundice simply means a yellow discoloration of the skin. It is a
description, like calling the sky blue. Some degree of jaundice is
extremely common — it occurs in more than half of all babies.

The cause of jaundice is elevated *bilirubin,* a yellow pigment
produced naturally in the body. Bilirubin is a normal waste product. In the womb, the placenta does the job of removing waste
from the body. But after delivery, the liver removes bilirubin from
the blood while the intestines get rid of excess bilirubin in the
stool. In a newborn baby, sometimes the liver is not yet fully
functioning, so it cannot get rid of the bilirubin effectively. The
bilirubin may build up faster than the liver can break it down and
the intestine can dispose of it in the stool. Other times the baby is
pooping too infrequently, giving the intestines time to reabsorb
the bilirubin rather than poop it out. And sometimes the bilirubin
that normally exists within the cells is released into the bloodstream, overwhelming the liver with too much bilirubin and causing a buildup of bilirubin in the blood. Any of these scenarios can
lead to jaundice.

CAUSES OF JAUNDICE

◆

Jaundice is very common — up to half of all babies become at least a little yellow in the first week of life. The most common causes of jaundice are listed here. Babies with more than one of these are likely to have more significant jaundice.

More than 10 percent weight loss from birth weight
Dehydration
Blood type incompatibility
Infection
Prematurity
Low birth weight
Feeding difficulty

When the cause of jaundice is slow liver function, it can take a few days of life before the liver functions fully, helping to remove bilirubin and other waste. In the newborn, therefore, bilirubin circulates in the bloodstream longer than usual, and this extra bilirubin causes the skin to look yellow.

When bilirubin is elevated because it is released from the cells into the bloodstream, this is usually a consequence of the destruction or death of red blood cells. All red blood cells age and die; it is a normal process. When this happens, the cells are broken apart by the spleen. They release the substances that had been stored inside, including bilirubin. About 1 percent of all red blood cells die every day, and after the first week of life, the body is equipped to deal with this. In newborns, however, up to 5 or even 10 percent of the red blood cells can break open every day. This happens especially when a baby and its mother have different blood types. A mother can form antibodies to her baby's blood, and these antibodies can react against the baby's blood, "attacking" it as foreign. This reaction is called *Coombs' positive hemolytic anemia.* It causes large numbers of red blood cells to die and large levels of bilirubin to be released into the bloodstream. Because the liver is already working slowly, it can take an extralong time to clear all of this bilirubin out of the blood. In these cases, babies can look very yellow very quickly! Babies of mothers with certain blood types (O-negative, O-positive, A-negative, B-negative, and AB-negative) will typically have their blood type checked at birth because the risk of Coombs' positive hemolytic anemia is much higher.

Another possible cause of jaundice is infection. When bacteria infect the blood, red blood cells can break apart more easily, releasing excess bilirubin. Infection can also impair liver function. For the same reasons listed previously, babies with infections can look quite yellow. Babies older than a week or two have other causes of jaundice, including liver disease, that are discussed in some of the Web links at the end of this section.

Amazingly jaundice in babies usually starts in the face and makes its way down the body. When it resolves, it moves in the opposite direction. Therefore the whites of the eyes are usually yellow when the jaundice first begins, and they are the last part of the body to remain yellow until the jaundice completely resolves. Jaundice may be more difficult to see in children of color. However, if the level is high and the jaundice is traveling down the body, then yellow discoloration can be visible in the palms and even soles of the feet. In general, though, jaundice is more difficult to see in darker-skinned babies.

What can I do?

The more a baby poops, the faster the jaundice will resolve. The more milk your baby consumes, the more he will poop. Therefore jaundiced, breast-feeding babies should breast-feed as often as possible. You can also give your baby supplemental formula to drink. This is often useful because breast-feeding moms (especially first-time breast-feeding moms) produce very little liquid in the first few days of life, so babies do not drink much. This initial form of breast milk is called *colostrum;* it is followed a day or two later by *transitional breast milk* and eventually (by day three to four) by larger volumes of breast milk. If a baby doesn't drink much in the first few days of life, then he doesn't poop much. Supplemental formula helps stimulate more stooling. You should not stop breast-feeding — instead the formula is used in addition to early breast milk. Once the breast milk is in, the formula can be stopped because the breast milk will do the job.

You can also place your baby in a direct beam of sunlight for about 10 to 20 minutes at a time, one or two times per day. He should be naked (except for a diaper) and should be held inside a window so he doesn't get too cold (rather than being held outside). Sunlight helps jaundice resolve more quickly by transforming the bilirubin into a form that can be pooped out more efficiently and can be urinated out as well.

Unfortunately indoor light such as a lamp or an overhead light does not work the same way that sunlight does. Therefore turning on the lights won't help to resolve jaundice any faster.

When does my doctor need to be involved?

Anytime your baby looks yellow, your doctor should check the child. This is especially true if the baby is younger than 24 hours *or* older than one month, or if the yellow discoloration is increasing over hours or days. Remember, the jaundice marches down the baby's body as the bilirubin level gets higher — so a yellow discoloration in the face represents a much lower bilirubin level than yellow discoloration all the way down to the toes.

What tests need to be done, and what do the results mean?

The level of bilirubin can be measured by a blood test that is described in chapter 29. If the level is high, it often needs to be rechecked over the next few days. If a baby is placed under special blue fluorescent lights — called *phototherapy lights* — to help the level fall, then the blood test must be repeated to make sure the number is decreasing appropriately. Sometimes the level is borderline, so it is rechecked a day or two later (without the baby being placed under lights) to make sure it is not rapidly going up. This is covered more extensively in the following passages.

There is a new technique that measures bilirubin levels without drawing blood. This method uses a sticker attached to the skin. While it is still experimental, *transcutaneous* (across the skin) bilirubin measurements may become much more common over the next few years.

What are the treatments?

The best way for a newborn to get rid of extra bilirubin is to poop it out, and the means for increasing stooling are described in the previous passages. It is common for doctors to recommend supplemental formula when significant jaundice is noted.

Mild jaundice is considered normal in babies older than 24 hours and younger than about nine or ten days. When the jaundice is not mild, however, then bilirubin in the blood is measured. The number value of bilirubin will correlate with the severity of the jaundice. The significance of the number varies with age. In other words, a baby who is 24 hours old is expected to have a lower bilirubin level than a baby who is 72 hours old. In general, when the number is above a certain level, your doctor will consider interventions such as phototherapy. The general American Academy of Pediatrics (AAP) guidelines for bilirubin levels in full-term infants are as follows:

Age of baby	Consider phototherapy (bilirubin level)	Start phototherapy (bilirubin level)
<24 hours	any visible jaundice*	
25–48 hours	≥12 mg/dL	≥15 mg/dL
49–72 hours	≥15 mg/dL	≥18 mg/dL
>72 hours	≥17 mg/dL	≥20 mg/dL

*At less than 24 hours of life, jaundice is always abnormal regardless of the bilirubin level.

These guidelines are currently being reviewed by the AAP. The committee stresses that any infant younger than 24 hours of age with jaundice must have his bilirubin level checked. The committee also states that any child discharged from the hospital in less than 48 hours should be seen for follow-up within two to three days of discharge. In some cases, follow-up as soon as 24 hours is necessary.

Light helps to get rid of excess bilirubin. If placing a baby in sunlight does not work or if the level of jaundice is too high, then a phototherapy light may be used. These lights simply imitate direct sunlight, helping to convert the bilirubin into a form more readily removed from the body. Unlike sunlight, though, the phototherapy lights can be on 24 hours per day, helping the jaundice to resolve more quickly.

In very extreme cases, when the bilirubin level is so high that it is dangerous, blood can be removed from the baby's body and replaced with donated blood or *saline* (a saltwater solution that is safe to run directly into a baby's veins). This method, called an *exchange transfusion,* lowers the bilirubin level by physically removing bilirubin from the body.

What are the possible complications?

The most dangerous complication of high bilirubin levels is called *kernicterus.* This is a situation where there is so much bilirubin in the blood that it crosses over into the brain. While bilirubin can be removed from the blood, it cannot be removed from the brain. If bilirubin deposits in the brain, then it can cause long-term problems with brain function. Because bilirubin levels can be checked easily, kernicterus has become extremely uncommon.

It is important to note that the bilirubin level must surpass a specific number to begin to risk entering the brain. For a full-term baby, kernicterus is a worry when the bilirubin level is greater than 25 to 30 mg/dL after three days of life. For a premature baby or a baby younger than 72 hours old, kernicterus can be a worry even at lower bilirubin levels. In all of these cases, a baby will look severely jaundiced whenever kernicterus is a concern.

Additional Resources

http://www.nlm.nih.gov/medlineplus/encyclopedia.html (Click on "N," then scroll down to "newborn jaundice.")

http://www.medem.com (Go to "search medical library" in upper right-hand corner and type in "jaundice.")

http://www.packardchildrenshospital.org (Go to "search" in upper right-hand corner and type in "jaundice.")

http://www.aap.org/policy/hyperb.htm

12

Head Shape

◆

In order for a baby to be able to travel through the birth canal, the head must be small enough and flexible enough to fit. Fortunately the brain is only a fraction of its adult size at birth. The bones that surround it are also able to mold into different positions. This explains why most babies that have been resting low in their mother's pelvis, waiting for delivery, have long pointy heads just after birth.

While the head must be extremely moldable, it must also be very sturdy. The skull is responsible for protecting the brain beneath it. It must be strong enough to endure bumps and bonks during delivery and thereafter. And, in order to grow and develop complex language and thought, the brain and its surrounding skull must be able to expand. Therefore both the brain and its protective shell are designed to change shape and grow over time. For something so hard to the touch, the bony skull is amazingly malleable.

Head growth is greatest in the first year of life. As the skull grows, it changes shape. Therefore, when a baby is placed in various positions over and over again, the pressure on one particular part of the skull can cause flattening of that area. While children and adults have relatively fixed head shapes, babies do not. The range of skull shapes and the speed at which the skull changes shape are remarkable.

POINTED HEAD (MOLDING)
(Birth)

What is happening inside my baby's body?
The bones that make up your baby's skull are designed to move around so that the head can pass through a tight space when the baby is born. In fact the skull bones look like big pieces of a puzzle: they fit together, but they are not firmly attached.

When a baby hangs upside down and low in her mom's pelvis for days (or weeks), the bones of her skull mold to fit the mom's pelvis. This is why many newborn babies have pointed heads — a phenomenon called *molding.* This is a good strategy for a delivering baby because it may help her to pass through a very narrow birth canal. Some babies do not hang upside down in the pelvis for long (or at all), so they have perfectly round heads at birth. This is especially true among babies born by cesarean section.

The fact that the bones of a baby's skull can move around allows humans to have rapid brain growth, not just while developing inside the womb but after birth as well. In the first two years of life, the human head grows an average of 40 percent, allowing a newborn to be delivered while her brain is still quite immature. In fact humans are the only species born with brains that are so immature that a baby is entirely dependent upon a parent. Think of horses — they are able to walk within hours of birth. Humans cannot even crawl yet. Why does this happen? Because humans are born with immature brains that can ultimately develop a level of sophistication that no other animals have. Again, this is all thanks to a moldable head and movable skull bones. The only alternative in evolution allowing for massive human brain size and sophistication would have been for moms to have gigantic hips!

Molding lasts only a few days after the baby is born. Remarkably the head rounds itself out quickly once a baby has been delivered. Within a week the head assumes a standard round shape, with a soft spot at the very top toward the front and another, smaller soft spot at the top toward the back. These spots — called *fontanels* — are simply normal spaces between the bones of the skull. They allow for even more growth of the brain and skull after birth. The fontanel at the back of the head typically closes between two and twelve weeks of life; the one at the top of the head usually closes sometime between six and eighteen months of age.

What can I do?
Parents do not need to do anything to resolve molding. The head will usually round itself out. However, in some cases, parts of the skull become flat over time. To avoid this, you should put your baby down to sleep on her back, with the head in slightly different positions throughout the day and night. Sometimes the head is turned to one side, sometimes to the other, and sometimes it is placed in the middle. This strategy, which allows the head to continue to round itself out, is covered in more detail in the section on *plagiocephaly* that follows.

When does my doctor need to be involved?
Doctors do not need to do anything about head molding. The changing shape of the head in the womb is normal and goes away quickly after birth.

What tests need to be done, and what do the results mean?
Tests are unnecessary in the case of molding because the shaping of the skull in the womb is normal.

What are the treatments?
Head molding does not require treatment; it will resolve itself. However, to avoid future flattening of certain parts of your baby's head, you should rotate her sleep position so that she is not continually resting on one part of her head. This is covered in the section on plagiocephaly that follows.

What are the possible complications?
There are no complications from head molding. It resolves quickly on its own.

Additional Resources
http://www.cdc.gov/nchs/about/major/nhanes/growthcharts/charts.htm

◆   ◆   ◆

FLAT HEAD (PLAGIOCEPHALY)
(1–9 Months)

What is happening inside my baby's body?
Just as the head was shaped in the womb by mom's pelvis, the
head is subject to reshaping after birth too. This is because the
plates of the skull are pliable, so positioning of the head can dramatically affect its shape over time. When babies are laid down to
sleep in the same position over and over again, specific spots on
the skull receive more pressure just from the weight of the head
on that area. If the position of the head is not rotated regularly,
then the part that repeatedly bears the weight will flatten. For
some babies the flat part is on the back of the skull, but for others
it is on one side or the other. Noticeable flattening is called *plagiocephaly.*

Plagiocephaly can also result from repeated positioning while
sitting up. When your baby sits in a car seat, his head flops to one
side or the other. Head-and-neck pillows help to keep him sup-
ported, but sometimes a baby prefers to turn his head in one particular direction, or the seat is arranged so that he is in the same
position each time. Again, gravity and the weight of the head can
put pressure on a specific part of the skull, and this can contribute to flattening of one side of the head.

Babies with *torticollis* have uneven neck muscles. These babies
hold their head cocked to one side. They are more likely to develop plagiocephaly simply because they position their own
heads in one direction most of the time. Torticollis is covered in
more detail in chapter 17.

What can I do?
You can rotate your baby's sleeping position regularly. Your baby
should sleep on his back, with his head turned alternately to one
side, then the other, and then kept in the middle. He can be slightly
propped up on his side using a *wedge* (triangular-shaped pillow)
or a rolled blanket tucked behind him. Any material used to position a baby should be placed below the shoulders so that, in case

he squirms and flips over, there is no chance that the material will block the nose and mouth. If a flat area has begun to form on the skull, then an effort should be made to avoid laying the baby on that side until the skull has rounded out again.

If you notice that your baby prefers to look in one direction and this is contributing to flattening of the head on one side, then try to provide entertainment in the opposite direction. Toys can be placed in the crib in such a way that the baby turns his head to look at them. In the car, a mirror can be placed on the backseat so that he will turn his head to catch a glimpse of himself. When trying strategies like these, you should remember to put the target objects in a place that entices the baby to look in the opposite direction from his favored glance.

When does my doctor need to be involved?
If you notice an area of flattening on the head, let your doctor know.

What tests need to be done, and what do the results mean?
If a baby has plagiocephaly, then tests are usually not necessary. The treatment will typically be the same regardless of any tests that may be done.

What are the treatments?
Helping your baby to round out his head can be difficult because once he has developed a comfortable flat place to rest his head, you will need to do some maneuvering to get him to sleep or to just hold his head in a different position. If repositioning and placing toys and mirrors have not helped, and if the head flattening has become severe, then a *helmet* may be used. This is unusual.

Helmets help to round out the head. They are firm, so they place gentle pressure on the parts of the skull that are more rounded and no pressure on the areas that are flat. Over time (usually months), the flattened parts of the head become round. Helmets are almost never used until a baby is 4 to 6 months old — the head will usually round itself out well before then. Helmets are rarely used after a child is 10 to 12 months old, because the bones of the skull are far less moldable by this point.

What are the possible complications?
The only complication of plagiocephaly is a cosmetic one: a permanently flattened head. This is usually hidden by hair, especially when the flat spot is in the back. But in rare cases, one side of the skull is significantly flatter than the other, and the cosmetic effect can be noticeable. If a person has very thin or sparse hair, then the flat spot is more obvious.

Additional Resources
http://www.hmc.psu.edu/neurosurgery/pservices/helmet.htm

◆　　◆　　◆

BALD SPOTS
(2–6 Months)

What is happening inside my baby's body?
Almost all babies develop bald spots on the back of the head, just above the neck. This was not the case when babies were put to sleep facing down, but now that they are placed on their backs, it is the norm. The cause of balding is repeated pressure and friction on one spot on the scalp. This spot will lose hair. The principle is similar to head flattening, but this problem is much easier to solve, because as a baby becomes stronger and lifts his head, he reduces the scalp friction and the hair grows back normally.

What can I do?
Parents can try to alternate a baby's sleeping position, but balding happens quite easily, with very little friction along the scalp. Therefore there is little a parent can do except wait.

When does my doctor need to be involved?
Doctors do not need to be involved because bald patches on the back of the head are normal and temporary.

What tests need to be done, and what do the results mean?
Because this is a normal phenomenon, tests do not need to be done.

What are the treatments?
Time is the only real cure for balding, but repositioning a baby so that different points of the scalp receive pressure and friction may help to minimize the bald spot.

What are the possible complications?
There are no complications. The hair will grow back.

Additional Resources
http://www.choc.com/dev/pediatric/hhg/hairloss.htm

◆   ◆   ◆

SOFT SPOTS (FONTANELS)
(Birth–12 Months)

What is happening inside my baby's body?
The soft spots (also known as *fontanels*) are the connections between the skull bones. There are actually four of them at birth, but only two are noticeable. The bigger one at the top of the head is called the *anterior fontanel;* the smaller one in the midline of the back of the head is called the *posterior fontanel.* The fontanel system allows a baby to be delivered with ease because it makes the head more malleable. With loose connections between the bones of the skull, the head can mold into a long narrow shape in order to travel more easily through the vaginal canal.

The soft spots may feel delicate, but they are remarkably tough. Many parents are afraid to touch them, but there is nothing to fear because the overlying tissue is very strong. The fluid surrounding the brain sits underneath the soft spots, so when you touch the area it can feel boggy.

The posterior fontanel closes first because it is the smaller of the two soft spots. On average, it closes between weeks 2 to 12. But the anterior fontanel stays open much longer, closing anytime between 6 to 18 months.

What can I do?
Nothing special needs to be done to the fontanels. You don't need to avoid touching the area or brushing the hair there.

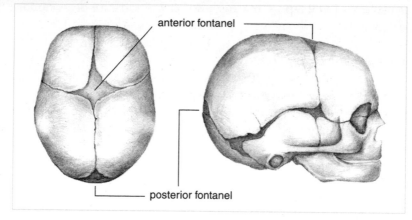

anterior fontanel

posterior fontanel

The newborn skull with its open fontanels

When does my doctor need to be involved?

Fontanels usually look flat or very slightly raised or sunken. Call your doctor if the fontanel is noticeably bulging or sunken. A *bulging fontanel* can be the sign of infection in the fluid surrounding the brain. A baby with an infection around the brain will usually look very sick — he will almost always be very fussy or sleepy (or both) and have a high fever. A *sunken fontanel* can be a sign of dehydration. A cushion of fluid surrounds the brain, and as the body gets increasingly dehydrated, fluid from every compartment diminishes. When this happens, the fontanel looks like a deep crevasse. A dehydrated baby usually looks quite ill. This is described in more detail in chapter 28.

What tests need to be done, and what do the results mean?

Normal fontanels require no tests. In rare instances, if the child is very sick or the fontanel is bulging, then a *spinal tap* may be considered. This test checks the fluid that surrounds the brain. The fluid is drawn from the lower back, where the base of the spinal cord sits. It is never drawn from the fontanel. Occasionally a CT scan or ultrasound of the head may be done as well. These tests look at both the fluid surrounding the brain and the brain itself. Ultrasounds are particularly useful in a baby whose anterior fontanel is still open. But once it closes, an ultrasound on the skull is useless. Spinal taps, CT scans, and ultrasounds are described in chapter 29.

What are the treatments?

A fontanel will close on its own and requires no treatment. If the fontanel is truly bulging or sunken, then the underlying cause requires treatment. An infection causing a bulging fontanel will usually be treated with antibiotics. Dehydration causing a sunken fontanel will be treated with fluids for hydration. Each of these is covered in more detail in chapter 28.

What are the possible complications?

A fontanel can close too early or stay open too long. If the fontanel closes too soon, then the shape of the head may be affected. Remember that the fontanels are open spaces between some of the skull bones; there are also *sutures* between all the skull bones that hold neighboring bones together tightly. If these sutures fuse too early, then the shape of the head can be pro-foundly affected. This is called *craniosynostosis*. If only the fontanels close early but the sutures remain normal, then the head will maintain a normal shape.

A fontanel that stays open too long may signal some other underlying problem. Babies with thyroid disease or malnutrition may have delayed closure of the fontanels. Some genetic syn-dromes also cause delayed closure. And bone diseases such as *rickets* may slow the process as well.

Additional Resources
http://www.nlm.nih.gov/medlineplus/encyclopedia.html (Click on "Cp–Cz," then scroll down to "cranial sutures.")

Eyes

No sooner do the eyes form than babies begin to perceive light in the womb. After birth, the eyes must learn to see. This is a gradual process. Right after birth, a baby cannot see much. In fact her vision is similar to that of a legally blind adult. But vision matures rapidly over the first few weeks of life, as the eyes receive stimulation in the form of thousands of images a day. The eyes are soon able to focus, and the brain integrates all the information coming through them. Remarkably quickly, a baby learns how to see.

The development of vision includes learning to focus on objects near and far, discriminating colors, and using both eyes to see "in stereo." Once a baby can see well, she can begin to acquire visual knowledge. She learns what her parents look like, the difference between day and night, and how to tell far from near. The eyes must coordinate their movements so that they deliver similar information to the brain. Sometimes they look like they are wandering or crossed, but this can be a normal step in the process of developing vision. Occasionally the eyes become scratched or infected, but they usually heal quickly.

EYE ROLLING AND WANDERING
(Birth–3 Months)

What is happening inside my baby's body?
Newborns are legally blind. If their vision were measured, it would be about 20/500. In other words, a baby can basically only see things that are the size and shape of a breast. This makes sense from an evolutionary point of view: it is all a newborn really *needs* to see. By six or seven months, vision improves to 20/50.

Newborns are also essentially color blind, able to see only black, white, and red. Again, this makes sense, as nipples on the human breast are red.

Vision improves over the first few months of life, as babies need to learn to see. With time, the eyes and brain begin to work together — the brain interpreting visual images from the two eyes "in stereo." At first, though, the brain accepts input from both eyes independently, so the eyes occasionally do funny things. The most common is eye wandering: one eye can roll in one direction while the other can be wandering off in an entirely different direction. This can be very disconcerting, but it usually stops by 4 to 6 weeks, when the brain and the eyes are much better at communicating. After that, the eyes will still occasionally wander or cross, but by 3 to 4 months, the crossing should be entirely gone.

What can I do?
Parents don't need to do anything — including worry — about occasional eye wandering in the first several weeks of life; it is entirely normal.

When does my doctor need to be involved?
A doctor does not need to be involved with random and occasional eye wandering seen in the first two months of life; this is completely normal. However, if one eye is not moving well, if the eyes look permanently crossed, or if the wandering eye movements are extremely frequent, then a doctor should check the

child. This is true even if the baby is younger than eight weeks old. If you are ever in doubt, talk to your doctor.

What tests need to be done, and what do the results mean?
Because newborns normally have occasional eye wandering, tests do not need to be done.

What are the treatments?
No treatment is necessary for normal eye wandering. As the baby learns to see, the movements will resolve.

What are the possible complications?
There are no complications of normal newborn eye rolling.

Additional Resources
http://www.kidshealth.org/parent/general/eyes/vision_p3.html
http://www.tinyeyes.com/
http://www.people.virginia.edu/~jyl8b/Percep/sensedev.html

◆　　◆　　◆

CROSSED EYES
(Birth–12 Months)

What is happening inside my baby's body?
There are three reasons why your baby may appear cross-eyed: (1) immature eye control causes the eyes to wander and occasionally appear to be crossed; (2) the eyes and nose are shaped in such a way that the eyes look crossed (but really they are not); or (3) the eyes actually cross (point toward the nose). Believe it or not, the third option — truly crossed eyes — is quite rare.

When babies look cross-eyed only some of the time, it is usually because their eyes randomly wander inward and point at the nose. This happens normally in the first few weeks of life, when the eye control is immature and the eyes and brain have not yet learned to work together. As your baby gets older, her eye wandering will become less and less frequent until one day it stops. If only one eye is crossed (or if it looks outward), and if this happens regularly beyond 2 to 3 months of age, then it is likely that one of the muscles responsible for controlling the eye movements is weak. This is called **strabismus.**

By far the most common reason for a baby to look cross-eyed is an optical illusion: if the eyes are widely spaced, if the bridge of the nose is wide and still undeveloped, or if the upper eyelids are particularly thick (called **epicanthal folds**), then the eyes can appear crossed even when they are actually perfectly aligned. This phenomenon is called **pseudostrabismus.** It is normal in infants of many ethnic backgrounds, especially Asian.

The best way to tell if your baby's eyes are not properly aligned is to look at the way light reflects on them. When light reflects at the same place on both eyes, they are aligned. When it reflects in different spots on the two eyes, they are not aligned. (Even though this test looks for how light "reflects," doctors refer to it as the light "reflex.")

What can I do?

Watch for a pattern to the crossing of the eyes. If your baby's eyes wander randomly, and this largely resolves by two months, then you needn't do anything. Even until three months of age, occasional eye crossing is acceptable.

If the crossing is an optical illusion caused by epicanthal folds, then there is nothing a parent can do. As the child grows, the eyes usually look less crossed.

When does my doctor need to be involved?

An ophthalmologist (eye doctor) needs to see a baby if one or both eyes turn inward (or outward) consistently beyond two months of age or occasionally beyond three months. Sometimes it can be hard for a parent to tell whether the eyes are turned in or out, so if there is any doubt, you should have the baby seen by your doctor.

What tests need to be done, and what do the results mean?

Your pediatrician or an ophthalmologist may do a **cover/uncover test.** This test checks eye alignment and identifies strabismus. In this test, an attention-getting object is held in the baby's line of vision. Then a cover is placed over one eye for at least two sec-

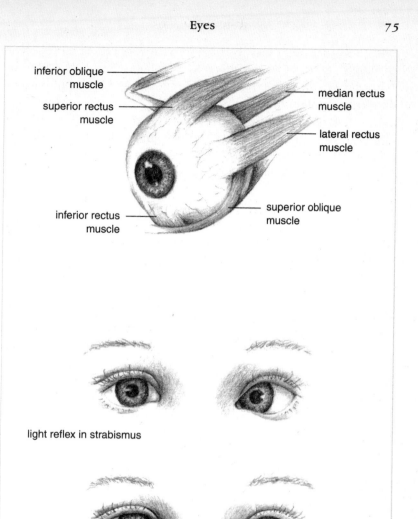

inferior oblique muscle

median rectus muscle

superior rectus muscle

lateral rectus muscle

inferior rectus muscle

superior oblique muscle

light reflex in strabismus

normal light reflex

Anatomy of the eyeball (*top*);
using the light reflex to test for strabismus (*bottom*)

onds and then removed. Normal eyes will continue to focus on the target. An eye that is truly crossed will move slightly when the other (normal) eye is covered. This crossed eye is trying to maintain focus on the object.

This test is far more sensitive when done in an older child or adult who can cooperate with the test. In babies, sometimes the only way to determine that their eyes are misaligned is to look at the light reflex previously described.

What are the treatments?

When strabismus is diagnosed early enough (before six years of age, although this is certainly not an absolute), it can usually be corrected with glasses. The glasses help to focus the eyes together on a single target and therefore help eye alignment. If glasses are worn early enough, then eventually the eyes may become aligned, or at the very least will align while the child is wearing the glasses.

When strabismus is diagnosed too late, the brain learns to see with misaligned eyes. The brain actually blocks out or suppresses images from the misaligned eye, so even with glasses, the eye continues to cross. Many of these children require eye-muscle surgery to treat the strabismus, and they usually continue to need glasses after the surgery.

What are the possible complications?

The worst complication of untreated strabismus is functional blindness in the crossed eye, also called *amblyopia*. This happens because the brain is designed to integrate the images from two eyes "in stereo." If one eye is wandering randomly or misaligned, then the brain cannot integrate the input from the two eyes, and it will categorically reject or suppress input from the misaligned eye. If the brain rejects input from one of the two eyes and only uses the dominant eye, then the nondominant eye will behave as if it were blind. Even though the eye itself is normal, the brain treats it as if it does not exist.

Amblyopia can be caused by a number of problems. If something such as a cataract blocks or blurs the vision from one eye for a long enough time, then amblyopia can result. It can also be caused by an improperly formed eyelid that obstructs a baby's view. Whatever the origin, when the brain cannot integrate the input from one eye with the input from the other, the result is functional blindness in one eye. Amblyopia is sometimes treated by patching the dominant eye, thereby encouraging use of the nondominant eye. But if it is not treated in early childhood, then amblyopia will not improve, even with glasses and patching.

While most doctors and parents can easily see strabismus, amblyopia without strabismus usually goes unnoticed by both. In fact only an eye doctor comfortable with examining young children and infants can diagnose this type of amblyopia.

Additional Resources
http://www.neec.com/Pedatric_Ophthalmology_Strabismus.html
http://med-aapos.bu.edu/aapos/pediintro.html
http://www.nlm.nih.gov/medlineplus/encyclopedia.html (Click on "Sq–Sz," then scroll down to "strabismus.")
http://www.nlm.nih.gov/medlineplus/encyclopedia.html (Click on "Ah–Ap," then scroll down to "amblyopia.")

◈   ◈   ◈

EYE MUCUS AND PINKEYE
(Birth–12 Months)

What is happening inside my baby's body?
Most babies do not make tears in the first couple weeks of life. Typically, around week three or four, parents will notice the eyes looking glassy, accompanied by an occasional tear with crying. Then the waterworks begin.

Once a baby can make tears, he must be able to drain them. Unfortunately the little holes underneath the eyelids (called *lacrimal ducts*) are often too small to do the job. They can be so narrow that they do not drain well, or they can be easily clogged with daily debris from the eye. In either case, the tears stay in the eye, making it look glassy or watery. A watery eye quickly collects white or yellow or even green goop made of mucus, or *discharge*. The medical term for this process is *dacryostenosis* — "dacryo" meaning "duct" and "stenosis" meaning small.

WHEN TO WORRY ABOUT EYE INFECTION

◆

Conjunctivitis — or pinkeye, as it is often called — is extremely common. However, the infection can spread. Here are some tips about when you should worry that your child's pinkeye is not just run-of-the-mill:

Eye is swollen shut, with taut red skin
Child cries when moving eye from side to side
Eyeball looks like it is bulging from the head and is
asymmetrical compared to the other side
Child cannot tolerate light because it hurts too much
Child has very high fever

There are other causes of goopy eyes. Infections (without dacryostenosis) can certainly cause a discharge. These infections — known as *conjunctivitis* — are extremely contagious. They are caused by viruses or bacteria, and are often passed along by relatives or children in school or day care. Some infections are also passed at birth, when the child is traveling through the vaginal canal. Classic viral and bacterial conjunctivitis look different: while both may cause the eye to look pink or red, viral conjunctivitis typically streams clear water whereas bacterial conjunctivitis tends to cause thick yellow or green discharge. In some cases, however, the two types of infection can look very similar.

Conjunctivitis can exist alone or together with an ear infection. The eyes and ears are actually connected via the sinuses. Therefore an infection in one place can spread to the other.

What can I do?

In order to get rid of the discharge, you must wipe your baby's eye clean. The best way to do this is to use a damp cotton ball, piece of gauze, or soft towel and wipe from the corner nearest his nose toward the corner nearest his ear. If there is dacryostenosis, then this wiping helps to temporarily unplug the tear duct.

With dacryostenosis, the goop will reappear every few hours because the duct is just too small to drain the tears — wiping isn't enough.

Believe it or not, a dropperful of special salt water called *saline* (available over the counter at most drugstores) or even breast milk (!) squirted in your baby's eye will rinse away the debris, clearing up the discharge relatively quickly. Breast milk is also filled with antibodies that get rid of lingering bacteria. But with dacryostenosis, the liquids work only as long as they are used. Once stopped, the discharge returns because the underlying problem has not been resolved: the duct is still too small or clogged.

In order to help remove the crusty discharge that collects around the eye, you can gently wash the eyelid with baby shampoo mixed with warm water. This mild soap helps to get rid of sticky discharge. Be careful not to get the shampoo inside the eye.

For babies with dacryostenosis, many doctors suggest massaging the tear duct. To do this, you can use one finger and gently rub between the nose and the corner of the eye. This massage helps to dislodge debris stuck in the duct. Massage, irrigation, cleaning, and wiping are often used in combination.

When does my doctor need to be involved?
Call the doctor if there is any persistent yellow or green discharge from the eye. A doctor needs to see your baby if the eyelid becomes increasingly swollen or red. This unusual circumstance can mean that the infection has moved into the skin around the eye.

You also need to contact your doctor if the discharge in the eye is not improving despite antibiotic eyedrops. This can signal that the infection has moved into the ears, so no matter how many eyedrops are used, the ear (via the sinuses) will continue to be a source of bacteria.

What tests need to be done, and what do the results mean?
Sometimes a culture of the eye discharge can determine the cause of the infection. This is especially helpful in newborns, because they have been exposed to very few bacteria, most of which live

in the birth canal. Specific bacteria require specific antibiotic treatment. So if a doctor can figure out exactly what is causing the infection, then treating it becomes relatively easy.

It is important to remember that, as a baby ages, bacteria begin to settle on the skin normally. Therefore the older the child, the less helpful a culture will be, because it becomes more and more likely that the culture will grow only the normal skin bacteria. Normal bacteria can cause conjunctivitis, but almost all common antibiotic treatments are effective against these. So, unless the eye continues to get worse and worse despite treatment, it is rarely necessary to prove exactly which bacteria is causing the infection.

When the eyelid swells and becomes infected, a CT scan or MRI scan may be necessary. These pictures determine whether the infection is on the outer skin only or has moved behind the eye. Infections within the eye are extremely rare and require significantly stronger medicines. If left untreated, these infections can lead to blindness.

What are the treatments?

When the cause of goopy eyes is an infection, medication may be needed. Bacterial conjunctivitis can be treated with antibiotic drops or gels. In order to prevent conjunctivitis in the first few days of life, standard practice is to give babies an antibiotic ointment directly after birth. This kills any potential bacteria that may have been present in the birth canal.

Unlike bacterial infections, viral conjunctivitis will not improve with antibiotics because viruses are not killed by antibiotic medications. Careful cleaning of the eye is all that can be done to manage the discharge. A virus resolves on its own over time.

Remember, a baby with dacryostenosis will have recurrent bouts of eye discharge until the duct opens up and drains properly. Repeated courses of saline, breast milk drops, or antibiotics may be necessary.

Some babies with dacryostenosis need antibiotic drops because the discharge gets progressively worse, and antibiotic drops are better at getting rid of large numbers of bacteria than are breast milk or saline drops. In cases of dacryostenosis where the discharge lasts months and months, a child needs to have a surgical procedure to open up the duct and help tear drainage. A pediatric ophthalmologist performs this procedure.

What are the possible complications?

Most eye infections are uncomplicated. However, if the infection moves deep into the surrounding skin or behind the eyeball itself — rather than remaining at the lid surface only — then it can spread rapidly. This secondary infection is called *cellulitis*, meaning that there is inflammation of the skin and deeper tissues. Two of the most worrisome complications of conjunctivitis are *periorbital cellulitis* ("peri" meaning "around"; "orbital" meaning "socket") and *orbital cellulitis* (infections within the eye socket behind the eye).

Periorbital cellulitis (also known as *preseptal cellulitis*) usually starts as a sinus infection. The infection moves to the skin around the eye, typically causing the top or bottom (or both) eyelid(s) to swell. A red rim can also appear where the infection is spreading. While periorbital cellulitis is far less serious than orbital cellulitis, periorbital infection can in some cases move behind the eye, causing orbital cellulitis.

Orbital cellulitis is far more worrisome than periorbital. This infection exists within the eye socket — behind the eyeball — involving the muscles, fat, nerves, or bones. Signs of orbital cellulitis include pain with movement of the eye, severe swelling, or high fever. Whenever there is a concern about orbital cellulitis, a CT scan or MRI should be done. An untreated orbital cellulitis can travel along the optic nerve into the brain, causing blindness or *meningitis* (infection of the fluid around the brain). Therefore children with these infections must be treated in the hospital using intravenous antibiotics.

Additional Resources

http://www.drhull.com/EncyMaster/D/dacryostenosis.html
http://www.nlm.nih.gov/medlineplus/encyclopedia.html (Click on "N," then scroll down to "neonatal conjunctivitis.")
http://www.nlm.nih.gov/medlineplus/encyclopedia.html (Click on "Bl–Bz," then scroll down to "blocked tear duct.")

◆ ◆ ◆

SCRATCHED EYE (CORNEAL ABRASION)
(Birth–12 Months)

What is happening inside my baby's body?
The *cornea* is a clear layer of tissue covering the front of the eye. It protects the eye from irritants and minor damage. A corneal abrasion refers to damage of this tissue. Many people think of it as a scratch on the eye.

Several things can cause a corneal abrasion. In babies, the most common include a baby's own fingernails, which can accidentally swipe across the eye, and any object — a piece of paper, some sand, or some clothing — that can get into the eye. Corneal abrasion is not contagious.

Babies with corneal abrasions typically have acute pain and may have a history of recent trauma. They may attempt to avoid bright lights by closing the eyes, produce an unusual amount of tears, or blink much more frequently than usual. The eye may look red and irritated, or it may look relatively normal.

When a baby is crying inconsolably, a scratched cornea may be to blame. This is especially true among infants under 2 or 3 months, whose hands and arms flail and whose fingernails grow rapidly. In these cases, it can be difficult to get a good look in the eye because it is often shut during screaming episodes.

What can I do?
Some parents patch the eye temporarily using a piece of gauze or other material to make the child more comfortable in bright light. Often, though, a child is more agitated than soothed by a makeshift patch placed by parents. It is much safer to let a health care provider patch the eye than to attempt to do it yourself.

When does my doctor need to be involved?
Anytime you suspect that the eye has been injured, you should consult a doctor immediately.

What tests need to be done, and what do the results mean?
An exam of the eye will involve looking underneath the eyelids
to check for a foreign body (such as a piece of dirt or sand). Many
doctors will use *fluorescein* — a fluorescent eyedrop — to light
up a possible abrasion. The fluorescein lasts only a few seconds,
is harmless, and does not cause any additional pain.

If a health care provider is unable to examine the eye thor-
oughly or if a more detailed exam is necessary, then an ophthalmologist (eye doctor) should be called. An extensive exam of the
eye, called a *slit lamp exam,* can be performed to make sure that
everything is normal.

What are the treatments?
If the cornea is truly scratched, then antibiotics will often be used
to prevent secondary infection. An antibiotic can be given in the
form of a drop or an ointment. Sometimes an eye patch is used to
make the eye more comfortable and to minimize rapid blinking,
helping to speed the healing of the abrasion. The most important
part of this treatment is to leave the patch in place for as long as
directed. Rubbing or pulling at the patch may loosen it and delay
healing. Patching the eye is somewhat controversial, but it can
make the child more comfortable. Most patches are used for only
24 hours. The larger the abrasion, the more likely a doctor is to
use a patch.

What are the possible complications?
The cornea typically heals itself within a few days. A deep abrasion, however, may become infected or scar, and a poorly healed
one may develop recurrent erosion. Scars and erosions cause a
range of symptoms, including tearing, mild discomfort, and blurry
vision.

In the most extreme cases, the cornea may be so damaged that
a new one may need to be transplanted. This is exceedingly rare.

Additional Resources
http://www.mckinley.uiuc.edu/health-info/dis-cond/misc/cornabra.html
http://www.packardchildrenshospital.org (Go to "search" in upper right-
hand corner and type in "corneal abrasion.")

14

Ears

◆

Babies can hear in the womb. They know the shushing sound of flowing blood and the pitch of their parents' voices. In fact the womb is a very noisy place. By some estimates, it is as loud as 90 decibels. That's similar to the volume at a rock concert.

When a baby is born, she can hear sounds quite well but is used to background noise. This is why total silence is not necessary for most babies, and instead having some sound in the background often lulls a baby to sleep.

A baby can recognize her parent's voice almost immediately, but she cannot tell where it is coming from. In fact localization of sound is not developed until about four months. Once a baby can localize, she will turn her head toward a clapping sound or toward the sound of shuffling feet in order to see who is coming. Before then, a sudden loud noise may simply startle her.

Hearing is critical to language development. A child cannot imitate sounds unless she has heard them. She cannot learn speech or intonation. Screening tests for hearing are now done routinely in the hospital to help identify, as early as possible, children with hearing impairments.

PITS AND TAGS
(Birth–12 Months)

What is happening inside my baby's body?
A *skin tag* is an extra piece of skin. It can appear anywhere on the body, but the most common spot for a baby is on the face, directly next to the ear (known as the *preauricular area*).

A *pit* is a small hole — about an eighth of an inch wide and usually less than one inch deep — in the skin. Sometimes the pit produces an oily substance called *sebum*. Again, the most common spot for a pit on a newborn is on the face, in the preauricular area. Preauricular pits and tags are usually normal.

What can I do?
There is nothing for you to do when it comes to preauricular tags and pits. These are normal variations and do not need to be treated in any special way.

When does my doctor need to be involved?
Your doctor needs to be involved if a pit or tag looks infected. Signs of infection include redness of the area, warmth when the skin is touched, and pus or fluid coming from the site of the pit or tag.

Sometimes parents want to have skin tags removed for cosmetic purposes. In this case, a doctor removes the tag. This is covered in the section on treatments that follows.

What tests need to be done, and what do the results mean?
Pits and tags typically do not require any type of testing. However, if a pit (or a tag) becomes infected, then bacteria are usually the cause. A culture can be done to determine what bacteria are growing within the pit. This is rarely necessary though, because the bacteria that normally live on skin are the ones that typically infect pits. Therefore, in most cases any antibiotic that treats skin bacteria will treat the bacteria living in pits.

What are the treatments?
Infected preauricular pits need to be treated with antibiotics. Repeatedly infected pits may require surgery.

Tags can be removed by being tied off if the stem is very narrow. To tie off a tag, a thin piece of string (usually the same string used to sew stitches) is tied in a knot at the base of the tag, as close to the face as possible. This cuts off the blood supply to the tag. Over a few days, the tag, together with the string, falls off.

When a parent wants a tag removed but it is too big to be tied off, the tag needs to be cut off by a dermatologist or surgeon. In this case, minor surgery is required.

What are the possible complications?

Pits can become infected because they can trap bacteria. If this happens once or twice, then antibiotics can be used to treat the problem. But if this happens regularly, then your child may require surgery to drain the infection and close the pit.

Rarely pits can be connected to other tissues beneath. When this happens, the connection is called a *sinus tract.* Sinus tracts can facilitate the movement of bacteria from the skin to tissues below. A sinus tract may be present when the pits are repeatedly infected; once the tract is closed, the infections usually resolve. Sinus tract closure requires surgery.

Pits can also suggest other ear problems. Although most children with preauricular pits have normal inner ears and normal hearing, there is a slightly higher chance that a child with a deep pit will have some hearing impairment. Hearing is now checked on most newborns just after delivery. Therefore you will usually know whether or not your baby can hear by the first or second day of life.

There are almost never any complications associated with isolated skin tags. However, when skin tags appear all over your baby's body, this can be the sign of dermatologic or (rarely) neurologic problems. You will need to consult specialists in these fields.

Additional Resources
http://www.nlm.nih.gov/medlineplus/encyclopedia.html (Click on "Pm–Pz," then scroll down to "preauricular tag or pit.")

◆   ◆   ◆

FOLDED EARS
(Birth–1 Month)

What is happening inside my baby's body?
The upper portion of the ear is made of *cartilage* — a firm but bendable substance. While a fetus is growing in the womb, she is squished into a tight space and the cartilage of the growing ear can be folded down. Then, when the baby is born, her ear may look misshapen. But this is entirely temporary. Once the baby is out of the womb, the cartilage is no longer pushed and the ear almost always flattens.

What can I do?
You do not need to do anything about folded ears because they will resolve on their own over time.

When does my doctor need to be involved?
Folded ears are normal and eventually go away, so your doctor rarely does anything about them. If the folding persists, then some doctors will become involved.

What tests need to be done, and what do the results mean?
No tests need to be done because this is a normal and short-lived phenomenon.

What are the treatments?
There are usually no necessary treatments. If the folding does not resolve over time, then some doctors will fashion a plastic cap to cover the outer ear, helping to hold it in place. This is especially useful when a baby continues to fold the cartilage by sleeping on her side.

In extreme cases, the cartilage may be adjusted with surgery. This is an entirely cosmetic procedure, so most surgeons prefer to wait until a child is older — unless the appearance is dramatic.

What are the possible complications?
There are no possible complications of folded ears. The baby's hearing will be normal.

Additional Resources
http://www.med.umich.edu/1libr/pa/pa_newbappe_hhg.htm (Scroll down
to "ears" section.)

EAR TUGGING
(2–12 Months)

What is happening inside my baby's body?
Many parents worry that ear tugging is a sure sign of an ear infection. But ears can be poked, tugged, pulled, and rubbed for any number of reasons. Some babies grab their ears when they are in pain. Others play with them simply because they are accessible. And still others will soothe themselves with ear rubbing. So how can you tell whether your baby is playing, self-soothing, or experiencing pain?

Babies discover their ears when they reach 3 to 4 months of age. Around this time, you may notice that your baby falls asleep fiddling with her ears or pulls on them in a playful manner during the day. The more often this happens — especially when the baby is happy and comfortable — the more likely it is that she is tugging simply to soothe herself. A happy baby who pulls her ears is not uncomfortable.

If your baby is grabbing and pulling her ear while crying, then she may be doing so from pain. The most common cause is *teething*. Teething babies will often poke at or pull on their ears when they are most uncomfortable. This is covered in some detail in the section on teething in chapter 16. Another cause of ear poking is *impacted earwax*. This is not too common, but some especially waxy babies will develop deep wax that becomes irritating after a while. You should never stick anything into the ear, including Q-Tips, even if you think the ear is waxy and may be irritating your baby. And finally there are *ear infections*, the most worrisome cause of ear tugging. These are uncommon in babies younger than six months. They are usually accompanied by a fever and cold symptoms — but not always. In fact there are many babies who do not pull at their ears even when the ears are infected. Sometimes the only sign of infection is a little bit of fussiness.

What can I do?

The very first thing to do is to distinguish whether or not your baby is in pain. If she is happy and comfortable, eating well and sleeping soundly, then the ear tugging should not worry you.

If your baby is uncomfortable, then see if she has a fever. Impacted earwax will not cause fever, but teething or an ear infection may. You can give her a fever reducer to help her feel more comfortable. A teething baby will often put as much in her mouth as possible — she will gnaw on her hands, her toys, a bottle nipple or pacifier, you, and just about anything else in sight. A baby with an ear infection will not do this. Sometimes a teething baby will be more uncomfortable when she is lying down. While this can also be true for a baby with an ear infection, ear infections tend to hurt regardless of the baby's position. Teething is covered in more detail in chapter 16.

If your baby has had wax before and you think this may be the problem, then you can try putting a few drops of oil in the ear. Any type of vegetable oil will work: olive, almond — you name it. First run the bottle under some warm water so that the oil becomes lukewarm. Two or three drops in each ear every night will help to soften the wax, making it easier for the doctor to clean out. Sometimes the wax will dissolve on its own. Never attempt to stick Q-Tips or other narrow objects deep into the ear.

While these general rules can help, you should remember that teething babies can get ear infections and vice versa, and they can have wax at the same time.

When does my doctor need to be involved?

If your baby is tugging her ears in pain, then you will probably want your doctor to take a look. Certainly if the fever is higher than 101°F or the baby is fussy, eating poorly, or sleeping too little or too much, then call your doctor. Anytime the ear itself is red or swollen, or if you see liquid draining from the ear, you should see your doctor.

What tests need to be done, and what do the results mean?

The best test for ear tugging is to have a doctor take a look. Beyond that, there are really no tests that need to be done.

What are the treatments?

Ear tugging in a happy, playful baby needs no treatment. Many babies will soothe themselves by rubbing their ears and will continue to do so all the way through childhood.

If the cause of the tugging is teething pain, then teething rings, gum rubbing, pain-relief medicines, and alternative treatments can be used. They are covered in chapter 16.

Ear infections do not always need to be treated. Viruses cause the vast majority of ear infections, and these cannot be treated with medicine because antibiotics work only on bacterial infections. Instead viral ear infections will usually go away on their own. If there is a bacterial infection, however, then antibiotics will be prescribed. You and your doctor should discuss whether or not your baby needs antibiotics.

Doctors or nurses can remove impacted earwax. The techniques range from using a tiny Q-Tip to scoop out the wax to irrigating the ear canal with warm water. For very hard wax, your doctor may have you use liquid drops for a couple of days to soften the wax, and then you may need to return for another round of cleaning.

What are the possible complications?

Multiple ear infections or untreated ear infections can eventually cause hearing loss. If your child has had multiple ear infections and cannot clear the fluid out of her inner ears, then your doctor may recommend *tympanostomy tubes.* These tubes are inserted surgically by an otolaryngologist (ear, nose, and throat doctor). Tubes are almost never used in infants; toddlers are the most likely group to require them.

Neither teething nor impacted wax has any long-term effect on the ears. Wax is often a lifelong problem, and many adults need to have their ears cleaned by the doctor.

Additional Resources
http://www.nlm.nih.gov/medlineplus/encyclopedia.html (Click on "W," then scroll down to "wax blockage.")
http://www.mayoclinic.com/takecharge/healthdecisionguides/childrensmiddleeearinjury/index.cfm

15

Nose

---◆---

A newborn baby uses his nose to breathe. His mouth is still busy learning how to suck and swallow, so the nose is responsible for air passage. In fact the nose is so critical that typically the very first thing that happens when a baby's head is delivered is that the amniotic fluid is sucked out of the nose with a handheld syringe called a ***nasal aspirator*** (also called a ***bulb syringe***). The obstetrician does this so that when the umbilical cord is cut and the baby must take his first breath, the nose is as clear as possible.

When a baby gets congested, the sound can be tremendous. This is often most dramatic during feeding, when a baby relies entirely on his nose (because his mouth is full). The snorting and gurgling can frighten some parents. The milk itself can travel backward and get stuck up the back of the nose, or a baby can have a cold or allergies. Regardless, the nasal aspirator usually clears the nose quickly.

Babies rely almost entirely on nasal breathing until about two months of age, when breathing is shared between the nose and mouth. This is why it is easier for an older baby to deal with nasal congestion.

CONGESTION AND NOISY BREATHING
(Birth–12 Months)

What is happening inside my baby's body?
For the first two months of life, a baby breathes almost exclusively through his nose. The mouth is for eating, not breathing. The medical term for this is *obligate nose breathing*. Because the nasal passages are small, even a tiny amount of mucus can cause congestion. And because a baby can only breathe through his nose, it can sound pretty dramatic when he is congested.

When the nose produces mucus, the fluid trapped at the back of the nose sounds like a washing machine. Mucus can be produced either when a baby gets sick or in response to irritants in the air — pollens, dust, mold, perfumes, and so on. Fluid can also be trapped at the back of the nose during and after a feeding, when some of the milk travels backward (up the nose) instead of down into the stomach. Teething, which starts anytime after the first couple months of life and results in increased drooling, can also provide a source of extra fluid that gets trapped in the back of the nose.

When there is mucus present, a runny nose is always best because the mucus (or milk or saliva) is draining out. When your baby's nose is not running and he is congested, the fluid is trapped in the back far reaches of his nose. If it drips down the back of his throat, it will cause the baby to cough and gag. This phenomenon is called *postnasal drip.*

What can I do?
Congested babies need to get their noses running. The easiest way for you to do this is to take your baby into a steam shower or steamy bathroom (make sure to avoid the hot water coming in direct contact with you or the baby). The steam will work its way up the baby's nose, and within minutes the baby (and you) will have a runny nose. Then use a *bulb syringe* — the plastic handheld nose-and-mouth sucker — and suck out the draining fluid. Another name for the bulb syringe is a *nasal aspirator.* One or two sucks from each nostril should do the trick. While steam is

fairly safe, you should not stay in the bathroom for too long. Five to fifteen minutes at a time should be plenty.

Humidifiers and vaporizers work similarly to the way steamy bathrooms do, just with a lot less intensity. Moisturized air can be helpful when a child is congested, but it doesn't always help the nose to run. Make sure the humidifier is not on for too long — when droplets of moisture collect on the walls and ceiling, mold can easily grow. Also, clean and disinfect the humidifier regularly.

Another way to get the baby's nose to drain involves squirting liquid up the nose. You can use saline (a saltwater solution available in most drugstores), plain water, or even breast milk. The key is to hold your baby upright so that the fluid is squirted as high up into his nose as possible. Otherwise, if his head is cocked back, the liquid will squirt through his nose and directly into the back of his throat. In this position, the baby will simply swallow or gag on the liquid, which doesn't help the nose to drain at all.

Positioning your baby can help with his breathing as well. When a baby is lying down flat on his back, the congestion and noisy breathing invariably get worse. Mucus pools where the back of the nose meets the throat. So prop him up and let him sleep at an incline, using for example a parent's chest for support or even positioning him in a car seat. In a crib, the mattress can be angled by placing a towel underneath the mattress. Do not put anything (towel, pillow, etc.) directly underneath the baby's head.

When does my doctor need to be involved?

Doctors need to be involved anytime a baby has difficulty breathing. This can be tough for a parent to determine, especially since babies can sound so noisy while actually having no trouble breathing at all. There are some objective ways to determine whether or not your baby is having trouble breathing. Each of the following is a technique to get extra oxygen into the body and therefore can be a sign of breathing difficulty. Call your doctor if your baby displays two or more of these features or if you have any doubt.

Flaring the nostrils with each breath. This allows more air to flow into the airway and lungs.

Visible flexing or contracting of the long muscles at the neck — between the jaw and the shoulders. This pulls on the tops of the lungs, increasing the size of the lungs and the amount of air they can hold. The notch between the collarbones, called the sternal notch, may also be pulling in with each breath.

Visible flexing or contracting of the muscles between the ribs. This pulls on the lungs to open them horizontally. It also increases lung size and capacity. In order to see these muscles pulling, you can draw an imaginary line from your baby's armpit to his hip. Halfway along that line, look for the ribs moving with each breath. They will seem like a row of bucket handles pulling up and down.

Moving the belly up and down in an exaggerated way with each breath. This forces the diaphragm down, increasing the depth of the lungs and their air capacity.

Breathing fast. This increases the flow of air into the lungs simply by speeding it up. Remember that babies who have a fever will breathe fast to blow off their fever. This is *not* a sign of difficulty breathing — in the case of fever it is a very good way to cool down the baby. When the temperature is normal, the normal rate of breathing is age dependent: newborns breathe 40 to 60 times per minute; babies breathe 25 to 35 times per minute; young children breathe 20 to 30 times per minute; and adults typically breathe 12 to 14 times per minute. If your child has a fever, then you may give a fever-reducing medicine. When the temperature is normal, reassess the respiratory rate.

All of these signs are helpful in assessing a (relatively) calm child. In a crying baby, however, they are not necessarily accurate indicators of difficulty breathing. This is because a crying child will flare his nostrils, open his mouth, pull at the muscles between his ribs, and breathe fast as part of crying. Breathing is discussed in further detail in chapter 18.

Whenever you are in doubt, you should call your doctor or 911 immediately. When your child is having difficulty breathing, *never* put anything in his mouth, including food or liquid.

What tests need to be done, and what do the results mean?

Very few tests need to be done in order to treat congestion. Environmental irritants are among the most common causes of congestion. If a baby is irritated by something in the environment — carpet dust, for example — then removing him from that environment is the best "test" of cause and effect. Other irritants such as foods can also cause congestion. Again, removing the food (or changing the formula type) may identify the cause of congestion.

Traditional allergy tests do not work well on infants; this topic is covered in more detail in the section on eczema in chapter 11. Therefore trial and error — removing the suspected cause of the congestion and seeing what happens — is often the best test in these cases.

When a baby has difficulty breathing beyond simple congestion, a battery of tests may be required. These are covered in more detail in chapter 18.

What are the treatments?

Your doctor may recommend various approaches to keep your baby comfortable. These include positioning him upright and using steam or nose drops to remove the fluid blocking the nasal passages. There are some medicines on the market that treat congestion, but these do not work much better than the home remedies. Many of the over-the-counter nasal sprays should be used with caution in babies, as these sprays can have chemical stimulants. Most pediatricians do not recommend cough and cold suspensions for babies under 6 to 12 months of age.

If the source of congestion is an irritant causing allergy — carpets, cats, cigarette smoke, and so on — then removing the irritant is the best treatment. Sometimes it takes a little trial and error to figure out what the allergen is.

What are the possible complications?

Nasal congestion rarely becomes complicated. If it lingers for too long, then the mucus congesting the nose can back up into the sinuses — the spaces in the bones above the cheeks, next to the nose, and surrounding the eyes. Babies have small sinuses, and these can become clogged with mucus. When this happens, infants can develop sinus infections or middle-ear infections. These are often accompanied by fever, irritability, and thick nasal discharge. In rare cases, postnasal drip can drain into the lungs, leading to bronchitis or pneumonia.

Additional Resources
http://www.nlm.nih.gov/medlineplus/encyclopedia.html (Click on "N," then scroll down to "nasal congestion.")
http://www.mayoclinic.com/invoke.cfm?id=PR00038

16

Mouth

In the womb, a baby sucks her thumb and swallows small amounts of her own amniotic fluid. Once the baby is born, she must use her mouth for much more. She will learn how to drink larger amounts at one time and how to coordinate a swallow. She will begin to make sounds and eventually will talk. She will come to rely on her mouth and not just her nose for breathing. A baby soothes herself with her mouth by sucking and lets you know when there is a problem by crying.

A newborn learns to use her mouth very quickly. However, there can be some hurdles. The tongue — critical to many of these functions — can be attached too tightly to the base of the mouth. This can make eating difficult for the child and sometimes painful for the mother. The mouth can also become infected, most commonly with yeast. This can cause pain with swallowing and can eventually limit a baby's ability to eat. And as a mouthful of teeth begin to erupt over the first several months of life, the pain of teething and the accompanying drool can cause some difficulties.

TONGUE-TIED (ANKYLOGLOSSIA)
(Birth)

What is happening inside my baby's body?
The *frenulum* is the tiny piece of tissue that attaches the tongue to the bottom of the mouth. Open your mouth and lift your tongue — it is easy to see the stringlike tissue. The frenulum is attached to the tongue at different points in different people. The closer it is to the tip of the tongue, the less the tongue is able to stick out because the frenulum anchors the tongue to the base of the mouth.

The term *tongue-tied* (also called *ankyloglossia*) refers to a frenulum that attaches so close to the tip of the tongue that tongue movement is severely limited. When this is the case, a baby can find it difficult to eat. Some tongues look V shaped at their tip because the attachment extends all the way to the front.

About 1 in 1,000 babies is born tongue-tied. Most babies feed well despite the attachment, so nothing needs to be done. However, if a tongue-tied baby has trouble sucking because he cannot move his tongue well or if breast-feeding is painful for the mother due to the position of the frenulum, then the frenulum must be clipped. This allows more movement of the tongue and will lead to more effective sucking.

What can I do?
You don't need to do anything if your baby is feeding well. There are many babies with mild cases of ankyloglossia who feed and grow well, in which case a doctor doesn't need to intervene.

When does my doctor need to be involved?
If the limited tongue movement is making breast-feeding painful or if your baby is not gaining weight well because of poor breast- or bottle-feeding, then this should be brought to a doctor's attention.

What tests need to be done, and what do the results mean?
No tests need to be done. If the baby is not feeding or gaining well, then the ankyloglossia is severe enough that it needs to be treated.

What are the treatments?
The frenulum can be cut — a procedure called a *frenectomy.* This is a simple clipping procedure that requires no pain medication. The tongue is held in one hand and the frenulum is clipped using a small blade. There is rarely any bleeding because the blood supply to this particular area is so small. There is minimal pain — babies are usually feeding within minutes after the procedure.

There is some controversy over how a frenulum should be cut, especially with specific types of ankyloglossia. Some surgeons worry that scar tissue may build up, reforming the frenulum and creating a bigger problem. These doctors usually recommend a frenectomy using a laser, which requires a visit to a specialist's office. Others recommend a *Z-plasty,* which is a style of cutting the frenulum (the cut is made in the shape of the letter "Z"). Z-plasties are more painful, sometimes requiring sedation. The most commonly performed frenectomy is a simple snip of the tissue, done in a pediatrician's office.

What are the possible complications?
The main complication of being tongue-tied is poor feeding with subsequent poor weight gain. Almost as common is pain for breast-feeding moms. Typically as soon as the frenulum is cut, the baby feeds better and the mom is far more comfortable.

The main (but rare) complication of frenectomy is scarring, with the tongue reattaching to the base of the mouth. A small surgical procedure removes the scar tissue.

Controversy exists over whether or not ankyloglossia can cause speech problems. Some argue that the pronunciation of certain sounds — such as "th" — may be more difficult for children with more limited tongue movement. There is no medical consensus on this.

Additional Resources
http://www.entcolumbia.org/tongue.htm
http://www.nlm.nih.gov/medlineplus/encyclopedia.html (Click on "To–Tz,"
then scroll down to "tongue-tie.")

◆　　◆　　◆

THRUSH (YEAST IN THE MOUTH)
(Birth–12 Months)

What is happening inside my baby's body?
Thrush is an infection often found in the mouth. It is caused
by yeast, the most common of which is known by its medical
name, *Candida albicans*. This organism is normally present in
the human body. It likes to grow in warm, dark, moist environments such as the mouth and the vagina. It can grow on a breast-
feeding mother's nipples, as well as on bottle nipples and pacifiers.
When yeast grows too rapidly, it can cause minor problems. The
warmer and wetter the environment, the more likely *Candida* will
grow out of control.

When a baby has thrush, white patches coat the tongue and
the sidewalls of the mouth. Sometimes breast milk or formula can
coat the tongue or inside of the cheeks — looking a lot like
thrush — but milk never sticks to the surface. Therefore, in order
to determine whether it is really thrush, you can scrape the white
plaque with a fingernail or tongue depressor. If it comes off, then it
is not thrush; if it sticks firmly to the inside of the cheek, then it is.

Yeast grows rapidly after the use of antibiotics. This happens
because antibiotics aimed at invading bacteria also kill the normal bacteria that live in the body. These normal bacteria usually
keep yeast in check; when they are not around, yeast grows out if
control.

Yeast infections are not painful for every baby, but some parents notice that when their baby's mouth is filled with white
plaques, she does not eat as well as usual. These babies often
wince or fuss with feeding. Breast-feeding moms will often report
itching or a small amount of burning on the nipple when the
baby has a yeast infection. This usually indicates that the yeast
has spread to the breast as well. Surprisingly, though the yeast

looks very white in a baby's mouth, it is largely invisible on the mother's breast.

What can I do?

Thrush can go away on its own. Parents can try scraping the side-walls of the mouth to make sure that the white plaque is truly thrush and not milk that has temporarily adhered itself.

In order to get rid of yeast anywhere on the body, you should keep the affected area as cool and dry as possible. This is largely impossible in the mouth, but moms can dry their nipples well after feeding, and bottle nipples and pacifiers can be sterilized and air-dried after use. This can be achieved using a sterilizer, or the bottle nipples and pacifiers can be placed in rapidly boiling water for one to two minutes and then air-dried. To dry the breast nipples after feeding, you can blow on them, fan them with your hands, or even dry them with a hair-dryer on the "cool" setting. Mothers who pump their breast milk should sterilize the pump parts as well.

When thrush affects older babies who put everything in sight inside their mouths, toys need to be washed too. Babies who are eating solids should be given fewer dairy products and sugar-containing foods, as these help to promote yeast growth. The one exception is yogurt with live cultures (also called *acidophilus*). Acidophilus is a bacteria that helps to stop yeast multiplication. Therefore, even though yogurt is a dairy product, if it contains acidophilus it may be helpful in the case of thrush.

When does my doctor need to be involved?

Notify your doctor when your baby has thrush so that treatment can be started. This consultation can be done over the phone, especially if you are sure that the plaques are indeed thrush. However, a doctor should see a baby with thrush who does not improve despite medical treatment or a baby who is in significant pain.

What tests need to be done, and what do the results mean?

Tests rarely need to be done in the case of thrush. In some in-stances of recurrent thrush, it may be helpful to scrape a bit of the fungus and send it to a laboratory. The lab can check the type of yeast and test it to see how sensitive it is to various medical treatments.

What are the treatments?

Because yeast loves warm, dark, and moist environments, the best way to get rid of it is to create a cool, bright, and dry climate. However, this is nearly impossible inside the mouth. Therefore, in addition to the approaches described above, there are antifungal medicines that help get rid of thrush. These include nystatin and miconazole, and other medicines ending in "-azole." The medicines must be used for several days. Most are applied directly to the involved areas — when yeast appears in the mouth, medicines are given in the form of a liquid, whereas when yeast appears in the diaper area as a rash, creams are used (see chapter 11). It is important for breast-feeding moms to remember to put the medicine on their breasts as well; otherwise the yeast will continue to be passed back and forth between mother and baby.

What are the possible complications?

Because thrush can be painful, the baby may eat significantly less than she normally does, leading to poor weight gain. If the thrush extends all the way to the back of the mouth, then it can grow down the esophagus — the tube that carries food from the mouth to the stomach. When this happens, swallowing is extremely uncomfortable. When a baby refuses to drink because of the pain, she risks becoming dehydrated. If yeast grows and grows, it can spread to other parts of the body. Dissemination of a yeast infection is very rare. In all of these cases, more aggressive antifungal therapy may be needed.

Additional Resources
http://www.mayoclinic.com (Click on the letter "T" under "find information fast," then click on "thrush, oral.")
http://www.nlm.nih.gov/medlineplus/encyclopedia.html (Click on "O," then scroll down to "oral thrush.")

◆   ◆   ◆

SUCKING BLISTERS
(Birth–4 Months)

What is happening inside my baby's body?
Many babies develop blisters in the middle of the top or bottom lip. These clear or white swellings are a result of positioning and sucking during feeding. They can be firm or soft, chapped or smooth.

These sucking blisters are normal and will go away with time. Sometimes they appear and then disappear, only to appear again. They do not cause pain or difficulty with feeding.

What can I do?
Parents do not need to do anything about sucking blisters. They will come and go, and they are completely normal.

When does my doctor need to be involved?
If other blisters appear elsewhere on the lips or inside the mouth, or if they seem to be associated with fever, irritability, or pain during feeding, then call your doctor. Blisters that appear in groups or along with other symptoms are not sucking blisters. They may be caused by an infection.

What tests need to be done, and what do the results mean?
No tests need to be done for feeding blisters because they are normal and will go away with time.

What are the treatments?
There are no treatments for normal sucking blisters. Over time, a baby will change his positioning while feeding. The upper lip will become less involved in the sucking process and the blister will slowly disappear.

What are the possible complications?
There are no complications with normal sucking blisters. Babies with these blisters feed normally and gain weight well.

Additional Resources
http://www.med.umich.edu/1libr/pa/pa_newbappe_hhg.htm (Scroll down
to "mouth" section.)

◆   ◆   ◆

TEETHING
(3-12 Months)

What is happening inside my baby's body?
When your baby is born, his primary teeth are largely formed and
stored inside his gums. In order for the teeth to emerge, they
must travel through the gum to the surface. The first teeth appear
anytime between birth and 18 months of age. Yes, there are (very
rarely) babies born with a tooth! But the most common time for
teeth to erupt is sometime between 6 and 12 months. *Teething*
refers to the entire journey of a tooth. It is often associated with
some pain, but some babies teethe without feeling any pain at all.

Contrary to popular belief, when a baby is teething, his tooth is
not necessarily ready to erupt and become visible. In fact the
signs of teething usually begin weeks — or even months — before a tooth ever appears, as early as two or three months of age.
And remember, a baby must cut 20 teeth before the process is
complete!

As the tooth moves its way through the gum, it cuts through
nerves and pieces of tissue, sometimes resulting in swelling and
inflammation of the gums. This may be painful for your baby,
causing soreness, tenderness, and excessive drooling. Teething
pain is thought to be most acute when a baby is lying down
because the discomfort from the gum may be felt in the baby's
ears. When a baby is propped up, the pain in the ears is less
severe.

The excessive drooling associated with teething results in swallowed saliva, which can fill the stomach and reduce the baby's
appetite. Saliva passing through the intestines may result in looser
stools.

What can I do?

Some babies can soothe themselves by gnawing on their fists or teething toys. This is effective the same way that rubbing a sore muscle sometimes eases the pain. Teething rings soothe the gums by gentle massage. They come in all shapes and sizes, and depending on the child, different teething rings work better than others. Some teething rings have a vibration option, adding another layer of massage to the irritated gum. Some babies prefer to gnaw on their fingers or fists (or their parents). This approach often works just as well as a teething ring.

Cool materials — such as refrigerated teething rings, spoons, or chilled damp washcloths — can also help to reduce the inflammation and swelling along the gum, alleviating pain. Note, however, that it is important to avoid frozen teething rings that can injure the gums or cheeks with freezer burn.

There are a variety of medicines available for teething. These include homeopathic remedies, gels, and general pain relievers. They are covered in the section that follows.

When does my doctor need to be involved?

Doctors rarely need to be involved in the care of teething. However, it may be difficult for you to determine the cause of your baby's fussiness — whether he has an ear infection or his teeth are just starting to make their way through the gums. The symptoms of ear infections and teething can be quite similar. In both cases, a baby can have fever, ear pain with subsequent tugging, decreased appetite, or fussiness.

Luckily, in some cases the two can be distinguished. The fever associated with teething rarely goes above 101°F (38.3°C), whereas the fever of an ear infection can be higher. The ear tugging associated with teething almost always occurs when your baby is lying down, whereas the ear tugging of an ear infection occurs in all positions (but is often worse when lying down). And finally, the decreased appetite associated with teething is often a direct result of massive saliva production. When swallowed, saliva fills the stomach and leaves room for little else. There is typically less drooling with an ear infection. Often it is impossible to tell the difference between teething and ear infection without a doctor taking a look.

Most babies are teething on-again, off-again until they are 18 months old, and simultaneous ear infections may occur coincidentally. Other conditions — such as a sore throat or fussiness due to a viral illness — can mimic teething pain. When in doubt, you should visit your doctor.

What tests need to be done, and what do the results mean?

No tests need to be done when a child is teething. Instead a doctor can take a look inside the ears with a light to determine whether the baby's symptoms are caused by an ear infection or simple teething. Sometimes a doctor will mention that the gums look swollen, but remember that gums don't have to swell for teething pain to occur.

What are the treatments?

Medical treatments for teething can be divided into three general categories: topical treatments that are rubbed onto the gums, oral pain relievers, and alternative therapies.

Topical treatments for teething usually come in the form of a gel. These gels have medicines that are meant to reduce swelling and pain in the gums. The most common ingredients include salicylic acid, lignocaine, tannic acid, menthol, thymol, glycerol, and ethanol. However, there is no evidence that most of these gels actually work. In addition, the ones that do seem to work only do so for a very short time. In fact the relief they provide may be due largely to how they are applied: gels are rubbed on, and the rubbing creates the same massagelike effect as gnawing on a fist or a teething ring.

Oral pain relievers come in two main types — acetaminophen (the active ingredient in Tylenol) and ibuprofen (the active ingredient in Advil and Motrin). Baby aspirin is a misnomer and should *never* be given to infants or children because it has been associated with **Reye's syndrome,** an illness involving liver failure and brain disease. Acetaminophen is safe for use at all ages and is dosed according to weight. It is a very effective fever reducer and also helps to relieve pain. Ibuprofen may be used in children older than six months. It too is dosed by weight. Ibuprofen is both an anti-inflammatory and fever reducer. More specific information about these medications can be obtained from your doctor.

Alternative remedies come in many preparations. There are drops, tablets, gels, and solutions, depending on the style of therapy. Many herbal remedies work because they have active ingredients that are potent anti-inflammatories, reducing the swelling and pain in the gums. Remember that even though these are non-prescription remedies, they are still drugs and therefore need to be mentioned when your doctor asks what medication you are giving your baby.

What are the possible complications?

Teething itself has very few complications. Because it stimulates excessive drool, the swallowed saliva may reduce your baby's appetite. This may also cause loose stools. Sometimes a little rash will form around the mouth.

Low-grade fever may result from natural chemicals that are released as the tooth moves its way through the gum. Fever associated with teething is almost never above 101°F (38.3°C).

Bleeding is a rare complication of teething. It occurs when the gum is very swollen and the tooth erupts through, breaking some tiny blood vessels. The bleeding usually lasts only a few seconds. Brief oozing of blood may also occur. Sometimes parents will notice it only because there is a spot of blood on the baby's sheets or clothes. Other times blood collects underneath the swollen gum and looks blue, like a bruise.

Excessive bleeding or oozing that does not stop on its own requires medical attention.

Additional Resources
http://www.medem.com (Go to "search medical library" in upper right-hand corner and type in "teething.")
http://www.dentistry.uiowa.edu/public/oral/infants.html
http://www.nlm.nih.gov/medlineplus/encyclopedia.html (Click on "T–Tn," then scroll down to "teething.")

17

Neck

◆

When a baby is born, the neck is floppy because its muscles are weak in the first few weeks of life. Gradually these muscles become stronger and are able to hold the head upright. But if the muscle on one side of the neck is shorter or weaker than its counterpart on the other, then the head will cock to one side.

The neck does more than just hold up the head. It is the passageway for both food and air. The *trachea* carries air from the mouth to the lungs while the *esophagus* carries food to the stomach. The trachea is surrounded by cartilage for strength. This cartilage, however, is not always formed at birth, so the trachea may be floppy or easily compressible. If the tissues of the neck weigh down on the trachea, then breathing sounds become loud and raspy. As both the neck and the trachea strengthen, the sounds usually disappear.

The neck is long and skinny at birth but rapidly fills out with fatty tissue. The neck develops skin folds that roll over one another, trapping drool or dribbled milk. These fat folds are a sign of health in a young baby, but when you investigate what's between them, you may find that the area often looks irritated.

TORTICOLLIS
(Birth–3 Months)

What is happening inside my baby's body?

Torticollis literally means "twisted neck." It is the medical term used to describe head tilting or turning to one side as a result of slightly unequal neck muscles. Torticollis is extremely common in newborns because fetuses are crammed into such a small space. During development, the neck bends to help the baby fit inside the womb. As a result of this positioning, one of a pair of neck muscles (called the **sternocleidomastoid** or **SCM**) stretches longer than the other. When a baby is born, he will prefer to hold his head to the side of the shorter muscle — if he holds his head straight or turns to the other side, then he must stretch the shorter muscle in his neck.

Sometimes a mass or swelling can be felt over the shorter muscle. This typically results from minor trauma during delivery, when one SCM is pulled and then becomes slightly inflamed. Over the next one or two weeks, the traumatized muscle swells and develops a lumpy appearance. In this case, the baby will prefer to hold his head tilted in the direction of the injured muscle to minimize stretching the swollen area. As the swelling resolves on its own (and it always does), the muscle might heal too well, forming a fibrous band. The band further limits movement at the neck because it is tough and not stretchy like the original muscle.

Torticollis can also be acquired after birth. This can happen when a baby prefers to hold his head in one position, either because the shape of the skull provides a flat surface that is comfortable to rest on or because a parent places the baby in the same position (during feeding or in a car seat) over and over again. These sources of **positional torticollis** result in the shortening of one of the neck muscles simply because the neck is repeatedly kinked in one direction.

What can I do?

If you notice that your baby holds his head preferentially to one side, then mention it to your pediatrician. Torticollis can be difficult for a pediatrician to see if your baby is feeding during the visit or if he spends most of the appointment in your arms.

Parents can do gentle stretching exercises with the baby to help increase mobility of the shorter muscle. Alternating the feeding position can also help to stretch the neck in one direction and then the other. Changing the position of the headrest pillow in the car seat can help as well.

You should rotate the head position of any sleeping baby, but especially a baby with torticollis. When the neck muscles are uneven, a baby will clearly prefer to sleep with his head turned to one particular side. Because the bones of the skull change shape dramatically over the first few months of life, if a baby sleeps in the same position day and night, then the skull can flatten in one spot (see the section on *plagiocephaly* in chapter 12). This can create a vicious cycle: if the baby prefers to hold the head in a certain position *and* there is a flat spot on the skull that serves as a nice shelf on which to rest the head, then fixing both problems can be twice as difficult. This is called *torticollis-plagiocephaly sequence.* So placing your sleeping baby on his back with his head sometimes turned to the right side and other times to the left and still other times straight in the middle will help resolve the torticollis and minimize head flattening.

When does my doctor need to be involved?

Your doctor should be aware of torticollis, but it often resolves on its own. If the neck muscles continue to be uneven past the first 2 or 3 months of life, a doctor will often introduce stretching exercises or refer the baby to physical therapy.

What tests need to be done, and what do the results mean?

The tests to check for torticollis are simply maneuvers done during a physical exam. A doctor will look at how the baby holds his head and then will rotate the head and neck gently from side to side, checking for limitations. Sometimes a small mass (that feels like an olive) can be felt along the shorter side of the neck.

What are the treatments?

Over the first several weeks of life, torticollis often resolves with gentle stretching exercises of the neck. If this does not solve the problem entirely, then your doctor may want you to consult a physical therapist. Physical therapists utilize coordinated exercises to stretch the SCM. The torticollis should resolve within three months of starting physical therapy.

In very rare cases, a baby may not respond to physical therapy. If the torticollis persists, then surgery may be necessary. The surgery involves cutting the tight SCM on the shorter side of the neck so that the muscles can stretch. Physical therapy is still required, even after surgery, in order to further stretch and strengthen the muscle.

What are the possible complications?

The main potential complication of torticollis is plagiocephaly, or flattened head. As described above, this can happen when a baby prefers to keep his head in one particular position. The bones of the skull change shape over the first several months of life, so repeatedly sleeping or sitting in the same position puts pressure on one specific part of the skull, often causing it to flatten. For more about plagiocephaly, see chapter 12.

Additional Resources
http://www.pedisurg.com/PtEduc/Torticollis.htm
http://www.nlm.nih.gov/medlineplus/encyclopedia.html (Click on "To–Tz,"
then scroll down to "torticollis.")

◆   ◆   ◆

NARROW AIRWAY AND STRIDOR
(Birth–12 Months)

What is happening inside my baby's body?

Stridor is the medical term describing a low-pitched or squeaky sound that can be heard when a child inhales. It is caused by narrowing of the airway — the tube carrying air from the mouth down to the lungs. The airway may be narrowed for a number of reasons: a foreign object (such as food or a small part from a toy) can get stuck in the airway, or the passageway can become swollen in the presence of infection or inflammation. Perhaps the most common cause of stridor in a young baby has to do with the way his airway is built.

The passage for air is made of floppy tissue, held up by tough cartilage. If the cartilage is not entirely formed, then the floppy tube can fold on itself and cause a squeaking sound when air is inhaled. The same can happen when the tube itself is too narrow. These conditions are generally referred to as *tracheomalacia* (narrowing of the lower part of the airway) or *laryngomalacia* (narrowing of the upper part of the airway). In these conditions, stridor shows up just after birth and typically goes away as the airway grows and strengthens.

Infections that cause swelling in or around the airway can lead to stridor. The most dangerous of these is called *epiglottitis,* in which an infection causes swelling of the epiglottis — a piece of cartilage located at the base of the tongue that is responsible for preventing food from entering the airway during swallowing. When this area gets infected, it causes sudden-onset breathing problems that can progressively worsen, potentially leading to complete airway obstruction. There is so much swelling that air cannot get in or out of the lungs, resulting in a medical emergency. A child with epiglottitis will look very sick and may be seated in a tripod position (sitting on his bottom, leaning forward onto his hands) in order to make himself most comfortable. The most common cause of epiglottitis is a bacteria called *Haemophilus influenzae* type B. Fortunately this bacteria is now very rare, as children are vaccinated against it (see chapter 31).

Another common cause of stridor is *croup.* Croup is the inflammation and obstruction that result from a viral infection of the upper airway. The stridor and barky cough of croup almost always get worse at night and resolve during the day, but in some extreme cases, the barking goes around the clock. Croup typically lasts three to five days. Because it is caused by a viral infection, it does not respond to antibiotics.

When the airway suddenly swells due to allergy — a phenomenon called *anaphylaxis* — stridor can result. A child with anaphylaxis will likely have swelling at the lips and hives on his skin. Lip swelling is considered a sign of potential airway narrowing.

Rarely a blood vessel or other structure in the neck inadvertently wraps itself around the airway during fetal development, applying pressure on the tube from the outside. This causes airway narrowing, resulting in the squeaking sound of stridor. Structures wrapped around a tube are called *webs* or *rings.*

Finally, abnormalities in the vocal cords can cause stridor. If one or both vocal cords are paralyzed, then the space in the airway becomes narrow because the normally mobile vocal cord cannot move out of the way to make room for air passage. Again, when air has to get through a narrowed passage, stridor can result.

What can I do?

You should alert your child's doctor when you hear a low-pitched or squeaking sound with each breath. Sometimes sitting the baby upright — in a car seat, chair, or swing — can help to take pressure off the air passage. If swelling from inflammation or infection (especially croup) is the cause of the stridor, then cool mist or cold air may help to reduce the swelling. The baby can be bundled in warm clothes or blankets and then taken outside into the cool night air (fog is ideal). Often, alternating for 10 minutes each between cool air and steam can help to decrease stridor significantly.

Anytime a baby is struggling to breathe, you should call 911 or your doctor immediately.

When does my doctor need to be involved?

A doctor should be involved anytime your baby makes unusual noises with every breath or is having difficulty breathing. The latter can be difficult for you to determine, especially since babies can sound so noisy while actually having no trouble breathing at all. There are some objective ways to tell whether or not your baby is having trouble breathing. Each of the following is a technique to get extra oxygen into the body and therefore can be a sign of breathing difficulty. Call your doctor if your baby displays two or more of these features or if you are in doubt.

Flaring the nostrils with each breath. This allows more air to flow into the airway and lungs.

Visible flexing or contracting of the long muscles at the neck — between the jaw and the shoulders. This pulls on the tops of the lungs, increasing the size of the lungs and their air capacity. The notch between the collarbones, called the sternal notch, may also be pulling in with each breath.

Visible flexing or contracting of the muscles between the ribs. This pulls on the lungs to open them horizontally. It also increases the size of the lungs and their air capacity. In order to see these muscles pulling, you can draw an imaginary line from the baby's armpit to his hip. Halfway along that line, look for the ribs moving with each breath. They will seem like a row of bucket handles pulling up and down.

Moving the belly up and down in an exaggerated way with each breath. This forces the diaphragm down, increasing the depth of the lungs and their air capacity.

Breathing fast. This increases the flow of air into the lungs simply by speeding it up. Remember that babies who have a fever will breathe fast to blow off their fever. This is *not* a sign of difficulty breathing — in the case of fever it is a very good way to cool down the baby. When the temperature is normal, the normal rate of breathing is age dependent: newborns breathe 40 to 60 times per minute; babies breathe 25 to 35 times per minute; young children breathe 20 to 30 times per minute; and adults typically breathe 12 to 14 times per minute. If your child has a fever, then you may give a fever-reducing medicine. When the temperature is normal, reassess the respiratory rate.

All of these signs are helpful in assessing a (relatively) calm child. In a crying baby, however, they are not necessarily accurate indicators of difficulty breathing. This is because a crying child will flare his nostrils, open his mouth, pull at the muscles between his ribs, and breathe fast as part of crying. Breathing is covered in more detail in chapter 18.

When in doubt, you should call your doctor or 911 immediately. When your child is having difficulty breathing, you should *never* put anything in his mouth, including food or liquid.

What tests need to be done, and what do the results mean?
There are several tests that may be done when your child is having difficulty breathing. These are reviewed extensively in chapter 18. In the case of stridor, an X ray of the neck may be done to look at how the structures are formed. Sometimes a liquid called *barium* is used during the X ray — this liquid is swallowed in the form of a drink and helps to outline different tubes that travel down the neck by distinguishing between the tube that carries food (esophagus) and the one that carries air (trachea).

In persistent or extreme cases of stridor, a neck specialist — called an otolaryngologist, or ear, nose, and throat (ENT) doctor — may perform more extensive tests. These tests involve placing a tiny camera down the baby's airway to look at how it is shaped from the inside. Pictures may also be taken using a CT scan or an MRI, which will show both the airway and the surrounding structures.

Sometimes blood tests are required in order to make sure that the baby is getting adequate oxygen. A pulse oximeter may also be used. The blood tests will usually include a complete blood count, a sedimentation rate, and a blood culture. These tests and instruments are reviewed in chapter 29.

What are the treatments?
The treatment of stridor depends on its cause. When a baby with tracheomalacia or laryngomalacia is stable, the most common approach is simply observation over time. As your child grows, his airway will get bigger and stronger. Eventually it should no longer collapse on itself. While waiting for your child to outgrow stridor, you may be able to help by placing him in a car seat (or some other upright position that keeps his head elevated) during sleep.

Medications can be used when difficulty breathing and stridor result from acute inflammation and swelling of the airway. One such medicine is a *steroid.* Steroids can rapidly reduce swelling inside the airway. They may be given by injection, as a liquid taken by mouth, or in a mist that is blown through the baby's mouth and down into his lungs (this form is called a *nebulized treatment*). In cases where the swelling is secondary to severe allergy, *epinephrine* may be used in addition to steroids.

Another type of medication is a muscle relaxant called *albuterol*. This medicine relaxes the muscles that line the airways in the lungs so that the tubes carrying air can open to their maximum size. This medication is only effective when the muscles are clenched tight or in spasm. Albuterol can be given in liquid or mist form.

In rare cases, the airway will be so narrow that a breathing tube must be inserted to allow oxygen to get to the lungs. The *endotracheal tube (ETT)* is rarely necessary and is covered in detail in chapters 18 and 28. Epiglottitis represents such dramatic swelling of part of the airway that a breathing tube may be temporarily required.

When stridor is caused by a bacterial infection, antibiotics must be used. Antibiotics are often given intravenously (directly into the bloodstream) because a child with a swollen airway will have trouble swallowing medications. Intravenous forms are also more potent and faster acting.

If the cause of airway narrowing is something pushing from the outside such as a blood vessel or other structure wrapped around the trachea, then that structure usually must be removed. This is a surgical treatment performed by an otolaryngologist or a pediatric surgeon. A surgeon may also choose to prop the airway open from the inside by placing a device called a *stent* inside the airway to hold it open.

What are the possible complications?

Stridor can be a sign that air is not able to get into and out of the lungs with ease. Therefore the complications of stridor are the same as the complications for any problem with breathing or low oxygen levels. These are covered extensively in chapter 18.

The most frightening complication is the cessation of breathing. This can happen when the airway or lungs are overwhelmed with infection or inflammation, when they are completely obstructed, or when the lungs get too tired to breathe after several hours (or days) of hard work.

Infection in the airway can spread to the lungs and then elsewhere in the body, causing infection in the blood, bones, urine, or even spinal fluid and brain. Other complications of lung infection are covered in more detail in the section on breathing in chapter 18.

Additional Resources

http://www.pedisurg.com/PtEducENT/Stridor&laryngomalacia.htm
http://www.lpch.org/DiseaseHealthInfo/HealthLibrary/respire/stridor.html
http://www.vh.org/Providers/Textbooks/ElectricAirway/Text/MICEpiglotitis.html

◆　　◆　　◆

IRRITATED SKIN FOLDS
(Birth–6 Months)

What is happening inside my baby's body?

As you will notice just after your baby is born, the skin on your baby's neck folds over onto itself. As she starts to gain weight, the folds become very fat and even more redundant. Add to this that a baby younger than 4 or 5 months does not hold her head up very well. Even as the neck grows stronger, her head flops from side to side, so the skin folds bunch up even more.

The deepest grooves of the neck may begin to look red and irritated. The irritation comes from the skin underneath the folds rubbing on itself. Because the baby cannot hold her head up on her own, the folded skin does not get much air. Some babies will sweat a little bit, which collects in the folds and irritates the skin even more.

When you separate the folds with your fingers, you may find a white cheesy film. This film may be made of old milk or powder that had been used to soothe the area or may even be an infection. Milk gets trapped in the skin folds after a baby spits up. If you don't clean the neck well, then it is easy for small amounts of milk to trickle in. Once there, the milk congeals slightly, forming a cheesy-looking substance. If the milk is left for a couple of hours, then it will start to smell. Powdering the area under the neck will also create a thick white film. The powder mixes with moisture trapped in the skin folds, and as the baby moves her head, the powder clumps. Again, after a while, the powder will begin to smell. Infections can also cause a white film, but this is rare. More often infections just look very red and irritated deep in the folds. If there is a white film, then it may be pus or broken skin.

The most common infection in the neck folds is *yeast.* This is the same infection that causes thrush in the mouth and yeast infections in the diaper area. Although thrush in the mouth looks white and thick, yeast on the skin usually just looks red and shiny. Yeast likes to grow in areas that are warm, moist, and dark. Therefore the thicker the skin folds, the deeper the creases and the more likely yeast will grow. Bacteria can also cause infections in the skin folds of the neck. Unlike yeast, these tend to cause breaks in the skin and rapidly spreading areas of redness.

What can I do?
Air out the neck. You can prop open the skin folds and gently wipe the deep crevasses with a damp cloth. Then continue to hold open the folds and dry the area by patting it with a dry towel, fanning it with your hand, or blowing on it. Some parents use a hair dryer on the cool setting to get the deepest, wettest sections dry. Air is the best way to minimize irritation and prevent infection, especially with yeast.

In general, avoid powdering the neck. If you must use a powder, then try cornstarch in small amounts. Hold open the folds of the neck and dust off any extra powder so that it does not congeal and form a white cheesy layer.

When your baby spits up, try to clean her off as quickly as possible. If you see milk heading into the neck creases, then gently clean between the skin folds.

When does my doctor need to be involved?
If the skin folds look bright red and cleaning the area is painful for your baby, then call your doctor. The skin may be infected with bacteria. Other signs of bacterial infection include peeling or blistering skin, pus, a foul smell that does not go away with

cleaning, and spreading redness. You should see your doctor if your baby has any of these. If the skin folds have yeast and airing out the area is not helping, then call your doctor.

What tests need to be done, and what do the results mean?

If the neck folds are infected with bacteria and you are using an antibiotic to no avail, then a culture may be done. The culture identifies the cause of the infection and can help determine the best treatment. With the exception of bacterial infections (and rarely in these cases), tests do not need to be done on irritated skin folds.

What are the treatments?

Most skin fold irritation is treated with time and air. As the baby learns to hold her head upright, more air will circulate under the neck and the skin will be less irritated. In the meantime, airing out the folds is the best treatment and the best means of preventing further infection.

Yeast infections are treated with antifungal creams. The most common of these include nystatin, terbinafine, or "-azole" (clotrimazole, ketoconazole, econazole, miconazole) in the ingredients. Because yeast thrive in warm, dark, moist environments, the antifungal creams work much better if they are used sparingly and in tandem with airing.

Bacterial infections are treated with antibiotics. Mild infections will be treated with creams or ointments, but more serious infections require oral antibiotics. Just like yeast, bacteria thrive in a wet area. So use the creams sparingly and continue to air out the area frequently.

What are the possible complications?

The only complication of irritated skin folds is spreading infection. Yeast can spread to other dark, warm, moist areas such as the mouth or groin. Bacteria can spread along the skin or can move deep beneath it, causing infection in the tissues of the neck or in the bloodstream. Yeast infections are typically easy to treat — even when they have spread — but migrating bacterial infections can be much more difficult to control.

18

Chest and Lungs

◆

A baby does not use his lungs until the moment he is born and the umbilical cord is cut. It is only then that he must take a breath of air, relying on his lungs to take in oxygen and release carbon dioxide. In order for this transition to go smoothly, the lungs must develop while the baby is still in the womb. They must be prepared to breathe from the first moment after delivery.

Lung development relies on two things: time and space. First, a fetus must have enough time in the womb for his lungs to grow and develop appropriately. In most cases, the lungs are sufficiently developed by 34 weeks of gestation so that a baby born after this time will be able to breathe effectively on his own. When a mother is in premature labor or there is a medical reason why the baby must be delivered early, a test of the amniotic fluid can check for lung maturity before the baby is delivered.

The second parameter for lung development is space. The lungs are surrounded by the head, neck, and shoulders on top; the ribs on the sides; and the diaphragm and intestines below. If these structures are improperly formed in such a way that there is not enough space for the lungs to grow, then the lungs will not develop normally. One classic example is a diaphragmatic hernia, or a hole in one of the diaphragms. The hole allows the intestines to move into and fill the space that should be occupied by the lungs, preventing the lungs from growing where they normally would.

Amazingly the formation of the lungs depends on swallowed fluid. The amniotic fluid swallowed by a fetus goes largely into the stomach and intestines, and eventually out through the kidneys. But a small amount trickles into the lungs, where it helps to weigh down the developing lung tissue. Like two water balloons, the lungs slowly inflate with the help of fluid. By the time a baby is delivered, most of this fluid must be gone — otherwise the baby will have difficulty breathing. In the womb, the fluid is gradually absorbed by the lung tissues, and during labor, the endorphins released by a laboring mother help to mop up the rest. People once believed that squeezing a baby out the birth canal squeezed extra water out of the lungs, but this probably isn't true.

DIFFICULTY BREATHING AND WHEEZING
(Birth–12 Months)

What is happening inside my baby's body?
Respiratory distress is the medical term used to describe serious difficulty breathing. It can be hard to tell whether or not your baby is having respiratory distress, and if she is, it can be even more stressful for you to figure out what to do. What if your baby simply sounds noisy with each breath, or what if she is working harder than usual to get the air in?

Babies have to learn how to breathe. As a newborn, a baby will be able to breathe mainly through her nose. Her mouth is busy learning to eat and doesn't help much with breathing until about two months of age. This is significant because air follows a path from the nostrils down the neck and into the lungs. Any blockage along the way can cause difficulty breathing. Once a child is old enough to use the mouth for breathing, obstruction in the nose can often be overcome with help from the mouth, and only obstructions from the neck down will cause respiratory distress. But when infants are only a few days or weeks old, blockages at the back of the nose alone can cause breathing troubles.

It is also important to remember that babies do not breathe with the same regular pattern of children and adults. Rather, they do something called *normal periodic breathing*. Their breaths are very slow and deep, often for a minute or two. Then they speed up their breaths and take several quick shallow ones. After several seconds (sometimes minutes), they slow down again. The breathing pattern is something like this: slow . . . slow . . . slow . . . slow . . . slow . . . quick, quick, quick, quick . . . slow . . . slow . . . slow . . . slow . . . quick, quick, and so on.

The three most common general causes of respiratory distress in babies are obstruction along the airway, infection of the airway, and immaturity of the lungs.

The most prevalent types of obstructions that can block the flow of air down to the lungs include overly narrow or absent passages at the back of the nose called *choanal atresia;* small or floppy airway in the neck called *tracheolaryngomalacia* (see the section on stridor in chapter 17); and small or unusually formed airways. A foreign object such as a small piece of food or a toy (usually courtesy of an older sibling) can obstruct breathing when it becomes lodged in the airway or lungs. Swelling in the airway, as in the case of severe allergic reactions *(anaphylaxis),* can also cause obstruction but is extremely uncommon in babies.

The second general cause of respiratory distress is infection. Any infection in the airway, from the nose and mouth down to the lungs — virus, bacteria, or otherwise — stimulates the baby's immune system to produce swelling and mucus in its own defense. The swelling can create areas of obstruction and the mucus can get stuck deep in the lungs. One or both of these can block the normal flow of oxygen to areas of the lungs, forcing the lungs to work harder to get an acceptable amount of oxygen into the body. Sometimes the ends of the lungs, responsible for air exchange, will also become inflamed. This further impedes the movement of oxygen into the body. Older children and adults have bigger airways, so the swelling is relatively less significant — the bigger the airway to begin with, the more swelling is necessary to obstruct it entirely. Older kids and adults are also better at coughing up mucus, whereas babies are not good at this at all. The body can fight off most infections, but if there is significant swelling, inflammation, and mucus overwhelming the lungs, then a cycle of breathing difficulty may result. The more inflammation and obstruction, the harder it is to breathe. This is especially true when the infection settles low in the lungs. An infection in the lung is called *pneumonia.*

The third common source of respiratory distress among babies is lung immaturity. A baby who is born before her lungs are ready to breathe can have ***respiratory distress syndrome (RDS).*** Her lungs will be filled with fluid, causing them to be stiffer and less compliant than fully mature lungs. When a baby has low oxygen levels and oxygen is pushed into the lungs using a bag-mask, the stiff lungs can pop a small hole. This punctured lung, also called *pneumothorax,* makes breathing even more difficult. Also, as in the case of infected lungs, immature lungs contain fluid that blocks the normal pathway of oxygen. If oxygen cannot get where it needs to go, then the baby will work harder to try to compensate. Most babies with RDS are premature.

Severe asthma can also cause difficulty breathing. This is so rare in young babies, however, that it is not covered in detail here. More information is available through the Web links at the end of this section.

What can I do?

You should contact a health care provider anytime you suspect respiratory distress. If your baby is not breathing or is struggling to breathe, then call 911 and start CPR immediately.

When inflammation is part of the problem and the breathing is stable, sometimes steam or cool mist can help to make a child more comfortable. Alternating between the two — 10 minutes in steam followed by 10 minutes in cool air (but wearing something warm) and then back to steam — is often helpful too. If a baby seems to be having difficulty breathing, then this suggestion should be followed only on the advice of your doctor and in conjunction with other treatments.

If a foreign body — such as a toy or a small piece of food — becomes lodged in a baby's airway, then ***back blows*** may be used. This technique is taught in CPR classes as the baby version of the ***Heimlich maneuver.*** The child is held in an adult's arm, facedown (the head cradled in the adult's palm) and straddling the forearm. The adult should give five back blows. Then the child is flipped over so that she is faceup, and the mouth is swept

ASTHMA

◆

Asthma is primarily a disease of toddlers and older children. It is rare to get the diagnosis of asthma before a child is a year old, because in order to be labeled with asthma, a child must have more than one episode of wheezing. Sometimes a child who has had multiple episodes of wheezing will still not be called asthmatic. The term "reactive airways disease," or "RAD," is used to describe babies and children who have wheezing but do not yet qualify as having asthma.

Asthma has three components: muscle spasm, inflammation, and mucus secretion. The muscle spasm occurs in the smooth muscles surrounding the airways in the lungs. When the muscles spasm, the airways constrict, making a wheezing sound when the child exhales. Sometimes this sound is audible to the parent, other times a doctor must listen with a stethoscope in order to hear it. Inflammation occurs at the ends of the lungs, where oxygen is transferred from the lungs into the passing blood. Inflammation makes this exchange less efficient, so less oxygen gets into the bloodstream. Mucus is secreted throughout the airways of the lungs. This mucus congests the airways, further reducing their diameter and restricting airflow even more.

for the object. If the object is not retrieved, then the process is repeated.

When does my doctor need to be involved?
Anytime you suspect difficulty breathing, call your doctor. If your child is struggling to breathe or appears not to be breathing at all, then call 911 and start CPR immediately.

The signs of respiratory distress are listed below. Each of the following is an expression of a baby's effort to get extra oxygen into her body and therefore can be a sign of breathing difficulty.

Call your doctor if your baby is demonstrating two or more of these signs. If there is any doubt, you should seek the advice of a doctor.

Flaring the nostrils with each breath. This makes the nostrils wider and allows more air to flow into the airway and lungs.

Visible flexing or contracting of the long muscles at the neck — between the jaw and the shoulders. This pulls on the tops of the lungs, increasing the size of the lungs and their air capacity. The notch between the collarbones, called the sternal notch, may also be pulling in with each breath.

Visible flexing or contracting of the muscles between the ribs. This pulls on the lungs to open them horizontally. It also increases the size of the lungs and their air capacity. In order to see these muscles pulling, you can draw an imaginary line from the baby's armpit to her hip. Halfway along that line, look for the ribs moving with each breath. They will seem like a row of bucket handles pulling up and down.

Moving the belly up and down in an exaggerated way with each breath. This forces the diaphragm down, increasing the depth of the lungs and their air capacity.

Breathing fast. This increases the flow of air into the lungs simply by speeding it up. Sometimes an infection or inflammation in the lungs will manifest only with rapid, shallow breathing. The nostrils and chest may look normal, but the baby may appear to be panting. Fevers will cause this too, because the lungs speed up when the body temperature rises — babies who have a fever will breathe fast to "blow off" their fever. In the case of fever, fast breathing is *not* a sign of difficulty breathing — rather, it is a very good way to cool down the body. When the temperature is normal, the normal rate of breathing is age dependent: newborns breathe 40 to 60 times per minute; babies breathe 25 to 35 times per minute; young children breathe 20 to 30 times per minute; and adults typically breathe 12 to 14 times per minute. If your child has a fever, then you may give a fever-reducing medicine. When the temperature is normal, reassess the respiratory rate.

All of these signs are helpful in assessing a (relatively) calm child. In a crying baby, however, they are not necessarily accurate indicators of difficulty breathing. This is because a crying child will flare her nostrils, open her mouth, pull at the muscles between her ribs, and breathe fast as part of crying.

Whenever you are in doubt, you should call your doctor or 911 immediately. When your child is having difficulty breathing, *never* put anything in her mouth, including food or liquid.

What tests need to be done, and what do the results mean?
A baby in respiratory distress is working too hard to get oxygen into her body. Oxygen levels should be measured. Either a pulse oximeter or a blood oxygen level may be used to measure the oxygen level. These are described in chapter 29.

An X ray is often helpful for looking at the lung structure. It will reveal immature or improperly formed lungs, fluid (seen in many infections, trauma, and RDS), a foreign body, pneumothorax, and even inflammation.

In order to determine whether or not the cause is an infection, a complete blood count and a blood culture can be checked. A positive blood culture will identify the bacteria causing the infection and will help to determine what antibiotic your doctor will prescribe.

What are the treatments?
The treatment will depend on the cause. If there is obstruction somewhere along the airway, then the obstruction will need to be removed. Foreign objects stuck in the lung, for example, almost always need to be taken out. In many cases of tracheolaryngomalacia, it is often a matter of waiting for the baby to outgrow the condition (see the section on stridor in chapter 17). However, if there is significant obstruction causing too little oxygen to get to the rest of the body, then a surgical or other invasive procedure may be needed.

If a bacterial infection is causing the respiratory distress, then your doctor will prescribe antibiotics. If a viral infection is the cause, however, then only time and the body's own defense system will help. When the infection causes inflammation, your doctor may start your baby on anti-inflammatory medicines. *Steroids* are the most common of these. They can be given intravenously, by mouth, or by inhalation. There are also medicines that help to relax and open up the airways (the most common is called *albuterol*) and to decrease mucus production (the most common is called *ipratropium bromide*). These are typically given by inhalation using a machine called a *nebulizer.*

Finally, if immaturity has caused RDS, then in time the body will mop up the excess fluid in the lungs, and the lungs will slowly mature. Sometimes these babies require significant support for their breathing, including the use of a breathing tube. These babies are also at increased risk for pneumonia. This is described in some detail in the section on blueness in chapter 28.

In all of these scenarios, supplemental oxygen may be needed. Oxygen can be given by a tube attached to the nose, a mask strapped over the mouth, a tent surrounding the baby, or a tube inserted directly into the lungs.

What are the possible complications?

The most frightening complication of respiratory distress is that it can lead to *respiratory arrest* (failure to breathe). This can happen when the lungs are overwhelmed with infection or inflammation, when they are completely obstructed, or when the baby gets too tired to breathe after several hours (or days) of hard work.

Infection in the lungs can spread elsewhere in the body, causing infection in the blood, bones, urine, or even spinal fluid and brain. An infected lung can also form an *abscess,* which is a walled-off collection of fluid, or an *empyema,* which is a collection of pus right outside the lung. These fluid collections compound breathing troubles and provide reservoirs for infection.

Infants with RDS are at increased risk for lung infection in the first year of life. Many babies with RDS at birth now receive a medicine called palivizumab (also called Synagis) to help prevent

HOW SUPPLEMENTAL OXYGEN IS DELIVERED

◆

Blow-by. Oxygen is blown through a plastic tube that looks like a small hose. The tube is about an inch in diameter. It can be held in front of the baby's mouth or placed next to him strategically so that the air blows directly onto his face. The highly oxygenated air is humidified, so you may see it coming out the end of the tube like a mist.

Face mask. A face mask is a mask strapped to a baby's nose and mouth. The mask is attached to the same tubing that supplies the blow-by oxygen. A face mask has much better delivery of oxygen because the air is blown directly into the baby's nose and mouth, with very little escaping to the surrounding environment. However, babies do not generally like having a face mask strapped on, so it can be a struggle to keep them from pulling and tugging at it.

Nasal cannula. A nasal cannula is a small tube, about a millimeter or two in diameter, that wraps around the face, above the mouth, and directly under the nose. Two small prongs exit the tube at the nostrils, directing air up the nose. The nasal cannula is often taped onto babies and

respiratory syncytial virus, also known as **RSV.** This is especially true of premature babies, who can become quite ill with this infection. Infants born with RDS also have an increased risk later in life of developing asthma.

Additional Resources

http://www.nlm.nih.gov/medlineplus/encyclopedia.html (Click on "Bl–Bz," then scroll down to "breathing difficulty.")

http://www.nlm.nih.gov/medlineplus/encyclopedia.html (Click on "Cp–Cz," then scroll down to "CPR — infant.")

http://www.packardchildrenshospital.org (Go to "search" in upper right-hand corner and type in "breathing difficulty.")

http://www.medem.com (Go to "search medical library" in upper right-hand corner and type in "choking.")

small children because they will typically try to pull it off. The cannula is more comfortable than the face mask, but it delivers less oxygen than the mask because it is blowing air only up the nose.

Tent. Sometimes a baby will not tolerate a face mask but needs a significant amount of oxygen. Placing the baby in a plastic tent and then blowing the oxygen directly inside can accomplish this. The tent is small, covering the baby's head and neck. It is placed in the crib, and the baby can move freely underneath it. While the baby breathes highly oxygenated air inside the tent, the loose flaps and free edges allow some oxygen to escape. For this reason, the face mask is a more efficient way of delivering oxygen.

Endotracheal tube. An endotracheal tube (ETT) is used when a child is unable to breathe effectively on his own. The tube is placed in the mouth and then down into the lungs. It is attached to a breathing machine called a ventilator. This is the most effective means of getting oxygen down to the lungs, but it is also by far the most invasive. Its use is reserved for very ill children.

◆   ◆   ◆

BREAST BUDS
(Birth–2 Months)

What is happening inside my baby's body?
While a fetus develops inside its mother, the mother passes hormones through the placenta to the growing baby. These hormones affect two specific parts of the body: the genitalia and the breasts of both males and females. The genital effects are covered in chapter 24. This section explains why maternal hormones cause all newborns to have a small amount of breast swelling for the first few weeks of life.

Breast tissue in all humans is sensitive to estrogen. Therefore, when this hormone crosses the placenta and moves into the developing fetus's body, breast tissue is stimulated. When a baby is born — boy or girl — there is a small, firm mound underneath each nipple that is about the size of a short stack of dimes (and sometimes even bigger). As the maternal estrogen slowly leaves the baby's body over the first few weeks of life, the tissue will shrink down.

What can I do?

Parents do not need to do anything about breast buds. They are normal, and they will disappear within the first few weeks of life.

When does my doctor need to be involved?

A doctor almost never needs to be involved. If the area under and around the nipple becomes red and hot, or if the swelling increases significantly so that one side looks much larger than the other, then call your doctor.

What tests need to be done, and what do the results mean?

Tests do not need to be done when a baby has normal breast buds. Rarely a bud will look much bigger and redder than its counterpart. This may signal an infection, and a blood test may need to be done in order to determine the exact cause. More often than not, however, antibiotics are started without any tests because a few well-known bacteria are the most common culprits.

What are the treatments?

There is no treatment for normal breast buds — they will shrink and disappear with time. Infected breast buds are extremely rare and require antibiotics. The antibiotics are almost always given by mouth rather than topically (as an ointment or cream rubbed onto the inflamed area) because the oral antibiotics get to the area much more quickly and efficiently.

What are the possible complications?

The only potential complication of breast buds is infection. As stated previously, this is extremely rare and — when it does happen — usually occurs on only one side.

Additional Resources
http://www.nlm.nih.gov/medlineplus/encyclopedia.html (Click on "Hg–Hz,"
then scroll down to "hormonal effects in newborns.")
http://www.nlm.nih.gov/medlineplus/encyclopedia.html (Click on "Bl–Bz,"
then scroll down to "breast lump.")

❖   ❖   ❖

CHEST-WALL SHAPE (PECTUS)
(Birth)

What is happening inside my baby's body?

The front half of the chest — as opposed to the back and spine —
includes the ribs and *sternum* (breastbone) that surround the
heart and lungs. This area is typically shaped like a semicircle,
smooth and rounded. When it looks sunken or pointed in the
middle, the shape is called a *pectus*. This shape is seen in about
1 out of every 300 babies, though it is more common in boys than
in girls.

When the sternum is sunken in so that the chest looks concave,
this is called *pectus excavatum*. Another name for this is *funnel
chest*. When the breastbone is protruding outward and the chest
looks pointed and convex, this is known as *pectus carinatum*, or
pigeon chest. Pectus excavatum is the far more common type,
accounting for 85 percent of all pectus deformities.

In general, pectus is thought to be due to overgrowth of the
tissue — called *cartilage* — that connects the ribs to the sternum. When this tissue grows too rapidly in the developing
fetus, the chest wall either pouches out or buckles in. Sometimes
the baby has other irregularities of the muscles, bones, or blood
vessels.

Pectus often becomes more obvious during puberty, when the
bones and muscles are growing rapidly. However, it is usually
diagnosed right after birth.

What can I do?

Parents generally do not need to do anything for pectus. Usually
the pectus is mild and its only significance is cosmetic. If the pectus is severe, then bring it to the attention of your pediatrician.

When does my doctor need to be involved?
If the pectus is extreme, then the organs protected by the rib cage may be crammed into a small, abnormally shaped chest compartment. This can have further consequences, so your doctor will need to follow it closely. In most cases of pectus, however, you do not need to call your doctor.

What tests need to be done, and what do the results mean?
With significant pectus, a chest X ray shows the position of the heart and the size of the lungs. These organs may be unusually shaped due to the atypical dimensions of a pectus chest. If the pectus is severe, then other tests may be necessary in order to check heart and lung function.

What are the treatments?
The main treatment for pectus is physiotherapy, with a goal of posture improvement. Therapists can work with children to help them sit up straight and hold their shoulders back. Babies, however, cannot participate in this form of treatment for obvious reasons.

In an extreme case of pectus, you might have to consider surgery. An operation can fix the orientation of the ribs to the breastbone but also requires adjustment of the underlying muscles. Surgery is usually considered only when the heart or lungs are affected by the shape of the chest, or in older children and teens when the pectus causes loss of self-esteem and warrants a cosmetic repair.

What are the possible complications?
Significant pectus excavatum can push the heart further to the left than it normally sits. This displacement can interfere with blood flow to and from the heart. Eventually, the heart works harder to move blood through the body and can become fatigued. The heart muscle gets tired of continually pumping more than it was designed to and as a result can become less efficient with each pump.

In these cases, the child's lungs also have to work harder to provide oxygen to the blood because the lungs are scrunched into a smaller space than they otherwise would be. In addition, if the heart grows tired and pumps blood less efficiently, then the lungs work less efficiently as well. This can lead to difficulty during exercise, including shortness of breath and fatigue.

Pectus carinatum does not push on the heart or lungs the way that excavatum does. However, significant pectus carinatum can prevent complete expiration of air from the lungs simply because of the way the lungs are shaped by the convex sternum. Again, the effects of this are seen mostly during exercise, when air exchange needs to increase.

The most common complication of pectus, however, is cosmetic. Over time, children and teenagers with pectus often become self-conscious about their bodies. This is extremely important to recognize and can be a very good reason for correcting the shape of the chest wall. The surgery to correct this is almost never done before the age of eight, unless the heart or lungs are severely compromised.

Additional Resources
http://www.pectus.org
http://www.hmc.psu.edu/childrens/healthinfo/c/chestwall.htm
http://web1.tch.harvard.edu/ (Go to "Child Health A to Z," then enter "chest wall deformity" under "Search the Encyclopedia" at the bottom of the screen.)
http://www.nlm.nih.gov/medlineplus/encyclopedia.html (Click on "P–Pl," then scroll down to "pectus carinatum" and "pectus excavatum.")

◈   ◈   ◈

BONY BUMP IN THE MIDDLE OF THE CHEST (XIPHOID)
(Birth–2 Months)

What is happening inside my baby's body?
The **sternum** — also commonly known as the breastbone — is a flat bone that extends from the base of the neck to the top of the abdomen. It is long and narrow, and it provides a place for each rib to attach in the middle of the chest. The combination of the ribs and the sternum protects the heart and lungs from injury.

The sternum has a pointed tip called the *xiphoid process.* "Xiphoid" literally means "sword shaped." Many parents are surprised to find an arrowhead-shaped bone visible under a baby's skin about halfway between the shoulders and the belly button. But rest assured, this is the normal xiphoid process, and over time it will become invisible.

What can I do?
Parents need not do anything about the xiphoid process.

When does my doctor need to be involved?
A doctor does not need to do anything about the xiphoid.

What tests need to be done, and what do the results mean?
No tests need to be done.

What are the treatments?
There are no treatments because the pointy xiphoid process is normal.

What are the possible complications?
There are no complications.

Additional Resources
http://www.drhull.com/EncyMaster/X/xiphoid.html

19

Belly Button

◆

The belly button is the only visible remainder of the umbilical cord. Throughout fetal life, the umbilical cord is the sole source of oxygen and nutrition. When a baby is born and the cord is cut, what was once the most life-sustaining part of her body is now just a stump. The series of events is remarkable: a newborn baby takes her first breath and blood is forced through the lungs so that it can be replenished with oxygen. The vessels that carried oxygen-rich blood from mother to baby for so many months shrink down quickly, becoming tiny fibrous strands with no blood flowing through them. Within minutes, the entire flow of blood through the body has changed, and a baby is able to rely upon herself to get oxygen.

The remaining umbilical stump heals over the first few weeks of life. It turns black and hard, often rubbing against the diaper or clothing around it. It can bleed or ooze clear fluid or even become infected. Eventually it falls off, leaving behind the belly button. Sometimes the belly button points inward, but other times it pouches out. These "outies" have nothing to do with the way the cord is cut — only with how the muscles of the belly attach to one another.

HEALING UMBILICAL CORD
(Birth–1 Month)

What is happening inside my baby's body?

The umbilical cord is the connection between the placenta — the provider of nutrition to the growing fetus — and your baby. As soon as a baby is delivered, the cord is cut and the baby no longer receives oxygen and nutrition from her mother's blood supply. A clamp is placed on the cord to stop it from bleeding, and in some hospitals, the stump is washed with an antibacterial liquid.

From then on, the cord slowly rots off. It changes from yellow to brown to black. After several days (sometimes weeks) the stump detaches itself from the skin and leaves behind a goopy belly button. Over the next few days (or weeks) the area becomes scabbed, and eventually the belly button heals entirely. The belly button is considered completely healed when the scab comes off and the skin underneath looks normal. When the belly button has completely healed, your baby is ready for her first bath.

What can I do?

In the past, wiping the umbilical stump — and once it had fallen off, the healing belly button — with isopropyl (rubbing) alcohol was advised. This was thought to dry out the stump, speeding the progression from falling off to healing. There is no proof, however, that this actually speeds the process at all. Therefore you can simply leave the area alone. The alcohol does not help keep the area sterile, so with or without it, the belly button will generally remain clean.

In order to minimize irritation to the healing belly button, the front of a diaper can be turned down so that it does not rub against the sensitive healing skin. Some newborn diapers are now made with cutouts at the front, minimizing the need to adjust for the belly button.

Remember, you should not submerge your baby in a bath until the belly button is completely healed. Instead, give sponge baths only and keep the healing belly button dry.

When does my doctor need to be involved?
Call your doctor if the area around the healing belly button becomes red and infected, or if there is a large amount of liquid coming from the healing belly button. These topics are covered in the sections that follow.

What tests need to be done, and what do the results mean?
Even though a healing belly button may look black and crusty, this is normal. As long as there are no signs of infection — such as redness or pus — and there is not a large amount of fluid coming from the stump, no tests need to be done.

What are the treatments?
There are no treatments for a normal healing belly button.

What are the possible complications?
The only complications of healing belly buttons are infection and persistent fluid leakage. Both are covered in the sections below.

Additional Resources
http://www.nlm.nih.gov/medlineplus/encyclopedia.html (Click on "U," then scroll down to "umbilical cord care in newborns.")
http://www.who.int/search/en/ (Type "umbilical cord care" in search box.)

◆　　◆　　◆

STICKY BELLY BUTTON
(Birth–2 Months)

What is happening inside my baby's body?
Often the healing umbilical stump oozes clear fluid. This fluid, with a consistency like molasses, is not at all worrisome. Rather, when the body heals a wound, the area often becomes filled with cells and fluid in an effort to minimize infection. The sometimes clear, sometimes straw-colored thickened fluid that oozes from a healing belly button is normal.

Fluid with a strong odor that smells like urine (or watery yellow fluid that looks like urine) or fluid that has a pungent odor is not normal. These can be signs of structural problems or infection.

What can I do?
Some parents wipe the umbilical area with isopropyl alcohol daily. The alcohol is thought to dry out the area, making the cord fall off sooner and then helping the skin to heal once the stump has fallen off. There is no proof, however, that this works. In fact, the alcohol can become trapped under folds of skin and may actually slow the healing process. Simply patting the region with dry gauze probably promotes healing just as much because it helps to keep the umbilical area dry.

When does my doctor need to be involved?
You are more likely to need your doctor after the umbilical stump falls off. When it is still attached to the baby, the stump typically protects the skin, preventing irritation the same way a scab protects a healing wound. Once the stump does fall off, some babies have scar tissue at the belly button that can ooze clear or yellow fluid or can look crusted over like a scab. This is called a *granuloma.* It can be up to a half inch in size, with a smooth or irregular surface. A slowly healing granuloma can produce fluid long after the stump falls off and may need some help to stop oozing.

If the belly button is ever leaking any other fluid, especially one that looks or smells like urine, then call your doctor. This rare circumstance can signal a connection between the bladder and skin called a *fistula.* Urine leakage is unlike normal oozing: it is yellow (instead of clear), frequent, and occasionally high in volume.

If the belly button is oozing liquid that looks like pus or has a pungent odor, or if the area surrounding it becomes red and inflamed, then it may be infected. This requires a doctor.

What tests need to be done, and what do the results mean?
When the belly button is leaking fluid, tests need be done only when there is a concern that a fistula exists or there is a serious infection.

If there is a possibility of infection, then other tests may be required. This is covered in the section on red belly buttons later in this chapter.

What are the treatments?

Normal oozing from a belly button will often resolve on its own.

In the case of a granuloma, your doctor may apply *silver nitrate* to the belly button with a long, sterile Q-Tip. The silver nitrate helps to heal the granuloma and stop the oozing. The treated granuloma will form a scab and then heal.

If there is a fistula between the bladder and the belly button, then surgery is required, tying off the connection between the bladder and the skin. Usually additional tests will be done to ensure that the rest of the bladder and urinary tract are normal.

If an infection is present, then antibiotics are typically started. This is covered in the section on red belly buttons later in this chapter.

What are the possible complications?

The most common complication of a persistently oozing belly button is a granuloma, and the most common complication of a granuloma is infection. Anytime fluid collects inside or outside the body, bacteria can grow. This happens because the fluid forms a stagnant pool. If infection occurs, then two things need to be done: the infection must be treated (usually with antibiotics) and the source of the fluid must be addressed. In the case of a persistent granuloma, the area may need to be drained or surgically removed.

Additional Resources
http://www.packardchildrenshospital.org (Go to "search" in upper right-hand corner and type in "cord care.")
http://www.caps.ca/guests/statements/umbilical.htm

◆　◆　◆

RED BELLY BUTTON (OMPHALITIS)
(Birth–2 Months)

What is happening inside my baby's body?

Once the stump of the umbilical cord falls off, the belly button is formed. During this process, the area around the belly button can look red. Usually this is simply a part of normal healing. But if a healing belly button gets infected, then the area can become fire-engine red and feel hot to the touch, with the skin surrounding the old umbilical cord looking like a bright red halo. Most likely, the bacteria that normally live on the skin have found their way into the belly button. An infection in the belly button is called *omphalitis.*

Bacteria normally live on the skin of all humans, and when there is an opening in the skin, the bacteria can sneak underneath. Here they can grow unchecked, creating an infection. The healing belly button provides easy entrance for bacteria because the skin has not entirely sealed.

Infection can be contained in a small area or it can spread. Spreading infection moves outward from the initial site — as a streaking line or an expanding circle. The infection can also move down into the abdomen below, or into nearby muscles or blood vessels. Infections that travel into the bloodstream can eventually spread to distant organs such as the heart.

What can I do?

You can minimize irritation or the risk of infection of a healing belly button by folding down the front of the diaper. This reduces rubbing at the site. Wiping the area with isopropyl alcohol may also help to prevent infection, though this is debatable. Often, though, infection of the healing belly button is just bad luck: bacteria move underneath the skin and there is not much you can do to prevent it.

When does my doctor need to be involved?

Whenever the skin around the belly button (on the abdomen) is red and warm, call your doctor. If the liquid oozing from the belly button has a pungent smell or looks white like pus or yellow like urine, then call your doctor.

What tests need to be done, and what do the results mean?

Tests are usually not needed. However, if the infection continues to spread despite treatment with antibiotics, or if a child becomes seriously ill, then a CT or MRI scan may need to be done to look for deeper, more extensive infection. If the fluid appears to be urine, then it should be sent to the laboratory for a urinalysis.

What are the treatments?

The primary treatment for an infected belly button is antibiotics. Since the most likely bacteria to have caused the infection are those that normally live on the skin, the antibiotics most commonly used are those that kill these bacteria. These include penicillins and cephalosporins. For very mild infections, topical antibiotics can be given in the form of ointments or creams. But for moderate or severe infections, oral antibiotics must be used. In extreme cases, antibiotics can be given directly into the vein (intravenously).

What are the possible complications?

The most serious complication of omphalitis is a spreading infection. If the infection moves into the bloodstream, then it can spread quickly throughout the body to distant organs such as the heart. It can also cause overwhelming infection called *sepsis.* Because it takes time for bacteria to get from the belly button to the blood, these complications are relatively rare. They are treated with intravenous antibiotics.

The infection can also move down into the muscles and organs of the abdomen below the belly button. This type of infection can be difficult to treat. It always requires intravenous antibiotics and sometimes even surgery.

Additional Resources
http://author.emedicine.com/PED/topic1641.htm
http://www.caps.ca/guests/statements/umbilical.htm (Scroll down to "neonatal omphalitis.")

◆   ◆   ◆

UMBILICAL HERNIAS ("OUTIES")
(Birth–12 Months)

What is happening inside my baby's body?

A pair of stomach muscles runs down the belly from the ribs to the pelvis. These muscles are the same ones that you can see on a bodybuilder's abdomen. The muscles are parallel and are joined together from top to bottom by their surrounding thick tissues.

Newborns have these muscles, but the connecting tissue is not entirely attached. This makes sense, because the umbilical cord comes out through the space between these muscles. When your baby was inside the womb, if these muscles had been attached, then they would have cut off the blood exchange between mother and child. The two muscles and their accompanying tissue attach above and below the belly button but remain unattached right around the umbilical cord until after delivery.

Once your baby is delivered and the umbilical cord is cut, it is safe for the muscles to attach themselves. If, after the umbilical stump falls off, the muscles still haven't attached themselves, then the intestines can protrude through this hole and the belly button will look like an "outie," also known as an *umbilical hernia*. The actual hernia is made of a sac protruding through this opening between the pieces of muscle and tissue in the abdominal wall. This opening is called the *umbilical ring*.

Some babies have small hernias and some have large ones. The hernia always pops out when a baby cries because the pressure generated by crying causes the intestines to push out through the umbilical ring. The hernia may also look quite prominent when a baby strains. Sometimes hernias can get stuck. This is worrisome and is covered in detail in both the following text and chapter 23.

Umbilical hernias are seen in more than 10 percent of normal Caucasian babies and an even higher number of African American babies. They are more common in premature than full-term babies.

What can I do?

You need not — and really cannot — do anything to help an umbilical hernia. It is an age-old myth that one can tie a coin to a string and wrap the contraption around a baby's waist to push the belly button back in. Given the reason why umbilical hernias exist in the first place, you can easily see why this does not work.

When does my doctor need to be involved?

Hernias pop out — sometimes a remarkable amount — but should be easily flattened: with gentle pushing, a parent should be able to maneuver the hernia back down. When a baby is crying, it is

> ## WHEN TO WORRY ABOUT A HERNIA
> ◆
>
> *A hernia that can be pushed in with ease is never an emergency. However, there are times when hernias need immediate medical attention. Call your doctor if the hernia is*
>
> *Red*
> *Warm to the touch*
> *Impossible to push back in, even when the baby is calm*
> *Sticking out and the baby is vomiting*
>
> *These can be signs of incarceration or strangulation.*

difficult to push the hernia in; but when a baby is calm, it should be quite easy.

Hernias need to be seen by a doctor when they cannot be pushed back in easily or when the area around them becomes red and hot. Sometimes they are *incarcerated* — the intestines get stuck in the muscle and cannot be pushed back in because they are swollen. When this happens, they can become *strangulated.* This is when the blood supply to the part of the intestine that is stuck is compromised and that part of the intestine is starved of important nutrients, including oxygen. This can cause vomiting and remarkable pain.

Both incarcerated and strangulated hernias are medical emergencies. Strangulated hernias must be treated immediately with surgery, because if the part of the intestine deprived of oxygen dies, then that piece of bowel must be removed before life-threatening consequences set in. Incarcerated hernias may not require urgent surgery, but they need to be examined by doctors (often surgeons) quickly in order to prevent strangulation.

What tests need to be done, and what do the results mean?
The only test is to apply gentle pressure to the hernia to see if it can be pushed back in (in medical terms this is called *reduced*).

You or your doctor can perform this test. If a hernia can be easily reduced, then it is normal. If it cannot, then it may be incarcerated or strangulated.

In the case of a strangulated or incarcerated hernia, an ultrasound my help determine whether or not there is still blood flowing to the part of the bowel stuck in the hernia.

What are the treatments?
The treatment for a normal, reducible hernia is time. By two years of age, 95 percent of all umbilical hernias close on their own. If a hernia has not closed by kindergarten, then you may choose to have it surgically closed for cosmetic reasons.

All strangulated hernias and some incarcerated hernias must be treated surgically. The piece of intestine stuck in the gap between the muscles needs to be pushed back behind the muscles, and then the gap can be sewn closed. Sometimes the bowel is swollen or has had minimal blood flow while entrapped. In very extreme cases, when a segment of bowel has been so severely deprived of oxygen that it is no longer functional, it needs to be removed.

What are the possible complications?
Incarceration and strangulation are very, very rare. Babies with trapped hernias will almost always have pain and vomiting. Remember, when a baby is crying, a hernia will *always* be difficult to push back in.

Additional Resources
http://www.packardchildrenshospital.org (Go to "search" in upper right-hand corner and type in "umbilical hernia.")
http://www.caps.ca/guests/statements/umbilical.htm
http://www.nlm.nih.gov/medlineplus/encyclopedia.html (Click on "U," then scroll down to "umbilical hernia.")

◆   ◆   ◆

BELLY BUTTON PIGMENT
(Birth–12 Months)

What is happening inside my baby's body?
As the umbilical stump heals, pigment often collects deep inside
the new belly button. Some babies look like they have dirt stuck
inside! The pigment may stay for life, or it may resolve over
months. Often the pigmented layer of skin flakes off and the belly
button goes from being dark to the color of the rest of the body.

What can I do?
Avoid trying to pick out the pigment in the belly button. This can
cause irritation.

When does my doctor need to be involved?
A doctor does not need to do anything about pigment in the belly
button.

What tests need to be done, and what do the results mean?
No tests need to be done.

What are the treatments?
There are no treatments necessary. The pigment usually goes
away with time.

What are the possible complications?
There are no possible complications of a pigmented belly button.

Stomach and Intestine

◆

The gastrointestinal (GI) tract starts at the mouth and esophagus, and goes through the stomach, into the intestines, and out the rectum and anus. In an adult, it is more than 29 feet long!

While the entire GI tract forms during fetal development, it is not used to process food until a baby is born. This is because the fetus gets all of his nutrition through the umbilical cord. But just after birth, the umbilical cord is cut, and almost immediately a newborn must figure out how to feed by mouth, how to digest the food, how to determine that he feels full, and how to poop out the waste.

Some babies use their GI tracts too early. The best example of this is when a baby poops inside the womb. This is not meant to happen, but when a baby is stressed, it can occur. Other babies are a bit slow to use their GI tracts. They are lazy feeders after they are born or they have trouble digesting the breast milk or formula they are given. Problems with the GI tract can manifest as diarrhea, constipation, foul-smelling or unusual-looking stools, or loss of appetite.

It can be difficult to tell if your baby is eating enough. The very best way to measure this is to weigh the baby. Initially almost all newborns lose weight. But after a few days, they begin to regain it at a speed of one-half to one ounce per day. A baby does not keep up this pace, however, because at that rate he would weigh forty pounds by a year! As a baby becomes a more efficient feeder, he will learn to take more at a time, to space out his feeds, and to sleep in longer stretches.

NEWBORN WEIGHT LOSS AND WEIGHT GAIN
(Birth–1 Month)

What is happening inside my baby's body?
When a fetus grows inside the womb, nutrition is provided 24 hours a day, seven days a week through the umbilical cord. This means that a growing fetus receives continuous nutrition. But when a baby is delivered and the cord is cut, he does not get fed around-the-clock anymore. Instead he has to work by sucking a breast or bottle every two to three hours. Many times parents cannot believe how often their newborn wants to eat, sometimes as often as every hour. But despite how frequent this feeding schedule may seem to an adult, it is far less than the constant nutrition the baby was used to receiving prior to delivery. For your baby, a couple of hours is a long wait between each meal.

Most newborns manage the two or three hour wait between feedings with no difficulty. There is one catch, however. Humans are not designed to produce breast milk until around the third day of a baby's life. Before then, the breast-feeding baby gets a very concentrated liquid called **colostrum**. Colostrum is packed with antibodies (which help fight infections), but very little comes out of the breast with each feed — an ounce at a time at best. Again, this is normal, so most babies do fine until the third day of life, when the milk comes in.

Because of this delay in breast-milk production, most breast-fed babies lose weight in the first few days of life. Newborns are built to deal with this by having as much as a pound of extra water weight at birth, as you can see in the swollen eyes and puffy cheeks of recently delivered babies. This extra water is gradually urinated out or burned off with lots of vigorous sucking (because sucking burns calories). Bottle-fed babies lose this extra water as well, but they usually drop less weight because they tend to drink more liquid at each feed over the first few days.

Therefore, newborn weight loss is normal . . . up to a point. There are two rules about weight changes in a newborn. First, because excess water at birth equals roughly 10 percent of a newborn's total weight, he shouldn't lose more than 10 percent of his birth weight. This water is meant to be lost, so there is no need to worry that the baby is becoming dehydrated when he loses it. Beyond 10 percent, however, the baby can get dehydrated and may need some extra fluid. The second rule of weight loss is that a newborn should regain enough to be back to his birth weight by two weeks of life. This essentially assures health care providers that the baby is eating well and gaining weight appropriately. Because the average baby gains between one-half to one ounce per day, the baby's body weight after two weeks should be at least the same as it was at birth.

Remember that gaining and losing weight for a baby is often a matter of an ounce or two. Therefore, if a baby is weighed on two different scales, or he is clothed (or diapered) for one weight and naked for another, then the results can be skewed. The weights may differ slightly between the hospital scale and the doctor's office scale — or even between two scales in the same office!

An otherwise healthy baby who has lost too much weight or who has not returned to birth weight by two weeks is likely dehydrated. He will look skinny and his lips and tongue will be dry. Sometimes the soft spot on the top of the head is even sunken in. Dehydrated babies need to be treated aggressively and followed closely. Information about dehydration can be found in chapter 28.

Most of the time, the baby handles the transition from continuous feedings in the womb to intermittent feedings outside fairly well. A newborn, however, can go from happy and content to seemingly starving in no time. This is especially true of big babies (large for gestational age, or LGA) born to moms with maternal diabetes. These infants are at risk for *hypoglycemia* (low blood sugar) because they can make too much of the hormone *insulin*.

Too much insulin will cause the glucose level to fall below normal. Other infants who are at risk for hypoglycemia include small for gestational age (SGA) babies, preterm babies, newborns with infections, newborns who are too cold, meconium-stained babies (babies who pooped in the womb before coming out), or infants with central nervous system or congenital metabolic abnormalities. All of these babies can get very hungry between feeds. These topics are covered more extensively in part one.

There are a few medical problems that can cause a baby to lose too much weight or regain it too slowly. A baby may become infected with a bacteria or virus, which can lead to weight loss or poor weight gain. A baby with jaundice who is placed underneath bright lights can become slightly dehydrated because of the heat from the lamps, and this can slow his weight gain. Other causes of slow weight gain — such as intestinal or thyroid problems — are even more rare.

What can I do?

A breast-feeding baby needs to work to get his mom to produce milk. Remember, this naturally takes time. If a mother puts the baby to her breast for 10 to 15 minutes at a time every two to three hours beginning the first day after delivery, then she will send a repeated message to her body that it is time to start producing the milk. The baby's suck, the sound of his cry, and the hormone shifts in the mom's body after delivery all contribute to the production of breast milk.

There is one important exception to this rule of putting a newborn to the breast at regular short intervals, and that is the very first day of life. After delivery, both mom and baby are often exhausted. It is not unusual for a full-term, healthy baby to sleep six or even eight hours at a stretch the first day of life. After 24 hours, though, even if the baby still seems to want to sleep a lot, the mother must put him to her breast every two to three hours. Otherwise the breasts will not be stimulated enough for the milk to come in. Milk is only produced after regular and frequent stimulation. If the baby is unavailable for breast-feeding (because he is in the NICU or has had some complications), then pumping must be done at regular three-hour intervals.

Because a baby loses weight initially, in the first few weeks of life he needs to eat often. In general, after the first day of life, a newborn eats 8 to 12 times per day. You should not let a baby under 4 weeks of age eat fewer than eight times, no matter how well the baby seems to be sleeping. If this happens, then invariably the baby will not gain adequate weight. As babies get older, they become more efficient feeders. When they can take more milk at each feeding, the frequency of feedings will decrease.

When does my doctor need to be involved?

Call your doctor if your baby is taking fewer than eight feedings per 24-hour period (for a baby younger than one month) or if he is feeding poorly. You should also notify your doctor if you think your child is so hungry that he may have low blood sugar. Signs of low blood sugar in an infant may include jittering, shaking, extreme fussiness, or even seizures. Anytime a baby is too sleepy to eat for consecutive feedings, contact your doctor.

A newborn baby can also become dehydrated. If you are worried about this, then notify your doctor. Signs of dehydration include dry lips, tongue, and inside walls of the mouth; extreme sleepiness (lethargy); and a sunken soft spot at the top of the head. Dehydration is covered in more detail in chapter 28.

What tests need to be done, and what do the results mean?

The best test to check newborn weight loss is simple: weigh the baby. Use the same scale for rechecking a baby's weight, or use a digital scale that can be zeroed before the baby is weighed.

If a baby is showing signs of low blood glucose (hypoglycemia), then a blood test should be done to check the actual level. This can be performed as a heel stick (see chapter 29). If the level is extremely low, or if it fails to increase despite giving the baby sugar water or formula, then more comprehensive blood tests must be done to look for the cause of the low sugar level. These include a check of the electrolytes or the serum glucose, a complete blood count, and sometimes a blood culture. These tests require drawing blood from a vein, not a poke of the heel. For more information about these tests, see chapter 29.

Opinions differ as to the actual numeric value of blood glucose that should qualify as hypoglycemia. Currently the standard of care is that if the blood glucose concentration is lower than 40 mg/dL, then the child is considered hypoglycemic. If the baby has absolutely no symptoms, then some centers will allow the level to go down to 30 mg/dL for full-term infants (and even lower for premature or small for gestational age babies) before intervening. These values can be measured using a finger-prick machine or a blood draw sent to the hospital laboratory.

What are the treatments?

A baby who loses too much weight in the first few days of life or who does not regain enough to reach his birth weight by two weeks often needs to get extra food. A breast-fed baby can be supplemented with pumped breast milk or formula. These supplementary feedings can be given with a bottle, with a feeding tube attached to the mother's breast (called a **supplementary nursing system,** or **SNS**), or even with a cup, dropper, or finger.

It is often easier to figure out why a baby has lost too much weight or failed to regain it if he is bottle-fed, because parents can actually measure how much the baby is eating on any given day. Often, increasing the total amount of milk will solve the problem. With breast-feeding, the volume of milk per feed is almost impossible to measure. In order to increase the amount of breast milk a baby receives, you can raise the frequency of feedings or a mom can try to produce more breast milk. Specific methods for increasing milk production include pumping frequently, drinking lots of liquids, and occasionally using herbs or teas that help milk production. Your pediatrician or obstetrician can provide more information about these products.

Babies with low blood sugar need to be given glucose to raise the blood-sugar level to the normal range. There are two ways to give sugar: orally or through a vein. The oral treatment involves feeding the baby. A baby can take sugar water — a 5 percent solution of **dextrose** (a form of sugar) and sterile water — or formula. If a child seems to need extra calories on a regular basis for the first few days of life, then giving formula is often better than

WHAT IS THE DIFFERENCE BETWEEN
SUGAR WATER AND FORMULA?

◆

If a newborn is becoming dehydrated or is just extremely hungry in the first few days of life and her mother's milk is not in, then a supplement may be necessary. The two choices are sugar water and formula. Sugar water is a solution of water mixed with 5 percent dextrose. While it provides a small amount of sugar, this solution has none of the minerals or nutrients found in breast milk or formula. Therefore it does not give a newborn the nourishment she needs. Instead of repeatedly relying on sugar water, you should probably use formula to supplement feeds. The formula can be stopped once there is adequate breast-milk production. But until then, the baby will get the minerals, nutrients, and calories she needs.

sugar water, because formula has other minerals and nutrients that the child needs.

If a baby cannot take the feedings by mouth, or if the feeds are not working to raise the blood-sugar level, then an intravenous line must be started and a sugar solution dripped directly into the blood. The sugar solution is continued until the baby can maintain his blood-sugar level by drinking breast milk or formula. Beyond immediate treatment of the low blood sugar, additional treatments will depend on the specific cause of the hypoglycemia. Hypoglycemia can result from a variety of problems, including infection, thyroid trouble, and too much insulin production.

What are the possible complications?
A hungry baby who is simply not eating frequently enough will lose more weight than usual in the hospital and gain it back more slowly. Remember, it is normal for a baby to lose up to 10 percent of his birth weight in the first few days of life. The general rule is

THE DEBATE OVER NIPPLE CONFUSION

◆

There are many who believe that a baby can become confused by multiple nipples, and they worry that if a baby is trying to learn how to breast-feed, then the introduction of a bottle nipple will make this difficult. Nipple confusion is probably a myth. More likely, babies have nipple laziness. On the breast, a baby has to learn how to latch and feed well. The feedings take work. Bottle feedings are much easier, requiring less effort on behalf of the baby. Therefore a baby may not learn to feed efficiently from the breast if he is constantly offered the bottle. On the other hand, a baby who is never offered a bottle before he is 6 to 8 weeks old is likely never to accept one. Therefore it is generally recommended that if you want your baby to learn to drink from a bottle, then you should introduce one no later than 3 to 4 weeks and use the bottle at least every few days to keep up the baby's bottle skills. There are alternatives to a bottle altogether. Some babies take supplemental feeds from a medicine dropper or even off a spoon! And as they get older, many babies who will not drink from a bottle will drink from a cup or straw.

that a child should start gaining weight around the fourth or fifth day of life, and he should be back to his birth weight by two weeks. The main complications of too much weight loss and slow weight gain are dehydration and hypoglycemia. A baby with low blood sugar can become jittery or agitated. In addition, because the brain depends on glucose as its main source of fuel, having too little glucose can impair the brain's ability to function. Therefore, in extreme cases, severe or prolonged hypoglycemia may result in seizures and serious brain injury. Dehydration is covered in detail in chapter 28.

Additional Resources
http://www.packardchildrenshospital.org (Go to "search" in upper right-hand corner and type in "newborn weight loss.")
http://www.cincinnatichildrens.org (Go to "health topics" and then "Your Child's Health." Scroll down to the section on "Endocrine, Metabolism, and Diabetes" and select category called "Hypoglycemia in the Newborn.")
http://www.quickcare.org/gast/dehydrate.html
http://kidshealth.org/parent/growth/sleep/sleepnewborn.html

◆   ◆   ◆

OVERFEEDING
(Birth–12 Months)

What is happening inside my baby's body?
An overfed baby simply eats too much. This is usually a result of the *suck reflex:* a baby is born knowing how to suck, and this is the *only* way she can calm herself. She cannot scratch an itch or blow her nose, but she can suck.

Parents will sometimes interpret this constant sucking as hunger, so shortly after their baby has finished feeding, they may offer more. This results in more milk than the baby needs. But because the baby is sucking, she is soothed; in many instances she doesn't care if there is milk there or not and will take whatever is offered. In fact, it can be quite difficult for a baby to determine that she feels full, and it can be equally difficult for parents to tell that the baby doesn't need any more for the moment.

An overfed baby will gain weight quickly, sometimes too fast. She is also more likely to spit up. The spitting results from overflow in the stomach. Because the stomach can only hold so much milk, if a baby drinks more than that amount, then she will spit up the excess.

Unfortunately, because there are several causes of spitting up after feeds, it can be difficult for some parents to determine whether their baby is overfed. Sometimes the baby is sensitive to something in the breast milk (something that mom ate) or formula. Other times the muscle that keeps food down in the stomach and prevents it from going back up to the mouth does not work as well as it should. This latter cause, called *reflux,* is covered later in this chapter. There are other reasons for excessive spitting up, such as inability to pass food into the intestine *(pyloric stenosis)*, that are also covered later in this chapter.

What can I do?

When a baby is overfed, the simplest intervention is to reduce the amount given with each feeding. Remember, babies don't always know when they are full, and they will suck almost anytime they are given the opportunity. Therefore, in order to reduce feeding amounts, the feeding must be slowed down and the baby must be given time to decide whether or not she is full.

When overfeeding is suspected in a bottle-fed baby, she should be fed more slowly, stopping after each ounce or two and waiting a few minutes. Burping the baby midfeed will help reduce gas and will slow down the feeding. Some bottle-fed babies drink quickly because the hole at the end of the nipple is large and it takes little effort to get a lot of milk. By choosing a nipple with a smaller hole, you can ensure that the feeding will require more vigorous sucking and will take longer.

Breast-fed babies can take a break between feeding on each breast. Sometimes, however, there is so much milk in one breast that one side is more than enough for the entire feeding. When this is the case, try to take the baby off the breast after five to ten minutes, burp her, and then let her continue feeding. There are some mothers who have very rapid letdown of breast milk (milk rushes out at the beginning of the feed). The flow can be so strong that the baby can gag. In this case, the mom can try to manually express milk at the beginning of the feed so that the letdown is less forceful.

If the baby still wants to suck even after a feeding is completed, then try satisfying her with a finger or pacifier. The sucking will soothe her, and once she registers that she is full, she will stop sucking or fall asleep.

When does my doctor need to be involved?

Sometimes it is hard to tell that the cause of spitting up is overfeeding. Anytime you are concerned about your baby's spitting up, call your doctor.

BREAST VERSUS BOTTLE

◆

Is breast-feeding really best? Breast milk and formula are very similar, with almost identical fats, proteins, carbohydrates, and minerals. The big difference between the two is that breast milk has antibodies while formula does not. Antibodies help to fight infection, so breast-fed babies are slightly better equipped to deal with infections, especially in the first few months of life. But breast-feeding has to work for both mom and baby. There may be physical reasons why a baby cannot breast-feed effectively, such as cleft palate in the baby or severely inverted nipples in the mom. The mother may need to take medications that are dangerous if passed through the breast milk. Or a working mother may have to leave the house to go to work shortly after delivery, which creates problems if a baby needs to feed frequently. Some mothers choose to pump their breast milk and store it so that the baby can get breast milk from the bottle. But this is not absolutely necessary. Remember that many healthy children have been raised on formula. A combination of breast milk and formula or just formula alone is safe and healthy nutrition for your child. Breast-feeding should be a pleasure, not a stressor.

Signs that the spitting up is *not* due to overfeeding include forceful spitting up or spit-up that travels several inches from the baby's mouth; green (bile-containing) or red (bloody) spit-up; spit-up that is increasing in frequency and volume; and spit-up accompanied by fever or decreased energy. If any of these symptoms appear, call your doctor.

What tests need to be done, and what do the results mean?
Tests rarely need to be performed in the case of overfeeding. Rather, when the amount of breast milk or formula is reduced,

the spitting up should resolve. If, however, other causes of spitting up are suspected, then tests may be required. This is covered in the section on reflux later in this chapter.

What are the treatments?

The only treatment for overfeeding is to reduce the amount given per feed. Strategies to accomplish this are outlined in the previous sections. There are no medicines given.

What are the possible complications?

The main complications of overfeeding are reflux (painful spitting up) and obesity. Reflux is addressed later in this chapter. As for obesity, a baby typically gains one-half to one ounce per day in the first three months of life, and then one-quarter to one-half an ounce per day in the next three months. An overfed baby can gain two or three times that. While there is evidence that childhood obesity is linked with adult obesity, there is no clear consensus as to whether overfed or overweight babies have any risk of becoming obese children or adults.

Big babies may have slower motor development simply because they have more weight to move around. They may experience mild delays in sitting, rolling, standing, and walking. This can increase a baby's size even more because a sedentary lifestyle does not burn many calories. However, once a big baby can maneuver herself around, she will spend more calories being active and her weight gain will slow down. She will also likely be more interested in her surroundings and less interested in eating so much. This combination often leads to rapid slimming down of a big baby in the second year of life.

Additional Resources
http://www.lpch.org/HealthLibrary/ParentCareTopics/NewbornQuestions/
BottlefeedingQuestions.html
http://www.fda.gov/fdac/features/596_baby.html
http://www.nlm.nih.gov/medlineplus/encyclopedia.html (Click on "I–In,"
then scroll down to "infant formulas.")

◆   ◆   ◆

NORMAL STOOL VARIATION
(Birth–12 Months)

What is happening inside my baby's body?
Infant stool varies dramatically from baby to baby and from day
to day. A wide range of normal stool variation exists — colors
and textures that should cause no concern to parents. These
include *meconium,* the black tarry stool seen in the first few days
of life; *typical breast-fed stool,* yellow in color and speckled with
solid pieces resembling mustard seeds; *typical bottle-fed stool,*
green and more uniform than the breast-fed stool; and even *colorful stool* ranging from orange to electric green. Abnormal stool
colors include either red and bloody or white and mucus filled.
Black tarry stool should not continue past the first few days of life
and should not recur later.

The consistency of infant stool can vary but is considered
abnormal if it is so watery that it soaks through a diaper *(diarrhea)* or so dry that it looks like dried-out toothpaste or pellets
(constipation). These are covered later in this chapter.

Meconium. Meconium refers to normal newborn stool. When the
intestines form in a growing fetus, waste collects inside them.
This waste is a mixture of old cells, swallowed liquids, and other
products made by the developing intestine. Therefore the first
stools a baby passes are made of this nine-month-old-waste collection, and they come out in the form of a thick, sticky greenish-
black paste called meconium. It can take up to two or three days
to get rid of all this meconium. Once all the old debris are gone,
the stool changes color and consistency.

Meconium is always normal. Some babies pass it too early —
while they are still in the womb — and some babies have trouble
passing it. When the meconium is firm like a rock, it does not
pass easily out the anus. This is called a *meconium plug* and can
be associated with a variety of illnesses, including cystic fibrosis.

Breast-fed stool. The typical stool of a breast-fed baby is often described as "yellow mustard-seed stool." Once the breast milk has come in (around the third day of the baby's life), the meconium thins and lightens until the baby is passing liquid yellow stools. The consistency is similar to a thin milkshake. Some mothers notice that when they eat certain foods, the color changes from yellow to green or brown. This is normal and is discussed in the following text.

Bottle-fed stool. Bottle-fed babies usually produce green stools with a uniform consistency. They are still watery like the breast-fed stools but typically lack the seeded appearance. Sometimes bottle-fed stools can look yellow or brown. If different formulas are used, then the stools will often change color.

Colorful stool. Though most babies have fairly similar stools from day to day, some days the color changes dramatically. For breast-fed babies, it may be a consequence of something the mother ate. But for bottle-fed babies, there is little explanation. Sometimes a child has mild stomach flu and the stool changes color until the infection has passed. Regardless, it is not worrisome for the stool to look intermittently electric green or orange.

There are, however, more worrisome colors. Red can be a sign of blood. Brown flecks that look like coffee grounds can be evidence of old blood slowly passing through the intestine. Black is expected during the passage of meconium but should not return thereafter — it too can be a sign of blood. (Blood in the stool is covered in a separate section in this chapter.) White stool or mucus-filled stool is not typical either, although teething babies who are drooling excessively will swallow some of the excess drool, and this can pass through the stool as mucus. If the stool has any of these colors, then call your doctor.

What can I do?
You do not need to worry about normal stool variations. However, you should contact your doctor if your baby's stool has any abnormal colors.

When does my doctor need to be involved?
A doctor should be involved if the stool has any signs of blood, including black, bright red, or coffee-ground discoloration. A doctor should also be contacted if the stool is white or filled with mucus.

What tests need to be done, and what do the results mean?
No tests need to be done on stool that has normal color or texture variation. A baby who has an occasional bright green or orange stool is fine.

Bloody or mucus-filled stool, however, may indicate irritation, infection, or inflammation somewhere along the gastrointestinal tract. This is covered extensively in the section on blood in the stool later in this chapter.

What are the treatments?
Stools normally vary in color and texture. Therefore there are no treatments for normal stool variation.

What are the possible complications?
There is nothing to worry about when the stool changes color to a normal variant. The baby is absorbing nutrients well and will continue to gain weight.

Additional Resources
http://www.packardchildrenshospital.org (Go to "search" in upper right-hand corner and type in "stool color.")

CONSTIPATION
(Birth–12 Months)

What is happening inside my baby's body?
Some babies poop seven times a day. Other babies poop once every seven days. It doesn't matter how often a baby poops as long as what comes out is soft. Constipation refers to firm stool

that is difficult to pass. It does not refer exclusively to the frequency of stooling — a baby who stools once every few days may have soft stools and therefore is not constipated. The longer stool stays in the colon and rectum, however, the harder it usually becomes. Therefore, when a baby holds on to her stool much longer than what is normal for her, the stool is far more likely to look pasty, dry, or even like little pellets.

Some parents will notice that when their baby has not pooped in a while, she will become uncomfortable, drawing her legs up to her chest and even taking less milk at her feedings. This can be a precursor to constipation, but when the baby stools, it is typically still soft. You will quickly get used to your own baby's pattern. When she starts pooping less often, her risk of constipation increases.

To complicate matters, at around 4 to 6 weeks of life, many babies drastically slow down their own stooling pattern. Those who pooped several times per day may slow it down to once or twice; those who went daily or every other day may go as infrequently as once a week. This is appropriate. Imagine if, as adults, we went to the bathroom as often as a newborn! Parents can easily confuse this normal transition to a mature stooling pattern with constipation.

A baby with true constipation has infrequent, hard stools, sometimes even pelletlike. The stools hurt coming out, occasionally tearing the skin around the anus when they pass (called an *anal fissure*).

Constipation is a source of concern among parents because it is associated with pain. As described previously, constipated children will often draw their legs up to their chests and cry and sometimes decrease their milk intake. Once the anus is torn, there are two more potential causes of pain: stinging or burning caused by stool or urine coming into contact with the torn skin, and spasm of the muscle in the anus (called the *anal sphincter*). The spasms of the anal sphincter can also slow down normal stooling, causing a baby to become even more constipated. This creates a vicious cycle because a baby with a fissure who is persistently constipated will continue to reinjure the torn anus. Stools must be soft in order to allow healing of the broken skin. Anal fissures are covered in more detail in chapter 25.

There are many causes of constipation: a narrowing at the anus can prevent the stool from coming out. The nerves that move the intestines may not work well, slowing down the passage of stool. But often a baby is constipated simply because the milk she is drinking is stopping her up. And contrary to popular belief, this can happen with breast milk just as it can with formula.

What can I do?

By drinking more water and eating foods that promote bowel movements, a breast-feeding mom can change her diet to help soften the baby's stools. Sometimes a breast-feeding mom can drink prune juice to help her baby stool. Both breast- and bottle-feeding parents can also give their babies prune juice in small amounts, as outlined in more detail in the following text.

When an infant begins solid foods — usually by six months — her new diet may lead to (or exacerbate existing) constipation. You may try to minimize this by adding sweet fruits (apricots, prunes, peaches, pears, plums) and certain fibrous vegetables (such as peas and spinach) to her diet.

Some parents find that baby massage helps to move the bowels. Gentle rubbing of the abdomen and cycling of the legs and feet are usually incorporated. There are many books about infant massage that teach parents how to use this effectively.

Beyond dietary changes and massage, there are medicines and remedies that work wonders for constipated babies. These are described in the following text.

For a baby that is painfully constipated, you can help move the bowels manually. One approach is to use a rectal thermometer, usually coated with petroleum jelly or some other mild lubricant. The act of taking a rectal temperature stimulates the anal sphincter and often causes a baby to poop shortly thereafter. Some parents will use their pinky finger (cut your nails!) instead of a thermometer. If this does not work, then there are suppositories that can be used in a similar manner. These are covered with the other medications that follow.

You should try only once or twice to help move the bowels with a thermometer or a suppository before speaking with your doctor. Parents who rely too heavily on this technique may find that their baby becomes dependent on it and cannot pass a stool without help.

When does my doctor need to be involved?

If your baby is in pain, then contact your doctor. Also call if the constipation is ongoing or getting worse. Vomiting or fever with constipation each warrant a call to your doctor.

The first time your baby has blood in the stool, you may find it difficult to tell whether it is from an anal fissure or from elsewhere in the intestines. Either way, call your doctor. Blood in the stool is covered in more detail later in this chapter.

What tests need to be done, and what do the results mean?

For normal constipation that is readily resolved with dietary changes, prune juice, rectal thermometers, or over-the-counter medical treatments, no tests need to be done.

However, if the constipation is not easily treatable or if it worsens despite attempts to treat it, then the cause of the constipation must be sought. An X ray can show how much stool remains in the intestines. It can also identify some structural abnormalities of the intestinal tract. In extreme cases, a colonoscopy or biopsy may need to be done. These are performed by gastroenterologists — doctors specializing in the intestinal tract. Both techniques can be used to look for a variety of causes of constipation.

Hirschsprung's disease is the absence of nerves at the end of the colon that are necessary to help keep the bowels moving. This uncommon problem, which can cause severe constipation, can only be diagnosed through biopsy. Constipation resulting from Hirschsprung's disease requires surgery.

What are the treatments?

The two main treatments for constipation are stool softeners and lubrication. *Stool softeners* are taken by mouth and are meant to pass through the stomach and into the intestines to soften the forming stool. The most readily available stool softeners are prune juice and pear juice. These fibrous fruit juices are sugary, and this sugar content helps the body draw water into the intestines as the stool is being formed. This works to alleviate constipation because the body likes to dilute sugary substances in the intestines. Therefore water will collect in the intestines along with the sugars, softening the stool. Breast- and bottle-fed babies alike can take one or two ounces of prune or pear juice every 12 hours until the stool softens. This is generally recommended only when the baby has reached at least two months of age; parents of younger babies should contact their doctor.

If juice doesn't work, then lactulose may help. Lactulose is a nonabsorbable sugar that works much the same way that prunes and pears work. Other stool softeners include milk of magnesia, which can be given to a baby as half a teaspoon every 12 to 24 hours (in lieu of juice), and dioctyl sodium sulfosuccinate (docusate).

The other approach to constipation is lubrication. Lubrication works by greasing up the anus so that the stool can slide by more easily. Any color-free, perfume-free lubricant — such as Vaseline or other petroleum jelly — may be used. A small amount is applied at the anus using a finger, not a Q-Tip or other narrow tool. This can be repeated every few hours or with each diaper change until a stool is passed with ease. This technique helps to prevent (or minimize) anal fissures.

Sometimes lubrication must be combined with an approach that will help move the stool out of the rectum quickly. This is especially true when a baby is crying with discomfort. The most effective way to do this is to use a suppository or enema. *Glycerin* suppositories (sized for babies) are gently inserted into the anus. The physical presence of the suppository stimulates the bowels to contract, often pushing stool out. Suppositories lubricate the anus because they melt inside it, providing a pool of glycerin to coat the stool. The alternative to a suppository is an *enema,* which is a liquid inserted directly into the anus. Infant enemas can be made with a variety of substances, including premelted glycerin. They stimulate the bowels to move by the same principle as the suppository but often coat the stool better, helping to move things along even more. The glycerin enema sold in markets and pharmacies is called Babylax.

Remember, stimulation of the anus in order to help move the bowels should not be done regularly without speaking with your doctor. You do not want your baby to become dependent on this as a means of moving the bowels.

What are the possible complications?

The most common complication of constipation is more constipation. Once a baby has passed a painful stool, she does not want to repeat the uncomfortable experience. Therefore — especially among older babies (and young children) — constipation begets constipation because they will hold their stool in. Among infants, this is more readily solvable, because once a baby returns to normal, soft, painless stools, she is likely to resume regular pooping.

Regular constipation can lead to slow weight gain (or none at all). This happens when the impacted stools impair your baby's appetite.

Severely impacted stools that cannot come out despite all efforts can lead to a *toxic megacolon*. This very rare but worrisome consequence of constipation can be life threatening and requires immediate medical attention.

Additional Resources
http://www.caps.ca/guests/statements/constipation.htm
http://www.drhull.com/EncyMaster/C/constipation_infant.html
http://www.nlm.nih.gov/medlineplus/encyclopedia.html (Click on "Ah–Ap," then scroll down to "anal fissure.")
http://www.nlm.nih.gov/medlineplus/encyclopedia.html (Click on "To–Tz," then scroll down to "toxic megacolon.")

◇　　◇　　◇

DIARRHEA
(Birth–12 Months)

What is happening inside my baby's body?

Diarrhea is loose, watery, and frequent stool. Because infant stool is already pretty soft and pretty frequent, you may find it difficult to tell whether your baby has diarrhea. If the stool has so much water that it soaks almost entirely into the diaper, or if a child is stooling two or three times as often as he typically does, then he is having diarrhea.

Diarrhea has a number of causes. Infections — such as viruses, bacteria, and parasites — can all cause loose stool. They do so either by releasing toxins in the intestine or by changing the normal balance of bacteria in the gut. It is important to remember that bacteria are normal inhabitants of the intestine, and when the numbers and types of bacteria change dramatically, the consistency of the stool will change too. Probably the most common cause of infectious diarrhea among young children is a virus called *rotavirus.*

Foods can also cause diarrhea. Some infants cannot tolerate certain food types, even when they are passed through the breast milk or are components of formula. This is covered in some detail in the section on eczema in chapter 11 and also in the section on blood in the stool later in this chapter.

Antibiotics often cause diarrhea, although this is uncommon among young babies because they are rarely put on antibiotics in the first place. Antibiotics generally cause loose stool in much the same way as some infections cause it — by changing the balance of the bacteria that normally reside in the intestine. Babies may also be allergic to the antibiotic, with profuse diarrhea (and more often, rash) as a sign of the allergy.

Once any diarrhea starts, it can be difficult to stop. This happens because the intestines become very irritated. The normally absorptive intestine cannot absorb as well, so more water and nutrients are passed through the stool than usual.

What can I do?

If the diarrhea is associated with other symptoms, such as vomiting or fever, then it is likely the result of an infection. There is little that parents can do if a baby is not yet eating solid foods, other than to give some extra fluid to keep up with the excess water and nutrients being lost in the stool. Babies younger than four months cannot process plain drinking water very well. Therefore your baby should not be given water or teas in lieu of formula or breast milk.

In an older baby, if the diarrhea is associated with a particular food — or at any age if a new formula was started just at the onset of the diarrhea or if the diarrhea seems to be associated with something a breast-feeding mother ate — then avoiding that type of formula or food should solve the problem.

There are rehydration drinks available in supermarkets and drugstores. These have electrolytes to replace what is lost during ongoing diarrhea. Unfortunately these drinks are not safe if they are the only liquid consumed for more than 24 hours. Also, babies and young children often don't like the taste of these drinks. As an alternative, you may find it more helpful to try supplementing breast milk or formula with white grape juice (not purple) or rice water. These suggestions are intended for children over four months of age. If your baby is younger, then contact your doctor.

RICE WATER

◆

To make rice water, boil one liter of water. Add about one cup of rice and cook for five to ten minutes until the water is starchy. Then pour the liquid into a container. Some people like to add one teaspoon of sugar and a pinch of salt to the liquid. After the starchy liquid has cooled to room temperature, give it to the baby in small amounts. When a baby has been throwing up, start with tiny portions, such as half an ounce every 15 to 30 minutes. If this is tolerated, then increase to an ounce, and then to two ounces. If the baby has only diarrhea, then you do not need to limit the amount you are giving. Remember, this is intended for babies older than four months. You can do whatever you like with the leftover rice.

When does my doctor need to be involved?

Anytime there is blood or mucus in the diarrhea, or when there is so much diarrhea that the child risks becoming dehydrated, call your doctor. Dehydration can happen if the diarrhea persists over an extended period of time and is not getting better. Signs of dehydration are covered in chapter 28.

If a medication is the suspected cause of the diarrhea, then your doctor should be called because the medicine may need to be changed or stopped.

What tests need to be done, and what do the results mean?

Tests are rarely necessary in the case of diarrhea. If infection is suspected, however, tests can be done on the stool to look for bacteria, viruses, and parasites. Tests to look for infection are usually not done unless the diarrhea has lasted longer than two weeks or has become bloody.

If allergy is suspected but a specific allergen cannot be identified by trial and error (changing the diet), then the stool can also be checked for *white blood cells* and certain cells called *eosinophils*. These two cell types may be passed in the stool in the case of inflammation or allergy, but they do not identify the exact cause of the allergy. For more on diagnosing allergies, see the section on eczema in chapter 11.

What are the treatments?

Infection is a common cause of diarrhea among children. Bacterial infections are often left untreated, as they will almost always resolve spontaneously. Viruses must also run their course. However, diarrhea resulting from parasites such as *Giardia* require specific antibiotics for treatment.

If allergy is the source of the diarrhea, then the best treatment is always to stop the offending agent. Breast-feeding mothers need to try to keep track of what foods seem to be associated with the problem. Avoiding these foods should stop the diarrhea. Bottle-feeding parents may try a different type of formula. The general classes of formula include cow's milk, soy, hypoallergenic, and lactose-free. Sometimes one brand is better tolerated than another; other times the type of protein (cow versus soy) makes the difference.

If an antibiotic is the source of diarrhea, then your doctor may reduce the dosage or stop it altogether.

What are the possible complications?

The most worrisome complication of diarrhea is dehydration. The best way to avoid dehydration is to supplement the child with extra liquids such as breast milk, formula, and rice water. Dehydration is covered in chapter 28.

Severe or persistent diarrhea can also cause diaper rash. The rash can become very red and angry quite quickly, as the stool touches already inflamed skin. The best way to minimize a diaper rash in this situation is to change the diaper as soon as the stool is passed. Washing the bottom with plain water instead of perfumed soaps or wipes will also help. Sometimes a thin barrier cream, especially one with zinc, will help heal the skin. Diaper rashes are covered in chapter 11.

Additional Resources
http://www.niddk.nih.gov/health/digest/pubs/diarrhea/diarrhea.htm
http://www.nlm.nih.gov/medlineplus/encyclopedia.html (Click on "B–Bk," then scroll down to "babies and diarrhea.")

◆   ◆   ◆

BLOOD IN THE STOOL
(Birth–12 Months)

What is happening inside my baby's body?

You may find blood mixed into the stool, coating the stool, or next to the stool on the diaper. The blood can appear bright red; as brown flecks resembling coffee grounds; or black like tar. The coffee ground and black colors result from old blood passing slowly through the intestine. The black color is expected during the passage of meconium but should not return thereafter. Bloody stool can also look uniformly maroon like the color of currant jelly.

The source of the bleeding can often be determined from its color — a sign of how old the blood is and how long it has been in the intestine. If the blood is mixed in with the stool, then it is likely that the bleeding is coming from the intestine. If it appears around or next to the stool, however, then it is more likely that it originated from the skin around the anus, appearing after the stool passed through the intestines. This is called an ***anal fissure*** and is covered in more detail in chapter 25.

Foods are among the most common causes of blood (or mucus) in the stool. Among foods, cow's milk is one of the biggest offenders. Formulas made from cow's milk, or breast milk from mothers drinking and eating dairy products, can be the culprit. This is especially true if the child has other signs of allergy, such as eczema.

Though cow's milk is among the most common food sensitivity, many different foods can cause blood (or mucus) in the stool. Some bottle-fed babies have blood with both cow's milk *and* soy formulas. These children often do well with ***elemental formulas,*** which are made with cow's milk but are predigested so that the intestines do significantly less work breaking down the milk. These formulas are also typically hypoallergenic, with fewer additives that can cause intestinal irritation.

What can I do?

The first time you see blood in the stool, you should call your doctor. If possible, save the diaper with the bloody stool so that the doctor can see where the blood is relative to the stool.

When does my doctor need to be involved?

Call your doctor anytime you see blood in the stool for the first time. If you see copious amounts of blood; if the blood persists; or if the child seems pale, lethargic, or significantly irritable, then contact your doctor immediately.

What tests need to be done, and what do the results mean?

Tests are done based on the appearance of the child and the way the blood looks in the stool. Blood that is around the edges of the stool or separate from it altogether is likely the result of an anal fissure. This requires little testing and is covered in chapter 25.

THE DIFFERENCE BETWEEN COW'S MILK
AND SOY FORMULA
◆

Cow's milk formula and soy formula have different proteins. Cow's milk protein is well tolerated by most babies. In some instances, though, it will cause diarrhea or rash (or both). Soy protein is derived from plants called legumes. If a baby is sensitive to cow's milk protein, then she may better tolerate soy protein. Some parents choose to give soy formula to their child regardless of sensitivity issues because they would like to avoid cow's milk. This is a personal choice worth discussing with your doctor. The other ingredients in the formulas — fats, minerals, vitamins, and so on — are almost identical in soy and cow's milk preparations.

Stool that looks like currant jelly in a child who seems ill is a worrisome finding. The stool should be checked in the laboratory, but the child may also need an X ray or an ultrasound (or both). Currant jelly stool is associated with **intussusception** — an uncommon condition in which one piece of bowel telescopes into another, cutting off the blood supply and causing significant pain.

Because a food allergy may cause the irritation, your doctor will often suggest modifying the diet before running any tests on the stool. This is a trial-and-error method whereby a food is removed from the diet to see if the bleeding (or mucus) will stop. For instance, a cow's milk formula may be switched to a soy formula, or a breast-feeding mother may be instructed to limit her dairy intake. If the stool returns to normal, then the baby has essentially tested positive for cow's milk sensitivity. The term **sensitivity** is used rather than **allergy** because many babies who have intestinal reactions to cow's milk, or any other food for that matter, will outgrow these responses. Therefore, the babies are considered sensitive in the early months and are only diagnosed with a true allergy if the symptoms persist or if there are concurrent symptoms such as rash, fussiness, or hives.

If the bloody stools do not resolve by the restriction of a breast-feeding mother's cow's-milk intake alone, then a mother may need to further restrict her diet. She can slowly add back one food at a time to determine the cause of the sensitivity. Your doctor can tell you which foods are most likely to cause problems. Some of the most common include citrus, berries, tomato, onion, and spicy foods in general. This trial-and-error test works well when the amount of blood or mucus is small, when the baby is continuing to gain weight well, and when there are no other severe symptoms.

Sometimes your doctor may check your baby's stool to determine whether the blood and mucus are related to food sensitivity or to infection. Stool is sent to a laboratory, where it is checked for infections ranging from parasites to bacteria to viruses. The stool may also be checked for cells — debris from the intestine. *White blood cells* in the stool tend to accompany all sorts of infections and inflammation. Cells called *eosinophils* are specific markers of food sensitivity or allergy. If eosinophils are present but white blood cells are not, then the likely cause of blood (or mucus) is allergy, not infection.

In extreme cases, a gastroenterologist (a doctor specializing in the intestinal tract) may suggest tests that take pictures of the intestines. X rays can show the general shape of the bowels, and X rays done after a baby drinks a liquid that illuminates the lining of the intestines *(barium)* can show the inside walls as well. A tiny camera can be inserted into the stomach via the mouth (called an *upper endoscopy*) or into the large intestine via the anus (called a *colonoscopy*) to take clear pictures of the bowel. These tests are quite invasive and are used only when necessary.

What are the treatments?
If the stool has blood or mucus, then the treatment will depend on the cause. If food sensitivity is the culprit, then the offending food must be removed. For breast-feeding moms, this means restricting the diet. For bottle-feeders, the formula may be switched.

If intussusception is the cause, then the bowel must be released from its telescoped position. This requires an enema using a liquid visible on X ray (called a *barium enema*) or sometimes even surgery. Intussusception is extremely rare among infants; it is more common among toddlers.

What are the possible complications?

The complications of bloody stool or mucus-filled stool include diarrhea, diaper rash (because bloody stool is more irritating to the skin than normal stool is), poor weight gain, and abdominal pain. Other possible complications depend on the cause of the blood or mucus.

> *Additional Resources*
> http://www.nlm.nih.gov/medlineplus/encyclopedia.html (Click on "I–In," then scroll down to "intussusception [children].")
> http://web1.tch.harvard.edu/ (Go to "Child Health A to Z," then enter "bloody stool" under "Search the Encyclopedia" at the bottom of the screen.)

REFLUX
(Birth–12 Months)

What is happening inside my baby's body?

Milk travels from the mouth, down the esophagus, and into the stomach. There is a muscle at the junction between the esophagus and the stomach called the *lower esophageal sphincter* (or *LES*). This muscle keeps food in the stomach and doesn't let it back up. The LES is notoriously weak in the first few months of life. So, when a baby is fed just a little too much or is laid down immediately after feeding, food travels right back up the esophagus, into the mouth, and onto the baby's chest or clothes (or yours). If the spitting-up is associated with pain or arching of the back, this sequence of events is called reflux. Another name for it is *GERD,* or *gastroesophageal reflux disease.* Frequent or voluminous reflux is often uncomfortable for the baby, so he may arch and cry before spitting up.

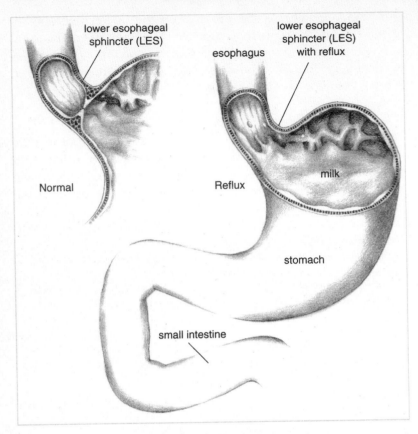

Normal lower esophageal sphincter (*left*)
versus lower esophageal sphincter that allows milk
back up into the esophagus in reflux (*right*)

The LES strengthens over time, so reflux typically resolves by three or four months of age. In the first few weeks of life, however, most babies have occasional episodes of reflux. When the milk that has gone down to the stomach comes back up, it is mixed with acids from the stomach. This acidic fluid burns, causing the baby to cry or wriggle with pain. The crying and movement can cause more juggling of the stomach contents, resulting in more reflux.

Infants who have had surgery or who are born with abnormal intestinal tracts have reflux more often than other children. The presence of acid in the esophagus caused by GERD can significantly increase airway reactivity, which can be a precursor to asthma.

What can I do?

There are a variety of things a parent can do to minimize reflux. You can hold your baby upright after feeds to allow gravity to help keep the milk down. Burp your baby well after each feed. Some babies need to be burped halfway through the feed as well. The amount of milk given at each feeding can be reduced so that the stomach doesn't overflow so easily. If this is done, then the baby may need extra feedings during the day so that he can continue to gain weight well.

Sometimes something in the milk exacerbates reflux. Breast-feeding mothers should try to keep a log so that they can track what they have eaten and correlate it with when the reflux is at its worst. Sometimes breast-feeding moms use a trial-and-error method by removing potential irritants from their diet and then adding them back to see if the reflux gets better or worse. This is similar to the strategy described in the section on eczema and food allergy in chapter 11 and in the section on blood in the stool earlier in this chapter.

Some babies are extremely sensitive to the protein in cow's milk. This sensitivity can cause the symptoms of reflux. Removing dairy from the mom's diet or choosing a dairy-free formula may help. Thickening the formula with a small amount of rice cereal may also help because it makes the formula heavier, allowing it to stay down in the stomach better. But using rice cereal to thicken milk does not always work. In some cases, it actually exacerbates reflux. Occasionally no standard formula is tolerated and an **elemental formula** is needed. Again, this is covered in chapter 11.

Medicines can help reflux in one of two ways. They can either reduce the amount of acid in the stomach so that the milk doesn't burn when it comes back up, or speed up the emptying of the stomach into the intestine. These are covered in more detail in the following text.

In general, the best treatment is time. Once the LES gets stronger and more coordinated, it does its job to keep milk in the stomach without letting it back up the esophagus.

FOODS FOR BREAST-FEEDING WOMEN TO AVOID
◆

If you are breast-feeding, then the foods (and drinks) you consume will make their way — in some form — into the breast milk. Some babies are fine no matter what their mom eats. Others are very sensitive, becoming gassy or rashy or fussy with certain foods. Below is a list of the biggest offenders, the foods most commonly associated with reactions in babies. If you think your baby is reacting to something in your milk, then try removing each of the following list items from your diet, one at a time. It may take several days to see results, but if the baby improves, then you've found the likely culprit. Some moms prefer to remove many of these things at once and then add them back one at a time to identify the source of the problem. Either approach will work.

Citrus: orange, lemon, lime, grapefruit
Berries: strawberries, raspberries, blueberries, cherries
   (this includes flavorings such as those found in yogurt)
Nuts
Shellfish
Wheat
Dairy
Tomato
Broccoli
Onions
Corn

When does my doctor need to be involved?

There are three reasons to call your doctor. First, call if you think your child has reflux — if your baby is arching and spitting up after feeds or seems to be in pain when laid down after feeds.

SPITTING UP VERSUS REFLUX

❖

It is normal for a baby to spit up. So how can you tell if your baby has reflux? In both cases, a baby can spit up a large amount and can spit up often . . . sometimes after every feed. The main difference is the degree of discomfort. A spitty baby will spit up and be fine. He will probably act as if nothing has happened — he won't cry or fuss. A baby with reflux, on the other hand, will be uncomfortable. He will arch his back when he is about to spit up, and he will often cry at the same time.

This call is nonurgent. Second, call if the baby is spitting up after almost every feeding, is spitting up more and more over time, or is spitting up forcefully. And finally, if the spit-up is green (bile colored), or red or brown (blood colored), call your doctor immediately.

What tests need to be done, and what do the results mean?
Reflux can often be diagnosed without any tests. If a baby improves with positioning — sitting up after feeds for 10 to 15 minutes — then mild reflux is the cause. When the reflux is more severe, especially if the baby is not gaining weight well or if he has remarkable pain after every feeding, then he may have to be put on an acid-reducing medicine to see if the symptoms improve.

In some cases, an X ray or ultrasound may be done to look at the stomach and intestine. A special X ray called an ***upper gastrointestinal (UGI) series*** can detect problems with the way the intestines are shaped. Other means of checking for reflux do not use X rays. ***Esophageal pH monitoring*** measures acid levels in the esophagus and can determine whether these levels are related to the reflux symptoms. ***Esophagoscopy*** is a technique where a tiny camera is inserted into the mouth and then down the esophagus. It videos the inside of the esophagus, and if an abnormal area is spotted, a biopsy can be performed at that time. When these more sophisticated tests are used, a gastroenterologist is involved. These tests are required very rarely in cases of reflux.

What are the treatments?

As described above, the main treatment for reflux is positioning. Keep your baby upright for at least 10 to 15 minutes after feeding. This can be difficult to do in the middle of the night, but remember that if the baby lies down, then the milk will often just come right back up. Some people keep a car seat by the bed and — after night feedings — prop the baby upright in the seat.

If positioning is not helping, then sometimes changing the mother's diet, altering the formula type, or thickening the milk with rice cereal may help.

There are medicines that can make the baby much more comfortable. One of the most common medicines is ranitidine (also known as Zantac), a type of *antihistamine*. This medicine reduces stomach acid so that when the milk *does* come back up, it doesn't burn quite as much. Then the baby won't arch and cry as often, helping to minimize the cycle of reflux. The baby will still spit up, but it won't hurt. Ranitidine is started at a low dose and can be increased — under medical supervision — until it becomes effective. There is a limit, however, to how much ranitidine a baby can take, so sometimes other medicines are needed. There are a number of acid-reducing medicines available.

There are also other classes of medicines that treat reflux. Some are *antacids,* such as Mylanta or Maalox. Others hasten the movement of food through the intestine. Metoclopramide (also known as Reglan) is one of these. In some children, it speeds the emptying of the stomach so that there is more room for milk at the outset of the next feeding. Discuss these with your doctor.

What are the possible complications?

Reflux can cause vomiting from acid irritation in the esophagus. It can also cause coughing because the regurgitated milk can gag a child. In rare instances, the refluxed milk comes up the esophagus and drains down into the neighboring airway (called *aspiration*). Repetitive episodes of this can cause asthma or pneumonia.

Children with reflux who vomit frequently may be slow to gain weight. Also, in time, the acid in the esophagus can cause inflammation or ulcers. Over the long term, chronic inflammation can result in esophageal scarring.

Additional Resources
http://www.kidshealth.org/parent/medical/digestive/gerd_reflux.html
http://www.packardchildrenshospital.org (Go to "search" in upper right-hand corner and type in "reflux.")
http://www.webgerd.com/GerdTreatmentInInfants.htm
http://www.healthsystem.virginia.edu/internet/pediatrics/patients/Tutorials/GERD/GERD.cfm

◇　　◇　　◇

SPITTING UP, VOMITING, AND PYLORIC STENOSIS
(Birth–12 Months)

What is happening inside my baby's body?
Spitting up is often normal. Vomiting is not. Distinguishing between the two is difficult, as both happen relatively frequently among infants.

The reason food tends to come back up in infants has to do with the anatomy of the stomach and intestines. Milk travels down to the stomach by way of the esophagus, a long narrow tube connecting the mouth and the stomach. Once the milk lands in the stomach, it must be emptied out into the intestine. Everything is meant to flow in one direction — down. In order to make sure digested food follows the right path, there are muscles along the way to direct the flow. There is one at the end of the esophagus where it meets the beginning of the stomach (called the *lower esophageal sphincter,* or *LES*) and another one at the outlet of the stomach where the stomach meets the intestine (called the *pyloric sphincter*). These muscles prevent food from reentering the area it has just left.

When the LES is loose and does not work well, food can flow easily from the stomach back up the esophagus. This spitting up is called *reflux* and is covered in the previous section.

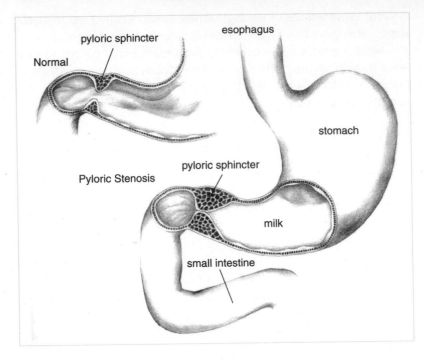

Normal pyloric sphincter (*left*) versus
pyloric sphincter that doesn't allow milk to drain
effectively out the stomach
in pyloric stenosis (*right*)

When the stomach itself is irritated — in the case of an infection or when the muscles of the stomach are in spasm — there will be vomiting. Compared with the spit-up of reflux, vomit is more forceful and sometimes more voluminous.

Finally, in infants the pyloric sphincter can cause a problem at the outlet of the stomach. The pyloric sphincter almost always works well — sometimes too well. It can become so thick and strong in some babies that the contents of the stomach have trouble passing through this muscle, and the milk gets backed up into the stomach. This is called *pyloric stenosis*. When the milk fills the stomach, it overflows into the esophagus. In this case, it doesn't just come out as spit-up — it comes out as remarkably forceful vomit. Many parents describe it as "projectile" and say that it can shoot up to ten feet from the baby's mouth! Pyloric stenosis occurs almost exclusively in infants.

What can I do?

Distinguish between spit-up and vomit. If your baby is vomiting, then stop offering liquids until the vomiting has subsided. After an hour or two, liquids can be reintroduced slowly, by the spoonful or dropper or in the form of a damp washcloth to suck on. If your baby can tolerate very small amounts of liquid without vomiting, then offer more. Even if your baby seems very thirsty and wants to drink a lot of liquid, remember that the more the baby drinks at a time, the more likely she is to throw it up again. Once your child is tolerating small amounts of liquid, you can gradually increase the amount offered.

When does my doctor need to be involved?

Call your doctor if your baby's vomiting is persistent or uncontrollable. This includes a baby who continues to vomit despite an empty stomach (called *dry heaving*) or who continues to vomit over several hours, unable to tolerate any liquids. Call if the color of the vomit is red, dark brown, or black. These are all colors associated with blood. Green vomit contains bile and is also worrisome — a doctor should evaluate any child who has it.

Anytime you think that the vomiting is becoming projectile, your baby should be evaluated for pyloric stenosis. This is covered in more detail in the following text.

What tests need to be done, and what do the results mean?

Vomiting rarely requires medical tests. In the case of bloody or green vomit, however, an X ray may be helpful to look at the bowels. X rays can show poor functioning in the intestines.

If there is blood in the vomit, then a complete blood count may be done to make sure that the baby is not losing too much blood. In extreme cases, if there is a significant amount of bleeding associated with the vomiting, then a small camera can be inserted through the mouth into the esophagus, stomach, and intestine in order to look for the source of the blood. This is called *endoscopy.*

If pyloric stenosis is suspected, then a physical exam may reveal a small round lump where the outlet of the stomach is. This lump, which feels like an olive, represents the actual thick and tight pyloric sphincter. To confirm the diagnosis, your doctor will do an ultrasound. Sometimes babies must drink some milk during the ultrasound so that the liquid can be followed down to the stomach and the outline of the enlarged pyloric sphincter can be seen.

What are the treatments?

The main treatment for most types of vomiting is time. If an infection (such as a virus or bacteria) is the cause, then the infection will typically pass and the vomiting will subside. Some infections — such as parasites — require treatment with specific medications.

There are medications available to stop acute vomiting. These medications, called *antiemetics,* are rarely used in infants but may be recommended if a child is becoming dehydrated. The most common of these is promethazine (also called Phenergan), given in the form of a rectal suppository since the oral form usually will not stay down in a vomiting child.

If pyloric stenosis is the cause of the vomiting, then the treatment is surgery. The surgery is a relatively simple procedure whereby the thickened, tight pylorus is cut to release the pressure on the outlet of the stomach. Children are often drinking within hours of the surgery, and the forceful spitting up resolves completely.

What are the possible complications?

The most worrisome complication of persistent vomiting or long-standing pyloric stenosis is dehydration. Dehydration can become quite severe, especially in a small baby with little reserve. This is covered in chapter 28.

Repetitive or forceful vomiting can also cause tears in the lining of the esophagus. When this occurs at the lower end of the esophagus, it is called a *Mallory-Weiss tear.* Its hallmark is bright-red blood with vomiting.

Additional Resources
http://www.packardchildrenshospital.org (Go to "search" in upper right-hand corner and type in "pyloric stenosis.")
http://web1.tch.harvard.edu/ (Go to "Child Health A to Z," then enter "pyloric stenosis" under "Search the Encyclopedia" at the bottom of the screen.)

◆   ◆   ◆

FAILURE TO THRIVE
(Birth–12 Months)

What is happening inside my baby's body?

Failure to thrive *(FTT)* is the medical term meaning poor weight gain. Some FTT babies actually lose weight, but most do not gain it with adequate speed. Weight gain is a critical measure of infant health. The better a baby gains, the better she will grow and the better her brain will develop. Of course, there is a limit — there is such a thing as too much weight gain. This is covered in an earlier section of this chapter.

Your baby will be weighed each time you visit your doctor. The weight is plotted on a growth chart so that the progression can be followed easily. The standard growth chart is divided into *percentiles:* 5th, 10th, 25th, 50th, 75th, 90th, and 95th. The percentile depends on both weight and age.

Percentiles are tricky to understand. First, do not get hung up on the absolute percentile. If your child was 50th percentile three months ago and has dropped to 25th percentile now, then there may be nothing to worry about. The rate of change, rather than the absolute value, is most important. Second, the percentiles are relative. Height, weight, and head circumference are all plotted on growth charts. The height and weight will usually travel together, so if a child has dropped a percentile in weight, then she will likely have dropped a percentile in height too. Look at all the numbers together. Third, babies tend to look like their parents. So a baby with long and lean parents will often have a lower percentile of weight than height. On the other hand, a baby with more short, stout parents may have a higher weight and a lower height. This is certainly not absolute, but in general thinner parents have thinner children. Finally, FTT is defined as a drop of more than two percentile categories over a short period of time. In other words, your child would have to go from the 50th percentile to below the 10th percentile in a short period of time in order to be called FTT. Weight change is often much more gradual than this.

There are many causes of FTT, but they can be boiled down to two general categories: too few calories coming in or too many calories being burned. The most common cause of too few calories coming in is underfeeding. Some babies cannot get as much milk as they want or need. In the case of a breast-fed baby, the mother may not be producing enough milk. In the case of a bottle-fed baby, the bottles may have too little milk at each feed or the baby may be receiving too few bottles over a 24-hour period. There are other, less common causes of inadequate caloric intake. For instance, some babies with nervous system problems or structural problems of the mouth or intestines have mechanical difficulties getting adequate food in. And very rarely, reflux can be so severe that a baby will not gain adequate weight. Reflux is described in the preceding section.

Sometimes FTT can occur despite normal caloric intake, or even when intake is excessive. This can result from *malabsorption,* the inability of the intestine to properly absorb food. Malabsorption may be caused by allergy to the milk (such as allergy to cow's milk or sensitivity to something that a breast-feeding mother is eating) or by failure to absorb the fats in breast milk or formula. Infection in the intestine can also lead to malabsorption, particularly in the case of parasites.

Sometimes FTT results when the baby burns through calories too quickly. Abnormalities in the infant's metabolism — including excessive thyroid or growth hormone levels — can cause FTT. Problems with any major organ system — such as the heart or lungs — can cause the body to burn calories inefficiently, leading to poor weight gain. And finally, there are chromosomal causes of FTT. Children with genetic diseases such as Down syndrome will often have poor weight gain early on.

What can I do?

It can be difficult to tell whether or not your child is getting enough calories. It is easier to discern this with a bottle-fed baby, because the daily milk consumption can be measured. Still, you may not be sure that the calories are getting in and staying in. In order to tell if your baby is getting enough with each feed, look for the signs of hunger (such as fussiness and glancing around for more food) when the feed is done. If your baby is furiously looking for food shortly after her last feed, then she may not have eaten enough.

If you think your child is not gaining weight adequately, then you can try feeding her more frequently or giving larger amounts with each feed. Keep a log of feeding, stooling, and sleeping patterns. This will help when you discuss the issue with your doctor.

Breast-feeding mothers can try to increase their milk supply by drinking lots of water and by feeding more frequently. Pumping the milk may help to stimulate more milk production. There are many remedies that can assist in increasing milk supply. Two of the most common include drinking a small amount of dark beer and taking the herb fenugreek.

When does my doctor need to be involved?

Call your doctor if you think your baby is not gaining adequate weight. Usually the doctor will suggest that you bring her to the office for a weight check. If your baby is taking significantly less milk with each feeding — leaving more behind in the bottle or pulling off the breast after a short interval — then talk to your doctor. Also call your doctor if your child has a dramatic increase in the number of stools per day or if the stools are watery, foul smelling, greasy, bloody, or filled with mucus.

If your doctor has told you that your child is failing to thrive, then you and your doctor will come up with a feeding and weighing plan. Follow-up will be fairly frequent, and you shouldn't hesitate to call with questions. Often a gastroenterologist will become involved with the care of your child.

What tests need to be done, and what do the results mean?
If increasing the number of calories solves the problem, then a baby with FTT may not need any tests. However, depending on the severity of the weight loss and the appearance of the child, tests may be done. A complete blood count looks for anemia and evidence of chronic problems. An electrolyte panel looks for problems in kidney function and imbalances in body minerals. Abnormalities on a liver panel may identify other chronic medical issues. Urine can be checked for infection and byproducts of metabolic problems. Stool may be tested for fat content — if there is fat in the stool, then there is some malabsorption. Stool can also be checked for infection (including parasites) and blood (a marker of allergy or intestinal inflammation).

An X ray may be done to look at the structure of the intestines. Occasionally the X ray is performed after the baby drinks a liquid that illuminates the lining of the intestines *(barium)*. Tiny cameras can also be inserted into the stomach via the mouth (called **upper endoscopy**) or into the large intestine via the anus (called *colonoscopy*) to take clear pictures of the bowel. These tests are invasive and used only when necessary. Most are described in detail in chapter 29.

What are the treatments?
If the cause of the FTT is too little caloric intake, then the treatment is to increase the amount of daily calories. Sometimes this is as simple as stepping up the frequency or volume of feedings. But other times — when there are physical or mechanical reasons for the poor intake, for example — these must be fixed. One example is cleft palate. A child with a cleft palate may have difficulty feeding effectively. Special bottle nipples can be used until the cleft is repaired.

If FTT occurs in the setting of high caloric intake, then the treatment will depend on the underlying cause. Malabsorption, for instance, may be treated by altering the diet. Hormonal abnormalities may require a specialist (endocrinologist). Infections can often be treated with medicines.

What are the possible complications?

The main complication of FTT is developmental delay. A child may not grow well and can eventually have short stature. The brain may not develop as well as it should, and in extreme cases this can lead to learning disorders or delayed mental development. The early gross motor skills — such as rolling, crawling, and walking — may be delayed as well. When FTT is identified and treated early, permanent long-term consequences are rare. However, the longer the FTT goes unrecognized or untreated, the more likely the child is to have long-term complications.

Additional Resources
http://www.nlm.nih.gov/medlineplus/encyclopedia.html (Click on "F," then scroll down to "failure to thrive.")
http://www.cdc.gov/growthcharts/
http://www.lpch.org/DiseaseHealthInfo/HealthLibrary/growth/thrive.html

Hips

The hip is called a ball-and-socket joint: it is a combination of two bones, one curving around the other to make possible a wide range of movements. The hips allow us to kick our legs, balance our weight, and walk.

Hips form both in the womb and after birth. The socket of the hip curves itself around the top of the thighbone while the baby is still in the womb. Once the baby is born, she begins to move her legs more freely. In order for the hip to continue to form properly, the top of the thighbone, which resembles a ball, must remain in good position.

Without normal hip joints, a child may have tremendous difficulty walking. For this reason, pediatricians check the hips many times throughout the first year of life.

HIP CLUNKS AND HIP DISLOCATION
(Birth–12 Months)

What is happening inside my baby's body?
At birth, the hip does not function like a perfect ball and socket. The socket is actually relatively flat at birth, and the ball (the head

of the femur, or long bone of the upper leg) must stay put in the correct place for the joint to deepen properly.

Your pediatrician will check your baby's hips just after birth by holding his knees and pushing down on the femurs, rotating the heads of the femurs in their sockets. If his femurs stay in place, then your doctor knows that the hip sockets have formed well. But if the hip joint makes a "clunk" because the femur falls too far back, then the socket is too flat. Flat hip sockets can create problems because the head of the femur can easily slip out of place. This, in turn, causes the joint to develop improperly — instead of becoming a ball and socket, it is more like a ball and plank. This is called *developmental dysplasia of the hip (DDH)*.

DDH was originally called congenital hip dislocation. However, it is now understood that infants may have dysplastic hips — flat joints that allow the femur to move easily — without having dislocated hips. The reverse is also true: some babies will have normal hips at birth, but shortly thereafter the hips will dislocate. Therefore, the new terminology encompasses both flattened and truly dislocated hip joints at birth and later in infancy.

DDH occurs in 1 out of every 100 babies; true dislocation occurs in only 1 in 1,000. It is more common among firstborns, females, and Native Americans. It is also more common among babies whose family members have DDH or extremely flexible ligaments. Dysplasia is found at an especially high rate among breech babies — by some estimates, up to one-quarter of all babies with DDH were breech deliveries. This is likely because the position of a breech baby's legs while in the womb can exaggerate the flattening of the hip sockets. Despite many theories, however, there is no complete consensus on why DDH occurs.

It is important to remember that not all cases of DDH are diagnosed at birth. All babies — especially those meeting any of the previously mentioned criteria — should be checked more than once for hip clunks. This is because not all newborns with DDH have hips that can be pushed out of the socket, and therefore not all cases are diagnosed at birth. However, in all cases of DDH, the hips can eventually be dislocated (and the problem diagnosed) during a later physical exam.

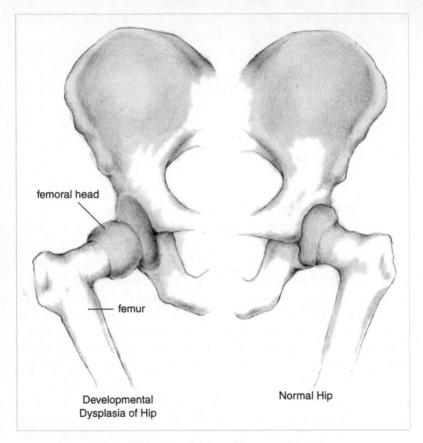

femoral head

femur

Developmental
Dysplasia of Hip

Normal Hip

Normal hip joint (*right side*) versus hip joint
as seen with developmental dysplasia of the hip (*left side*)

What can I do?

When a hip clunk is discovered in the hospital or in the first few
weeks of life, you may be instructed to double-diaper: instead of
using one diaper at a time to keep the baby clean, you might use
two, one on top of another. The extra bulk may assist in holding
the legs and hips in a stable position so that the head of the femur
can help the hip socket to round out.

Some doctors find double-diapering useless because hips that
feel loose at birth will sometimes tighten up spontaneously over
the first week of life. These doctors believe that double-diapering

The most extreme complication of untreated hip dislocation is that one leg is effectively much longer than the other. The leg lengths are actually equal, but the hip asymmetry makes one leg look (and act) as if it were shorter. Initially, this may be noticed by looking at the back of a child's legs — if the skin folds below the buttocks are noticeably unequal, then there may be a difference in leg length. Later, the length discrepancy may cause the child to limp. Eventually, untreated DDH can cause pain and an obvious limp. One foot may also point outward.

Additional Resources
http://www.packardchildrenshospital.org (Go to "search" in upper right-hand corner and type in "DDH.")
http://home.coqui.net/myrna/dysp.htm
http://www.ucsf.edu/orthopaedics/patientedu/img/ddh3.jpg

22

Bladder and Urinary Tract

◆

The urinary tract includes the kidneys, the ureters (tubes that carry urine from the kidneys to the bladder), the bladder, and the urethra (tube that carries urine out the body). The tract is fully developed early on in fetal life. In fact, the urine produced by a fetus forms the amniotic fluid surrounding a growing baby.

The urinary tract is one of the primary sources of waste removal in the body. The kidneys are in charge of a remarkably elaborate system of filtration — separating minerals, salts, and proteins that must be recycled by the body from those that can be tossed out. The bladder acts as the storage vault for urine, saving it until it is urinated out. Even though babies are not potty trained, they already have some bladder control. If they didn't, they would be urinating small drops continually throughout the day and night. Anyone who has ever changed a baby's diaper knows that a fair amount can be stored in the bladder . . . and then released on you when you try to change the baby.

Though the urinary tract is full of waste, it is meant to be sterile and free of infection. However, this portal to the outside becomes infected in many babies because the entrance to the urinary tract (the tip of the urethra) is often covered by stool in a dirty diaper. Stool will often contain bacteria. In fact, given how many times a day a young baby has a stool-filled diaper, it is amazing that the urinary tract does not get infected more often than it does.

PINK URINE
(Birth–12 Months)

What is happening inside my baby's body?
A healthy baby's urine may range in color from almost clear to yellow to dark amber. Just like in adults, this is a reflection of how much water is in the urine. The less water there is, the more concentrated the urine and the darker its color.

Healthy babies occasionally have pink urine. This may result from heavy concentration — sometimes the urine is so concentrated it looks pinkish instead of dark yellow. Other times the concentrated urine mixes with the superabsorbent chemicals in the diaper. This mixing in the diaper can cause the formation of pinkish crystals or a fine pink powder.

Rarely a pink tinge to the urine indicates blood in the urine. Typically any blood in the urine — even a small amount — makes the urine cranberry or red colored. Therefore it is very uncommon for pink urine to be the result of blood. Red urine is covered in the next section.

What can I do?
You do not need to worry about an occasional diaper with pinkish urine. To see whether the discoloration is due to superabsorbent chemicals in the diaper, try a different brand or a cloth diaper. If increased concentration of the urine is suspected as the cause of the pink color, then the baby may not be getting enough to drink. Try offering more breast milk or formula to see if the color resolves.

When does my doctor need to be involved?
Occasional pink urine is not worrisome, but persistent pink urine may be. If every diaper has a noticeable pink color, then call your doctor. If you suspect that your baby is dehydrated and the pink

color is a result of increased concentration of the urine, then contact your doctor. If the color changes from pink to red — indicating possible blood — then contact your doctor immediately.

What tests need to be done, and what do the results mean?
Tests are not usually necessary when a child has an isolated incident of pink urine. Some doctors, however, will choose to check the urine using a urinalysis for screening purposes. If the discoloration persists, then this test will almost certainly be done. The urinalysis determines whether the urine has any blood or other atypical components. For more about this test, see chapter 29.

If dehydration is the cause of pink urine, then other tests may be considered. For more on dehydration, see chapter 28.

What are the treatments?
Occasional pink urine does not need to be treated. However, if the cause of the pink urine is mild dehydration, then increasing the amount of breast milk or formula that the baby drinks will often solve the problem. If the pink urine persists, then the treatment will depend on the cause.

What are the possible complications?
There are almost never complications with sporadic pink urine, so there is no reason to worry about long-term complications.

Additional Resources
http://www.nlm.nih.gov/medlineplus/encyclopedia.html (Click on "U," then scroll down to "urine — abnormal color.")

RED URINE
(Birth–12 Months)

What is happening inside my baby's body?
When urine is red — not pink — blood is often present. In medical terms, this is called **hematuria.** The causes of red urine vary widely; the most common are covered here.

Blood seen in the diaper can be mixed into the urine or separate from it. If the blood is only in one spot and can be distinguished clearly from the rest of the urine, then the cause is likely irritation on the skin or just inside the urethra (tube that carries urine from the bladder out the penis or vagina).

If the blood is mixed into the urine such that the urine looks like a red puddle, then the bleeding might be coming from anywhere along the urinary tract. Irritation along the urethra, inside the bladder, or all the way up to the kidneys can cause bloody urine. Other causes include inherited blood disorders such as hemophilia or sickle-cell anemia; inherited kidney disease such as polycystic kidneys; problems with blood clotting; tumors; stones that cause bleeding as they move down the urinary tract; other sources of obstruction along the urinary tract; trauma; and child abuse.

Infection is one of the most common causes of blood in the urine. It can cause blood to appear in one of two ways. First, the urine itself may be infected. This is called a *UTI*, or *urinary tract infection*. UTIs can occur because bacteria (often from the stool) get up into the urethra and then grow rapidly in the warm urine. These are more common in girls than boys, because the urethra in a girl is shorter (a boy has the added length of the penis). When the bacteria multiply in the bladder, the walls of the bladder become inflamed. This is called *cystitis* and is a cause of blood in the urine. UTIs are covered in more detail in another section of this chapter.

Infection can also indirectly cause bloody urine. Sometimes there is an infection elsewhere in the body — such as strep throat — and as the body tries to clear that infection, it deposits the waste materials in the kidney. The kidneys are like sieves, filtering out the waste and saving the materials that need to be recirculated in the body. An overload in the kidney can cause the sieve to malfunction, allowing the kidney to spill blood into the urine. This is actually the most common cause of hematuria in children of all ages. It is known as *glomerulonephritis*.

It is important to note that blood in the urine is often invisible — that is, there is too little of it to see. This is called *microscopic hematuria*. It can only be diagnosed by testing the urine (with urinalysis) or by looking at the urine under a microscope.

The causes of microscopic hematuria are different from gross (or visible) hematuria.

What can I do?

You should try to assess whether or not your baby is having pain, whether or not she has a fever, and whether the blood is mixed into the urine or is sitting separately in the diaper.

When does my doctor need to be involved?

Call your doctor whenever you think there is blood in the urine. Even if you are not sure, it is better to call.

What tests need to be done, and what do the results mean?

Anytime the urine looks bloody, a urinalysis must be done to confirm the presence of blood. There are some foods and medicines that can make the urine appear red when actually there is no blood. Among the most notorious are beets and an antibiotic called rifampin.

A urine culture should also be done to determine whether or not there is an infection. If the urine culture is positive, then your doctor can identify the specific bacteria causing the infection — and hence the bleeding. Antibiotics will be started to treat the infection.

Many physicians will check electrolytes and perform other blood tests to look at kidney function. These tests can help determine whether the kidneys are filtering well or have begun to "leak." Blood tests look at substances in the body that are normally excreted or retained by the kidneys. If the balance of these is off, then there is evidence that the kidneys are malfunctioning. The cause of malfunction can usually be determined by blood and urine tests. Only in very rare and specific instances is an invasive procedure, such as a kidney biopsy, necessary to diagnose the cause of hematuria.

Finally, images of the urinary tract may be helpful. Your doctor may order an X ray, ultrasound, CT scan, or MRI to check the actual anatomy of the kidneys, ureters, bladder, and urethra. Stones or masses causing the bleeding can often be seen in one of these images.

All of these tests are described in more detail in chapter 29.

What are the treatments?

Treatment depends entirely on the cause. Infections are treated with antibiotics. Kidney malfunction may be treated with a variety of medications, from *steroids* (to help with inflammation) to *diuretics* (to help with urination). Masses may require surgical removal. Because there are so many potential causes of hematuria, the litany of treatments is long. Many are covered in the Web links at the end of this section.

What are the possible complications?

Most people with glomerulonephritis or other causes of hematuria recover and have no long-term problems. However, there is occasional permanent kidney damage. In the most extreme cases, kidney failure can result. When the kidneys fail to work, the body lacks an effective way to get rid of waste. In lieu of working kidneys, patients can have *dialysis,* where the blood is filtered using a machine. Usually this must continue for the rest of the patient's life or until a kidney transplant can be done. Occasionally kidney function may spontaneously return. Again, it is important to stress that this is exceedingly rare among babies.

Additional Resources
http://www.med.stanford.edu/school/Urology/Patients/hematuria.html
http://www.nlm.nih.gov/medlineplus/encyclopedia.html (Click on "U," then scroll down to "urine — bloody or dark.")
http://web1.tch.harvard.edu (Go to "Child Health A to Z," then enter "glomerular disease" or "blood in urine" under "Search the Encyclopedia" at the bottom of the screen.)

CRYSTALS IN THE DIAPER
(Birth–12 Months)

What is happening inside my baby's body?

Dirty diapers typically have yellow urine or green, yellow, or brown stool. So what if you see white or pink crystals? This is actually fairly common.

The crystals look like large grains of salt. These so-called *urate crystals* can be clear or have a faint color to them. They are formed

when there is too little water in the urine, causing the substances
in the urine to crystallize into tiny little stones. There are two
main causes of crystal formation: either the urine is very concentrated (having less water in it than usual) or the diaper is so
superabsorbent that it wicks away most of the water in the urine,
leaving behind substances that then crystallize. The crystals are
painless to the baby.

What can I do?
If the cause is mild dehydration leading to concentrated urine,
then try increasing the amount of breast milk or formula that the
baby drinks.

When does my doctor need to be involved?
If there are other changes in the color or smell of the urine, then
call your doctor. If your baby just has crystals in the diaper, then
don't worry.

What tests need to be done, and what do the results mean?
A urinalysis can be performed to check how concentrated the
urine is, but this is rarely necessary. Most of the time, no tests are
done.

What are the treatments?
There are no treatments for crystals. However, if the cause is mild
dehydration, then increasing the amount of breast milk or formula
the baby drinks can make the urine more watery. In turn, crystals
are less likely to form. Likewise, switching to a less superabsorbent diaper may result in less crystal formation. The latter is not
necessarily recommended, however, because the less absorbent a
diaper is, the more exposure the baby has to a wet puddle of
urine and the more likely he will be to get a mild diaper rash.

What are the possible complications?
Crystals themselves cause no complications. They will go away
either when the type of diaper is changed or when the baby
begins to drink a bit more fluid. They are not at all associated
with kidney stones or other urinary problems.

◆   ◆   ◆

INFECTED URINE
(Birth–12 Months)

What is happening inside my baby's body?

Urine provides a means to filter waste out of the body. More often than not, baby urine is clear in color and relatively odorless. Occasionally it will look dark yellow, especially during the first few days of life or when a child has not had enough to drink. Urine can also have a strong smell, because some waste products carry an odor. While a single episode of pungent-smelling or dark urine can be normal, persistent smelly or discolored urine can signal the presence of bacteria. When the urine is infected with bacteria, it is called a *urinary tract infection,* or *UTI.*

The urinary tract starts with the kidneys, where the urine is made. The urine flows from each kidney down a tube called a ureter and into the bladder, which functions as a urine-collection bag. The bladder stores the urine until your baby is ready to urinate, and then the urine flows out of her body via the urethra.

If the kidneys, ureters, bladder, or urethra are abnormally formed, obstructed, or irregularly connected to one another, then urine is more likely to pool or reflux (go backward) than to follow its typical steady route. When urine pools, it is no different than any stagnant body of water (like a pond at the park): bacteria will prefer to grow there. This is why babies with atypical anatomy of their urinary tract are more likely to have UTIs than other children.

Likewise, if there is a blockage of normal urine flow somewhere along the tract, then the urine above the blockage will pool and stagnate. Again, this is a setup for infection.

If urine actually flows backward — from the bladder up the ureters and toward the kidneys — then a UTI can result. This condition, known as *vesicoureteral reflux,* or *VUR,* occurs in 30 to 50 percent of children with UTIs. It can result from a number of anatomical abnormalities, the most common of which is abnormal insertion of the ureters into the bladder. Of note, reflux can cause a UTI and a UTI can cause reflux: when the infected urine pools in the bladder, it can reflux up the ureters much more easily than when normal urine collects in the bladder.

Finally, if the stool gets into the urethra, then urine can become infected with bacteria that live in the intestine. The bacteria that normally live in the intestine are often contained in the stool. If the stool gets into the urethra, the bacteria can move up the urethra and into the bladder, where they will multiply rapidly. This source of UTI is much more common among girls than boys because girls have a shorter urethra, giving the bacteria a smaller distance to travel in order to get to the bladder.

What can I do?
The only way you can help to prevent UTI is by practicing good hygiene. When cleaning a girl after a stool, try to avoid getting the poop into the urethra, which can happen when you wipe back to front. Because stool can easily spread itself throughout the diaper, it can get into the urethra despite practicing good hygiene. There is no way to prevent any of the other causes of urinary tract infection, since most of these have to do with the anatomy of the urinary tract.

When does my doctor need to be involved?
If the urine is persistently dark or foul smelling, then consult your doctor. UTIs can cause fever. Anytime a baby younger than six weeks old has a fever, call your doctor. (For more about this, see the section on fever in chapter 28.) At any age, the combination of fever, pain with urination, and dark, smelly urine often signals a UTI and should prompt a visit to the doctor.

What tests need to be done, and what do the results mean?
The urine can be checked for infection with a urinalysis and a urine culture. These are described in detail in chapter 29. A urinalysis takes only minutes and can indicate a likely infection. The culture can specify the exact bacteria that is causing the infection, and this, in turn, will dictate which antibiotics should be prescribed. Urine cultures take two or three days, so a urinalysis is a helpful initial step to determine whether or not the urine is infected in the first place.

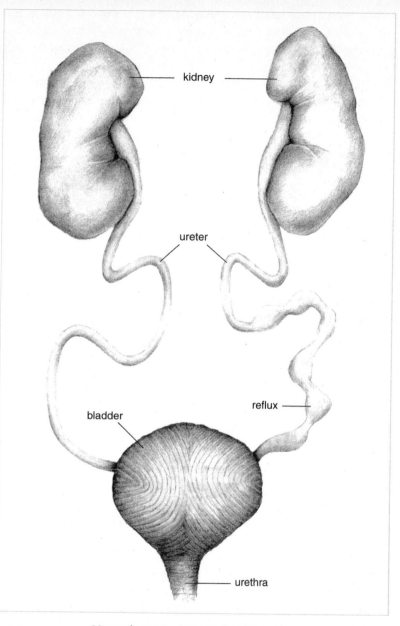

Normal urinary tract (*left side*) versus
urinary tract with urine refluxing back
up toward the kidney (*right side*)

When an infant has a UTI, tests need to be done to look at the structure of the urinary tract. This is because a UTI in an infant suggests an increased chance of a structural abnormality. Over time, anatomic abnormalities can result in multiple UTIs.

An ultrasound can look at the size and structure of the ureters and kidneys. A *voiding cystourethrogram (VCUG)* is a test that uses a special dye to light up the bladder, ureters, and sometimes kidneys. A tube is inserted into the urethra, and the dye is injected directly into the bladder. A special X ray device (called a *fluoroscope*) takes pictures to see if the dye stays in the bladder or refluxes back up into the ureters and even the kidneys. Another type of imaging study is a *Tc-dimercaptosuccinic acid scan (DMSA scan)*. This scan uses a chemical that is injected into a vein and is filtered out of the bloodstream through the kidneys. The filtration of this material can be followed with specific images, outlining the urinary tract and any abnormalities.

Regardless of which of these imaging studies is used, the test should be done only after the UTI is treated completely. This is because the infection itself can cause reflux of the urine from the bladder up the ureters and even into the kidneys. Therefore, if the urine is infected, then these tests may show falsely positive results suggesting abnormal anatomy of the urinary tract when in fact the urinary tract is structurally normal. If the infection is gone, however, then the tests will accurately represent the structure of the kidneys, ureters, bladder, and urethra.

What are the treatments?

The treatment for UTI is an antibiotic. The precise antibiotic depends on the bacteria causing the infection. A urine culture can reveal both the bacteria present and the specific antibiotics to which the bacteria is sensitive.

If the underlying cause of the UTI is abnormal anatomy, then surgery may be needed. This depends on the type of anatomical abnormality and the severity of the infections. Some anatomical problems get better on their own as a child grows. But sometimes a urologist (a surgeon specializing in the urinary tract) must fix the problem.

A baby who has had two UTIs may be placed on prophylactic antibiotics. This means that your doctor may prescribe a daily low dose of an antibacterial medicine (antibiotic) to keep the urine from getting infected. A child with a mild problem often outgrows the need for prophylactic antibiotics, but initially the antibiotics may prevent recurrent UTIs and sometimes even help to avoid surgery.

What are the possible complications?

The most worrisome complication of a UTI is spread of the infection from the urine into the kidney and then to other parts of the body, including the bloodstream. When bacteria multiply in the bladder and travel up the ureters to the kidneys, the kidneys themselves can become infected. This is called *pyelonephritis*. Infection of the kidneys can lead to scarring and damage of the kidney tissue, and ultimately (but very rarely) kidney failure.

The bacteria causing a UTI can move to other parts of the body, infecting the lungs (pneumonia) or even the fluid around the brain (meningitis). When the infection spreads throughout the bloodstream, it is known as *urosepsis*. While this is uncommon, it is most worrisome among children under six weeks of age, and is one of the reasons why infants six weeks and younger who have a fever will usually be hospitalized and started on antibiotics immediately. This is covered in more detail in the fever section in chapter 28.

Additional Resources
www.packardchildrenshospital.org (Go to "search" in upper right-hand corner and type in "urinary tract infection.")
http://www.duj.com/peduti.html
http://web1.tch.harvard.edu/ (Go to "Child Health A to Z," then enter "urinary tract infection" under "Search the Encyclopedia" at the bottom of the screen.)

23

Penis and Scrotum

———————◇———————

The penis and scrotum range in size and shape. Both are fully formed in the womb, but the testicles that fill the scrotum actually develop in the abdomen and then descend into the scrotum late in the pregnancy. Sometimes a baby is born with one or two undescended testicles. Other times the testicles have descended but the scrotal sac is filled with extra fluid.

The penis also varies depending on whether or not a family chooses to circumcise. Regimens for cleaning and caring for the penis will differ slightly between circumcised and uncircumcised boys.

There is much debate over whether or not to circumcise. This is a very personal decision. There is little medical evidence suggesting that one is better than the other. The biggest study to date suggests that 1 in 500 boys who are uncircumcised will have a urinary tract infection sometime in the first year of life as a direct result of being uncircumcised. This seems to be the only difference and is not all that significant. If you are looking for guidance to decide whether or not to circumcise, then your social and cultural circumstances, as well as your personal opinions, are much more important factors.

CIRCUMCISION
(Birth–1 Month)

What is happening inside my baby's body?

Circumcision involves cutting off the *foreskin* that covers the head of the penis. It can be done anytime in a boy's life, although after the first month or so, the procedure becomes painful enough to require sedation. Therefore, it is safest to do a circumcision in the first 2 to 4 weeks of a baby's life.

In the hospital, either obstetricians or pediatricians perform circumcisions. Once a baby has left the hospital and gone home, pediatricians or specially trained religious figures may do the circumcision. Urologists — doctors who specialize in the genital and urinary systems — almost always perform the circumcisions done later in life.

Depending on who performs the procedure, different techniques are used. A *Plastibell* is a plastic dome affixed to the head of the penis. It separates the penis and the foreskin, and then cuts off the blood supply to the tip of the foreskin. After a few days, the foreskin falls off. An alternate approach is to trim the foreskin directly. This method utilizes a metal clamp to separate the penis from its foreskin so that the person performing the circumcision can cut off the foreskin without damaging the head of the penis. There are several tools available to accomplish this, but the two most common are called the *Mogen* and the *Gomco.*

What can I do?

Parents do not typically participate in circumcisions, although you may choose to stay with your baby to observe the procedure. Once the circumcision is complete, you will need to care for the circumcision site.

When does my doctor need to be involved?

Once in a great while, the person performing the circumcision will discover that the urethra (where the urine comes out of the penis) does not exit at the top of the head of the penis. This is called *hypospadias.* If this is discovered, then the circumcision

should not be completed. Boys with this anatomy need to be
seen by a urologist.

What tests need to be done, and what do the results mean?
Usually no tests need to be done prior to circumcision. The only
exception to this is a bilirubin level for babies with significant
jaundice. Because a baby with a high bilirubin level is more apt
to have problems clotting blood, a circumcision will often be
postponed until the jaundice has resolved. For more about jaundice, see chapter 11.

What are the treatments?
There are a variety of ways to reduce the pain of circumcision
and to treat the penis afterward. Many people who perform circumcisions use anesthetic creams or injections to numb the site
prior to the circumcision. When the procedure is done, the area
almost always looks more painful than it feels.

There are times when a doctor should check the circumcision
site. This is especially true if the area continues to bleed or looks
bright red and feels warm to the touch.

In order to prevent infection at the circumcision site, you
should use water to keep the area clean. Little or no soap is necessary. Ointments or creams — such as Vaseline, vitamin A and D
ointment, or antibiotic cream — can also be applied to the penis.
The person performing the circumcision will suggest one or more
of these. A gauze pad is typically used in the first couple of days
to gently cover the tip of the penis. After a day or two, simple
cleaning is all that is necessary.

What are the possible complications?
Sometimes the penis bleeds for several minutes after the circumcision. Bleeding usually stops with gentle pressure. When it continues for an extended period, this can indicate a problem with
blood clotting.

If the area is not kept clean, then the penis can become infected. This is quite rare. Stool should be gently wiped off the
healing penis to reduce this risk.

Additional Resources
http://www.packardchildrenshospital.org (Go to "search" in upper right-
hand corner and type in "circumcision.")
http://www.cirp.org/library/procedure/

◆ ◆ ◆

UNCIRCUMCISED PENIS AND
FORESKIN QUESTIONS
(Birth–12 Months)

What is happening inside my baby's body?
A baby boy is born with a covering over his penis called the *foreskin.* Circumcision is the process of removing this covering. Many
boys are not circumcised, and therefore they retain their fore-
skins.

The area under an infant's foreskin never needs to be vigorously cleaned. It may collect some normal debris, but the body
manages this on its own. In fact, pulling the foreskin back in an
effort to clean — called **retraction** — can cause irritation and
swelling. In extreme cases, the foreskin can become so swollen
that it cannot be returned back over the head of the penis. This
condition is called *paraphimosis,* and it requires emergency
intervention by a doctor.

The foreskin may retract on its own at any age, but more often
than not, this doesn't happen until a boy is older — usually around
two or three years old (or older). Then it becomes easily mobile
and can be retracted for cleaning.

Sometimes the foreskin is not at all retractable because its
opening is too narrow. This is called *phimosis.* Phimosis is normal among uncircumcised infants and toddlers, and usually resolves itself by school age. If you push the foreskin back too soon,
though, then the tip of the foreskin can form a scar and phimosis
can become permanent.

What can I do?
You should never do anything special with an uncircumcised
penis. Employ a hands-off policy. The diaper area is cleaned with

each diaper change, but the foreskin should never be forcibly pulled back in order to clean the penis. Of course, your baby will soon discover his penis, so the hands-off policy applies only to parents and caretakers.

When does my doctor need to be involved?

Your doctor needs to be called immediately when there is paraphimosis (the foreskin is pulled back over the head of the penis and cannot be returned to its usual position). Your doctor also needs to be involved if there is ever bulging of the foreskin with urination. In this case there is phimosis — the opening of the foreskin is too tight and urine becomes trapped behind the foreskin. Each time the baby urinates, the area swells with more urine. Trapped urine is a breeding ground for infection.

What tests need to be done, and what do the results mean?

If there is phimosis — and infection of the urine is suspected — then a urine culture should be done to determine the appropriate antibiotic treatment. Otherwise, tests are unnecessary.

What are the treatments?

In some cases of paraphimosis, when the foreskin is stuck below the head of the penis, a lubricant can be put on the penis to allow the foreskin to slide back into its original position. If the swelling is extreme, however, then a doctor needs to cut a small hole in the foreskin so that the tension can be released and the foreskin can be moved back into its usual position. If that does not work, then an emergency circumcision may need to be done.

For phimosis, a steroid cream can be applied to the tip of the foreskin to reduce the inflammation and break down the tight opening. This treatment needs to be applied several times a day for a few weeks. If phimosis causes a urinary tract infection, then the child will need to be treated with antibiotics. This is covered in more detail in chapter 22.

What are the possible complications?

The most worrisome complication associated with an uncircumcised penis is paraphimosis because it can limit the penis blood drainage, causing the head to swell. As the head engorges, the foreskin further restricts blood flow to the head of the penis. Reduced blood flow results in less oxygen. Eventually this may cause tissue death (also called *necrosis*). This is why paraphimosis is a medical emergency and requires immediate treatment.

Phimosis can cause urinary tract infection. Urinary tract infection is relatively uncommon in boys (compared to girls). According to some studies, the risk of infection in uncircumcised boys is up to 10 times that in circumcised boys, with about 1 in 500 uncircumcised boys having a urinary tract infection in the first year of life. These infections are easily treated with antibiotics.

Additional Resources
http://www.packardchildrenshospital.org (Go to "search" in upper right-hand corner and type in "phimosis.")
http://www.cirp.org/library/treatment/phimosis/
http://www.cirp.org/library/normal/aap/
http://www.urologychannel.com/emergencies/paraphimosis.shtml

◆   ◆   ◆

UNDESCENDED TESTICLE
(Birth–12 Months)

What is happening inside my baby's body?
When the testicles develop inside the growing fetus, they are all the way up in the belly. They do not descend into the scrotal sac until about the eighth month of gestation. Sometimes they do not descend at all. When a testicle has not come down into the sac, the medical name is *cryptorchidism*. This usually happens only on one side, but about one in three cases involves both testicles.

Remember that because the testicles do not normally descend until a baby is at about eight months' gestation, many premature babies have undescended testicles. These testicles tend to descend as the babies reach their original due date. Other causes of undescended testicles include hormonal imbalances, nervous system issues, genetics (dad with undescended testicle), or lack of testicular development in the first place.

What can I do?

The pediatrician usually diagnoses an undescended testicle during the first exam in the hospital. However, sometimes parents or other diaper-changers are the first to notice. There is nothing you need to do other than to bring it to the attention of your pediatrician.

When does my doctor need to be involved?

Your pediatrician should evaluate an undescended testicle. If the testicle is not felt, or if it is felt in the groin (the *inguinal canal*), then your pediatrician will often wait weeks or months to see if the testicle eventually descends into the scrotum. This usually happens by six months of age. However, if the testicle is still not felt at that point — either in the groin or scrotum — then your doctor will refer the baby to a urologist (a surgeon specializing in genital and urinary issues).

What tests need to be done, and what do the results mean?

In the past an ultrasound, CT scan, or MRI was done to look for the testicle. These techniques were not helpful, however, and therefore are no longer routinely used. Today, tests are typically not done.

What are the treatments?

Hormones can be given to stimulate the testicles to drop down. This form of treatment is rarely used today but can be considered when the testicle is stuck in the canal (as opposed to when no testicle is felt at all).

Surgery, called *orchiopexy,* can be done as well. In this procedure, the testicle is located, brought down into the scrotal sac, and then affixed to the scrotum so that it stays where it needs to stay.

What are the possible complications?

When left untreated, undescended testicles can cause infertility. This is much more common when both testicles are undescended. There is also a significantly increased risk of testicular cancer in adult years in an undescended testicle. Other complications include inguinal hernia and testicular torsion, both covered in detail later in this chapter.

Additional Resources
http://www.packardchildrenshospital.org (Go to "search" in upper right-hand corner and type in "cryptorchidism.")

◇   ◇   ◇

HERNIA
(Birth–12 Months)

What is happening inside my baby's body?
The word *hernia* means a bulge through an abnormal opening. Usually one organ — such as the intestine — bulges through a muscle. In the groin, the intestines can push through a muscle in the floor of the pelvis, poking through anywhere along the groin all the way down to the scrotum. This is due to the fact that before the testicles normally descend into the scrotum (around the eighth month of gestation), they are preceded by an out-pouching of the abdomen called the *processus vaginalis.* Initially the processus vaginalis is an open tubelike structure. Normally it shrinks down and closes before birth. But when it fails to close, it provides a conduit through which the intestines can slip down into the scrotum, resulting in a hernia.

Inguinal hernias are named for the region of the body where they are located (the inguinal canal) and account for 80 percent of all hernias in humans. About 2 percent of all children develop an inguinal hernia, with boys far outnumbering girls. Other common hernias include bulges through the muscles of the abdomen (called *umbilical hernias* [see chapter 19]) and bulges through the diaphragms that separate the lungs and the belly (called *diaphragmatic hernias*). The bulge through a diaphragmatic hernia is not visible because it exists entirely inside the body.

When the hernia appears in the scrotal sac, its most common path is through the processus vaginalis, the sac that carried the testicles from the abdomen (where they developed) into the scrotum. This sac usually shrinks down to a little scarlike string; but if

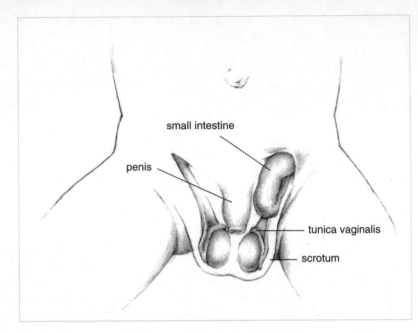

Inguinal hernia on right side with segment
of small intestine bulging through

it stays open, it provides a conduit through which bowel can easily slip down from the belly compartment into the scrotum.

What can I do?
Hernias often come and go: the intestine bulges through the hole
in the muscle when there is pressure exerted, such as when a
baby cries, strains, or coughs. However, most hernias pop themselves back in, or if they remain pushed out, parents should find
it easy to apply gentle pressure and push the bulge back in. If
you notice a hernia, gently apply pressure to push it back in. This
is called *reduction.*

When does my doctor need to be involved?
Call your doctor if your child's hernia will not go back in even
when the baby is calm. Remember, with pressure from crying or

straining, the hernia pops out. If the area around the popped-out hernia is red, hot, or swollen — and especially if the child is inconsolable, has vomiting, or develops fever at the same time — call your doctor. Vomiting is especially worrisome with hernias because when part of the bowel pops through a hole in the muscle and gets stuck, the intestine can become functionally blocked. Therefore, a hernia can cause intestinal obstruction, which in turn can cause vomiting.

If the hernia is reducible, you should still let your pediatrician know in a nonurgent manner. A doctor should evaluate any suspected hernia.

What tests need to be done, and what do the results mean?
Tests will rarely be done in the case of a reducible hernia. Your doctor will try to gently push on the hernia, making sure it is not stuck between pieces of muscle. If it is stuck, then it may be incarcerated or strangulated.

An *incarcerated hernia* is one in which the intestine becomes stuck in the muscle because of swelling, and it cannot be pushed back in. A *strangulated hernia* is an incarcerated hernia whose blood supply has been partially or entirely cut off. Without blood flow, the strangulated piece of bowel is starved of important nutrients, including oxygen. The part of the intestine deprived of oxygen can die, becoming nonfunctional and a potential site of infection. This is a surgical emergency. Although less critical, an incarcerated hernia also needs immediate evaluation by a doctor (often a surgeon) in order to prevent strangulation. It is impossible to tell the difference between an incarcerated and a strangulated hernia just by looking. An ultrasound can be done to check for bowel swelling and blood flow in the area of the hernia.

What are the treatments?
The most common treatment is simply pushing the hernia back in (reduction). If the bulge cannot be reduced, then the bowel may be incarcerated or strangulated, and the child needs to be seen by a surgeon.

Some pediatric surgeons prefer to operate on all inguinal hernias as soon as they are diagnosed, including those that are easily reduced, even if there are no symptoms. Others prefer to wait until a child with no symptoms is at least three months old in order to reduce the risks of anesthesia during surgery. All surgeons operate immediately in the case of incarcerated or strangulated hernias. And they generally agree that it is better to operate on a hernia soon after it is diagnosed than to wait for it to become incarcerated or strangulated.

Because inguinal hernias tend to appear on only one side, a controversy exists over what to do about the other side. Some surgeons believe that if one side is repaired, then the other side should be operated on as well. When the processus vaginalis is sewed closed on the opposite side, a future hernia and its complications can be avoided. Other surgeons disagree, opting only to operate on both sides if the child is at known risk for having two hernias.

What are the possible complications?
The most severe complication of a hernia is incarceration or strangulation. Often the skin around the incarcerated or strangulated hernia will become red and hot. A child may vomit because the part of the bowel stuck through the muscle is blocked, and therefore food cannot pass. Babies with strangulated hernias will almost always have pain. These complications are quite rare.

If your child has a hernia, you should feel comfortable that you know what signs to look for. Remember, when a baby is crying, a hernia will *always* be difficult to push back in.

Additional Resources
http://www.pedisurg.com/PtEduc/Inguinal_Hernia.htm
http://www.cincinnatichildrens.org (Go to search box in upper right-hand corner and type in "inguinal hernia.")
http://www.caps.ca/guests/statements/hernia.htm

◆   ◆   ◆

SWOLLEN SCROTUM
(Birth–12 Months)

What is happening inside my baby's body?
The most common cause of a swollen scrotum is a *hydrocele,* a collection of fluid around the testicle. The fluid fills the pouch — called the *processus vaginalis* — that carries the testicle down from the abdomen into the scrotum. When the pouch seals itself off so that the testicle can stay put in the scrotum, fluid sometimes gets locked in. This is called a *noncommunicating hydrocele.* Other times the pouch seals itself off incompletely so that there is room for fluid to leak slowly from the abdomen down into the scrotum and then up again into the abdomen. This type of hydrocele is called a *communicating hydrocele,* and it grows and shrinks throughout the day and night. About 2 percent of all males are born with a hydrocele of some sort.

The other causes of swollen scrotum include testicular torsion (see section in this chapter), infection, or a mass such as a hemangioma or tumor. These are exceedingly rare among infants. Unlike hydroceles, which are present from birth, most of these other causes of swollen scrotum suddenly appear weeks, months, or even years after birth.

What can I do?
You do not need to do anything with a hydrocele. In fact, most hydroceles — at least the noncommunicating type — go away by the time the baby turns a year old.

When does my doctor need to be involved?
Doctors help diagnose hydroceles. A doctor typically becomes involved when the hydrocele is communicating or when it persists after a child is a year old. In these cases, a urologist (doctor specializing in the genital and urinary systems) will likely consult in the baby's care.

What tests need to be done, and what do the results mean?
The easiest test to diagnose a hydrocele is the flashlight test, also called *transillumination.* A light is held up against the skin on one side of the scrotum. The light will travel through the water in the scrotum but will be blocked by the solid testicle. Therefore, transillumination outlines the testicle, fluid, and any other masses (such as hernias) in the scrotum.

If a testicle is not easily felt on exam because the hydrocele is so large, then a scrotal ultrasound can be done to look at the testicles. This is rarely necessary in an infant.

What are the treatments?
A noncommunicating hydrocele needs no treatment other than time. Almost all noncommunicating hydroceles are gone by a child's first birthday. However, a communicating hydrocele will usually persist after the first year of life. This type requires a small surgical procedure to drain the fluid and then seal the connection between the abdomen and the scrotum.

What are the possible complications?
Communicating hydroceles can develop hernias — loops of intestine can slip down into the scrotum. The worry here is that the bowel can get trapped. For more about hernias, see the section in this chapter or chapter 19.

> *Additional Resources*
> http://www.pedisurg.com/PtEduc/Hydrocele.htm
> http://www.nlm.nih.gov/medlineplus/encyclopedia.html (Click on "Hg–Hz," then scroll down to "hydrocele.")

◆   ◆   ◆

TESTICULAR TORSION
(Birth – 12 months)

What is happening inside my baby's body?
This painful swelling results from twisting of the testicle. The testicle is contained within a sac called the *tunica vaginalis,* and together the sac and its testicle hang from a stringlike structure

called the *spermatic cord.* The tunica vaginalis attaches to the back surface of the testicle, limiting the testicle's mobility. If the tunica vaginalis is attached too high, then the testicle can rotate freely from its spermatic cord.

The spermatic cord holds within it nerves and blood vessels. Therefore, when the testicle twists, the spermatic cord and its contents twist too, like a mop being wrung out. The blood that normally flows easily up and down the spermatic cord cannot move freely anymore. Instead, the blood supply to the testicle is cut off, resulting in loss of oxygen and other nutrient resources. When this happens, the area may become red or swollen. Eventually, without proper blood flow, the starved testicle can die. This process is extremely painful.

Testicular torsion is very rare. The majority of cases are seen in adolescents and adults. However, it can also occur in young boys, especially under one year.

What can I do?
Anytime a testicular torsion is suspected, you should call or visit your doctor immediately.

When does my doctor need to be involved?
Testicular torsion is a true surgical emergency. Symptoms of torsion include pain, swelling or redness of the scrotum, and vomiting. The maximum time from diagnosis to surgery is four to six hours; beyond that, the testicle is usually not salvageable. Testicular torsion is one of those better-safe-than-sorry situations — call the doctor even if you are not sure you need to.

What tests need to be done, and what do the results mean?
The *cremasteric reflex* causes one testicle to leave the scrotum and rise into the pelvis when the inner thigh of the same leg is stroked. This reflex is lost when the testicle becomes twisted. Therefore, loss of the cremasteric reflex is one simple test used to determine whether there may be testicular torsion.

A complete blood count is often done. In many cases of torsion this blood test is normal.

An ultrasound can be done to look at the testicle. If the ultrasound has *Doppler* — a mode that detects blood flow — then it can help determine if the testicle has actually twisted and cut off its own blood supply.

If the diagnosis is still uncertain, then a *radionuclide scan* of the testicle can be helpful. This test looks at the testicle and its blood flow, and can be more helpful in differentiating torsion from other conditions. A radionuclide scan is 90 to 100 percent accurate. Therefore, if the test shows decreased uptake in the affected testicle, then this suggests that there is no blood flow to that side — an almost certain diagnosis of torsion.

What are the treatments?

If the testicle is twisted, then it is sometimes possible to untwist it manually by rotating the testicle in the scrotal sac, a technique called *manual detorsion*. When this works, it resolves the problem immediately. Often pain relievers are given prior to this procedure — testicular torsion itself is extremely painful, but the untwisting of a testicle is painful as well. Rotation of the testicle may need to be attempted two or three times before complete detorsion is accomplished, making good pain relief even more important. The benefit of this procedure is that it requires no surgery and is successful in 30 to 70 percent of patients.

If manual detorsion is not successful, however, then surgery is required. During surgery, the testicle is untwisted and then visually examined to ensure that blood flow remains adequate. Then, an *orchiopexy* is performed. This procedure attaches the testicle to the scrotum so that it cannot twist itself again. Because the underlying cause of the problem is abnormal attachment of the tunica vaginalis, and there is a tunica vaginalis on each side of the scrotum, the other testicle usually needs to be treated with orchiopexy as well. Otherwise there is a high risk of future torsion on the opposite side. Therefore most surgeons do orchiopexies on both testicles.

What are the possible complications?

The most severe complication of testicular torsion is testicular death. This can happen when the blood supply to the testicle is cut off for a long enough time, usually longer than six hours. When the testicle dies, it must be surgically removed because it becomes a potential source of infection. Testicles that have died cannot produce sperm. Therefore, there is an increased chance of infertility among men who have lost one testicle.

Additional Resources

http://www.packardchildrenshospital.org (Go to "search" in upper right-hand corner and type in "testicular torsion.")

http://www.nlm.nih.gov/medlineplus/encyclopedia.html (Click on "T–Tn," then scroll down to "testicular torsion.")

24

Vagina

◆

The female genitalia fully develop — and actually overdevelop — in the womb. With so much estrogen from mom, the lips of the newborn baby's vagina (labia) look swollen like an adult's. Over the next few weeks, with no more blood supply from the placenta, the estrogen level drops and the labia shrink. As a result of this hormone drop, some girls have a bloody discharge similar to a miniperiod.

The vagina is easy to clean with diaper changes, but a white cheesy discharge or stool will often collect inside the labia. Vigorous cleaning of the area is not necessary. Instead, gently wipe the labia and try to remove debris. The discharge does not need to be scraped off — if it sticks, leave it.

LABIAL SWELLING
(EXTERNAL FEMALE GENITALIA)
(Birth–2 Months)

What is happening inside my baby's body?
During pregnancy, the growing fetus receives its mother's blood through the placenta. The blood contains a number of hormones

that are important in keeping the pregnancy healthy. One of these hormones is *estrogen.*

Among its many developmental roles, estrogen stimulates the lips of the vagina, called *labia,* to swell. This happens slowly during puberty, as estrogen levels in the female body rise. During development in the womb, the fetal labia respond the same way — estrogen makes the lips of the vagina swell. Therefore, all full-term newborn girls have large, puffy labia.

However, as the mother's estrogen slowly disappears from her baby's body over the first few weeks of life, the lips shrink down. After a month or so, the labia look like a typical little girl's. They do not swell again until estrogen levels rise in the preteen and teen years.

What can I do?
You do not need to do anything about swollen labia in the first few weeks of life because this is normal and will go away.

When does my doctor need to be involved?
Call your doctor only if the labial swelling persists beyond 6 to 8 weeks of life.

What tests need to be done, and what do the results mean?
No tests need to be done.

What are the treatments?
There are no treatments other than time. As estrogen leaves the baby's body, the swollen labia shrink down.

What are the possible complications?
There are no complications from this normal process.

Additional Resources
http://www.choc.com/pediatric/hhg/newbappe.htm (Scroll down to "Genitals, Girls.")

◆   ◆   ◆

VAGINAL DISCHARGE
(Birth–3 Months)

What is happening inside my baby's body?
Vaginal mucus, also called *discharge,* is a clear or white substance that comes out of a newborn girl's vagina. During fetal development, a mother's hormones (such as estrogen) pass into the baby via the placenta. The hormones stimulate the baby to produce discharge from the vagina during the first week of life. As the hormones gradually disappear from the baby's body, the discharge lessens and then eventually ceases.

Sometimes the discharge looks bloody. As the hormones that had traveled across the placenta slowly disappear from the baby's body, some newborn girls have bleeding from their vagina. This is essentially a miniperiod. A grown woman gets her period when her hormone levels drop below a certain limit. The same happens to an infant girl: she has received high doses of hormones from her mom during the pregnancy, and when the levels drop a few weeks after she is born, she can get a period-type bleeding. The blood is typically mixed with mucus and can appear anytime between birth and six weeks of life.

What can I do?
You do not have to do anything for mucus discharge or bloody vaginal discharge because both are normal. When cleaning the vagina during diaper changes, you should — as a matter of basic hygiene — always wipe the baby from front to back.

When does my doctor need to be involved?
If the discharge is green or foul smelling, or if it persists beyond the first few weeks of life, then call your doctor. Clear, white, or yellow discharge is normal.

Blood-tinged discharge is normal. However, if blood-tinged discharge persists beyond 6 to 8 weeks of life, then contact your doctor. Your doctor also needs to be involved if the blood is bright red and flowing the same way it would if the skin were cut.

This is not bloody discharge; it is bleeding. Anytime blood is mixed with urine, your doctor should be called.

If you suspect that a foreign object such as a small toy has been placed inside the vagina, then call your doctor. Foreign objects can cause infection and discharge. Sometimes an older sibling will place one inside the vagina of a younger sibling. Or, as babies get older and become mobile, they gain access to small objects and can put them just about anywhere.

What tests need to be done, and what do the results mean?
If the mucus is green or foul smelling, then a culture can be done to check whether or not there is a bacteria causing the problem. Otherwise tests are unnecessary.

What are the treatments?
With time, normal vaginal discharge will stop. Bloody discharge resolves as the hormone levels drop. If it persists, however, then the source of bleeding needs to be found. The cause of the persistent blood will determine the treatment.

If the discharge is green or foul smelling and an infection exists, then antibiotics may be used to treat the bacteria causing the discharge.

If a foreign object is present, then it needs to be removed. Often antibiotics will be given as well.

What are the possible complications?
There are no long-term complications of normal vaginal discharge, whether it is bloody or just plain mucus.

Additional Resources
http://www.rch.unimelb.edu.au/clinicalguide/pages/vulvovaginitis.php
http://www.choc.com/dev/pediatric/hhg/newbappe.htm (Scroll down to "Genitals, Girls.")

◆   ◆   ◆

VAGINAL (HYMENAL) SKIN TAGS
(Birth–3 Months)

What is happening inside my baby's body?
A vaginal skin tag is a small piece of skin that appears to be protruding from the vagina. The skin can look swollen and red, or it
can look the same as the skin elsewhere on the body. A vaginal
skin tag is often discovered with a diaper change: suddenly a
piece of tissue seems to appear that wasn't there before.

Vaginal skin tags are normal. The skin is often sensitive to
maternal hormones during fetal development, so the tag grows
rapidly while the baby is in the womb. Once the baby is delivered, the maternal estrogen slowly leaves the baby's body. As this
happens, the skin tag usually shrinks down until it is nearly — or
entirely — invisible.

What can I do?
Routine care should be taken while cleaning during diaper
changes. The skin tag is no more sensitive than the rest of the
genital area. When cleaning, you do not need to wipe more carefully here than anywhere else.

When does my doctor need to be involved?
Your doctor needs only to be involved if the skin tag bleeds. This
is very rare and usually occurs only when the skin is irritated with
overly vigorous cleaning.

What tests need to be done, and what do the results mean?
No tests are done with skin tags.

What are the treatments?
Almost all vaginal skin tags disappear with time. There are no
creams or ointments for vaginal skin tags, no special medicines to
make them shrink down faster. If a prominent tag remains for
several years, then you may choose to have it removed surgically
for cosmetic purposes.

What are the possible complications?

The only complications of vaginal skin tags are irritation and bleeding due to excessive rubbing or cleaning. This is uncommon and goes away when the vigorous cleaning stops.

Additional Resources

http://www.choc.com/dev/pediatric/hhg/newbappe.htm (Scroll down to "Genitals, Girls.")

◈   ◈   ◈

LABIAL ADHESIONS
(Birth–12 Months)

What is happening inside my baby's body?

The inner and outer lips of the vagina are called the *labia*. While they form as two separate pieces during fetal development, they can attach at their ends prior to delivery. Occasionally they stick together too much. When the inner lips are joined together in this manner, it is known as a *labial adhesion.*

It is estimated that between one-quarter and one-third of all girls are born with some degree of labial adhesion. Most are minor — extending only a millimeter or two — and often go unnoticed by both parents and doctors. The larger adhesions can extend from the back part of the vagina, near the anus, all the way up toward the clitoris.

The adhesions are usually caused by inflammation or irritation of the labia. The surface becomes sticky and a small scar forms. Girls can have labial adhesions at birth, but it is much more common for them to appear between three months and six years of age.

Most labial adhesions disappear on their own over time. Hormones such as estrogen help to dissolve the adhesions, so a girl going through puberty will often notice that the adhesion has resolved on its own.

What can I do?

If you notice an adhesion, then bring it to the attention of your doctor. There is very little you can (or need to) do to care for the adhesion, short of applying cream if a doctor prescribes it.

When does my doctor need to be involved?
Most labial adhesions do not require medical attention. However, if the adhesion is large, covering the majority of the vaginal opening, then there is an increased risk of infection or bleeding. Your doctor should be involved anytime infection or bleeding occurs.

What tests need to be done, and what do the results mean?
Tests are done only if there is a suspicion that the urine is infected. Large adhesions can cause urine infections by providing a place for urine to pool inside the vagina. Stagnant urine, just like any other stagnant fluid, is more likely to breed infection. Think of the still pond at the park covered with pond scum as opposed to clean flowing water in a stream.

If a ***urinary tract infection (UTI)*** is suspected, then your doctor will order a urinalysis and a urine culture. If the urinalysis shows signs of infection, or if the urine culture grows bacteria, then a UTI is present. UTIs are covered in chapter 22, and these tests are covered in chapter 29. A UTI must be treated with antibiotics.

What are the treatments?
Labial adhesions can be treated with direct application of an estrogen cream. Because hormones help to dissolve the adhesions, locally applied estrogen works quickly and easily. If the adhesion returns, then the estrogen is reapplied. Estrogen creams are typically used only when the adhesion is significant enough to cause potential bleeding or infection.

What are the possible complications?
Labial adhesions are known to recur even after several rounds of treatment with cream. Repeated use of estrogen cream can result in a change of the pigmentation (color) of part of the labia. Given the location of the tissue, the loss of pigmentation is generally not considered a significant side effect.

If a UTI occurs, the UTI itself can cause fever, burning with urination, foul-smelling urine, and frequent urination. For more on UTIs, see chapter 22.

Back and Anus

The spinal cord ends in the region between the lower back and anus. It begins to form by the 18th day of gestation, and the spinal canal closes by day 35. When there is a problem with formation of the end of the spinal cord, it can protrude through the skin of the lower back. This is called a *myelocele* or *meningo-myelocele*. It is also known as spina bifida.

Obstetricians can see large defects in the area on prenatal ultrasounds. Subtle problems, however, are not detectable until after birth. In fact, they can be so subtle that there is only a mild defect in the skin of the lower back. Your pediatrician may notice discoloration, dimples, hair tufts, or patches of irregular skin. An abnormality of the skin overlying the spinal cord can suggest an abnormality of the cord underneath.

ANAL FISSURES
(Birth–12 Months)

What is happening inside my baby's body?
The tissue around the anus can tear easily. In medical terms this is known as an *anal fissure*. A large, hard stool (constipation) or excessive wiping can result in an anal fissure. In fact, any

aggressive irritation at the area can cause tearing. The small cuts in the skin result in bright-red spots of blood. The blood is visible *next* to the stool in the diaper or on wipes, but it is not mixed into the stool at all. Up to 80 percent of babies will have an anal fissure before they are a year old, with mild constipation being the most common cause. Constipation is covered in detail in chapter 20.

The tearing of the skin around the anus is uncomfortable. Then, once the anus is torn, there are two more potential causes of pain. The first is stinging or burning because stool or urine comes into contact with the torn skin. Perfumed baby wipes can cause the same painful sensation. Though the skin heals relatively quickly in the anus, a baby with a fissure will often cry each time he urinates, stools, or has his diaper changed until the skin is completely healed.

The second source of pain is spasm of the muscle in the anus, called the **anal sphincter.** This muscle often spasms when there is irritation in the anus; it can also spasm when there is stool waiting to be released. The spasms may cause immediate pain. They can also create a vicious cycle by slowing down normal stooling, thereby causing a child to become increasingly constipated. Therefore a child with a fissure may become persistently constipated and will continue to reinjure the torn anus each time he passes another hard stool. Stools must be soft in order to reduce tearing of the anus and help promote healing of the irritated skin. In order for stools to remain soft, they must be passed with relative frequency.

What can I do?

Shining a flashlight onto the baby's anus can often identify the source of bleeding. Close inspection should reveal a small, slitlike tear of the skin just inside. Sometimes the area will be slightly red or there will be a spot of dried blood at the site.

To ease the pain of the fissure, apply a small amount of petroleum jelly to the anus. This will lubricate the skin, making the passage of the next stool easier. It is equally important to treat constipation if that is an associated problem. This is covered in chapter 20.

When does my doctor need to be involved?
If the source of bleeding is not obvious or if the bleeding continues beyond a drop or two of blood, then call your doctor. You should also consult your doctor if the bleeding persists or increases, or if blood is mixed into the stool itself. If you are at all unsure, ask your doctor.

What tests need to be done, and what do the results mean?
Anal fissures do not require any tests. But if the blood is mixed into the stool rather than coating it or sitting beside it, then the source of bleeding is more likely somewhere deep inside the intestines rather than an anal fissure. If intestinal bleeding is suspected, then a stool sample should be tested for infection, inflammation, and other causes of intestinal bleeding. This topic is covered in chapter 20.

What are the treatments?
The two main treatments for anal fissures are lubrication of the anus and treatment of constipation, if that is the underlying cause. Lubrication works directly at the site of the bleeding. When the area is greased, the stool can slide by more easily. Any color-free, perfume-free lubricant — such as Vaseline or other petroleum jellies — may be used. Apply a small amount at the anus using your pinkie finger — not a Q-Tip or other narrow tool. This can be repeated every few hours or with each diaper change until a stool is passed without accompanying blood.

Other treatments include gentle cleaning of the anus and the avoidance of perfumed baby wipes. These wipes will cause stinging when they contact an open cut. *Sitz baths* are also helpful — these warm-water baths contain various mild agents that help soothe the skin.

If constipation is the underlying cause of the fissure, then it must be treated. For information on treating constipation, see chapter 20.

What are the possible complications?
The most worrisome complication is a *chronic fissure* — one that will not heal. This happens when the same cut is continually

reopened before it has time to heal. In extreme cases, chronic fissures require surgery. Excessive bleeding and infection are extraordinarily uncommon with anal fissures, despite how frequently babies normally stool.

Additional Resources
www.drhull.com/EncyMaster/C/constipation_infant.html
http://www.nlm.nih.gov/medlineplus/encyclopedia.html (Click on "Ch–Co," then scroll down to "constipation.")
http://www.nlm.nih.gov/medlineplus/encyclopedia.html (Click on "Ah–Ap," then scroll down to "anal fissure.")

◆   ◆   ◆

SACRAL PITS, DIMPLES, AND HAIR TUFTS
(Birth–12 Months)

What is happening inside my baby's body?
A *sacral* (also known as *pilonidal*) *pit* is a small hole on the lower back between the bottom of the spine and the top of the buttock. A shallow pit is likewise called a sacral (or pilonidal) dimple. A hair tuft is a patch of hair overlying that same region. All of these are usually normal, simply marking the bottom of the spinal cord. Regardless, these and other lower back irregularities need to be checked by a doctor.

The spinal cord forms during the first trimester of pregnancy. As it develops, the skin covering the back is also developing. Therefore, if the bottom end of the spinal cord does not develop perfectly, then the overlying skin can look uneven. Sometimes a piece of the spinal cord actually gets "stuck" to the growing skin, and the spinal cord tugs on the skin in this area. In its most extreme form, the spinal cord can drag the skin all the way down to its endpoint, forming a deep pit, or the skin can drag the spinal cord out to the surface of the body and beyond, creating a *myelocele* or *meningomyelocele,* also known as *spina bifida.* Most of the time, when the end of the spinal cord is abnormal, there is an indication on the skin in this region.

Think, however, of family members and friends you know. Many have patches of hair or slight dimples or discolorations on this part of the lower back. In fact, it is extremely common to have variation in the skin at this precise point on the body and to be completely normal — more than 1 in every 50 normal babies is born with a pit, dimple, or abnormality of the skin on the lower back. In fact, it is far more common to have a normal pit, dimple, or tuft than to have anything wrong with the spinal cord below. Therefore the simple presence of a dimple or some hair at the base of a child's spine usually means nothing.

On the other hand, when the spinal cord and its overlying skin are attached, problems may arise as the child gets older and the cord tries to grow. This affects the nerves to the lower half of the body, including the legs and feet, bladder, and bowels.

Deep pits can also become infected. If the pit is deep enough, then the infection can track right down to the spinal cord.

What can I do?

You do not need to do anything about pits, dimples, or hair tufts other than to bring them to the attention of your pediatrician. The area should be kept clean with regular bathing. No special care is required for a normal pit, dimple, or tuft.

When does my doctor need to be involved?

If the base of the pit is visible when the surrounding skin is gently pulled aside, then the pit is shallow and you should not worry. If the base of the pit is not visible, or if there is a tuft of hair arising only from the pit — rather than a patch of hair generally distributed in the region of the lower back — then your doctor needs to be involved. You also need to contact your doctor if the area has a thick tuft of hair sprouting from a relatively small patch of skin, or if the irregularity is in the form of a skin tag, skin swelling, or an unusual mark.

If a pit or dimple looks red and irritated, swollen, or tender, then it could be infected. Clear or yellowish fluid draining from the pit may be the fluid normally surrounding the brain and spinal cord. White fluid may be pus, signaling an infection. Your doctor should see your baby if he has any of these problems.

Most pits, dimples, and tufts are at the base of the spine, just above (or even tucked within) the crease of the buttocks. When a pit is visible much higher on the back, a doctor should be involved. Your doctor should also evaluate the pit if it is off to one side (not in the midline) or if there are other skin abnormalities in the general area.

Finally, when a child has any other visible defects, especially along the midline of the body, bring them to the attention of your doctor. The midline of the body is the imaginary line that connects the belly button up to the nose, travels up and over the head to the middle of the back of the neck, and then goes down to the crease in the buttocks. This "line" separates right from left. Structures on either side should be fairly symmetric, and structures along the line should be intact. Some examples of *midline defects* include cleft palate and hypospadias.

What tests need to be done, and what do the results mean?

Most sacral dimples, pits, or tufts are normal, so testing is usually not necessary. If a test is done, then an ultrasound is typically the first choice. The ultrasound is placed on the baby's lower back so that a doctor can see whether or not the spinal canal and the skin are connected in any way. If the ultrasound is too difficult to interpret, or if the baby is older than 6 to 12 months, then an MRI may be done.

The ultrasound or MRI can help to show whether or not there is a direct connection between the skin along the lower back and the spinal column below. An MRI can also illustrate the structure of the spinal cord. A normal result shows no connection between the spinal column and any surrounding structures.

What are the treatments?

A child with a connection between a sacral pit, dimple, or tuft and the underlying spinal cord requires surgery. Eventually this connection can limit spinal cord growth, damaging the nerves of the cord. In some cases, it can also lead to infection of the spinal cord or the fluid surrounding the spinal cord *(meningitis)*.

If the skin around the pit is infected, then antibiotics are usually necessary. These must be taken by mouth; they cannot be applied to the site of the pit. If there is a large amount of fluid or pus, then drainage may be required. If the spinal cord or the

cord's surrounding fluid becomes infected, then intravenous antibiotics will likely be needed.

What are the possible complications?

When the area looks red or irritated, it could be infected. Infection may just involve the skin, or it may involve the deeper tissues, including muscles, nerves, the fluid around the spinal cord,
and the brain.

The area of the dimple — or a neighboring area, for that matter — can become filled with fluid. At this stage it is called a
pilonidal cyst and often requires drainage.

If the sacral pit or tuft reaches down to the spinal cord and
involves those nerves, then bowel and bladder function can
become impaired. The most common manifestation is urinary
tract infection caused by inability to effectively drain the bladder
due to poorly functioning nerves. The resulting stagnant urine in
the bladder breeds infection. If nerves that go to the bowel are
involved, then chronic constipation may also result.

Additional Resources
http://www.nlm.nih.gov/medlineplus/encyclopedia.html (Click on "P–Pl,"
then scroll down to "pilonidal dimple.")
http://www.sbaa.org/docs/spotlights/occulta.pdf

Legs and Feet

The legs and feet form early in the pregnancy, their bones clearly visible on ultrasound by 16 weeks of gestation. They kick for the next several months, at first unnoticed by the mom but soon unmistakable. Movement helps the limbs form. In fact, as space becomes more and more cramped in the womb, the legs and feet can get pushed into awkward positions that affect their growth.

The legs and feet continue to change after a baby is born. The legs often look bowed, sometimes right at birth. The lower leg has a C-shaped curvature that is entirely normal. By the time a baby masters walking, her legs will likely begin to straighten. Until then, though, some babies have long straight limbs while others have wide curved ones.

The feet look like puddles early on, with no obvious arch. Like the legs, the feet will develop as they need to, once they bear weight and become responsible for walking. Some babies point their feet inward, others turn their feet out. All of this evolves over the first several months and years of a child's life.

BOWLEGS
(Birth–12 Months)

What is happening inside my baby's body?
It is normal for a baby's legs to look bowed — like he just got off a horse — until two to three years of age. There is often a C-shaped curvature between the knee and ankle from birth, and in most children, maximal bowing of the legs actually occurs when they are newborns. This curvature (also called *varus deformity*) is natural and almost always resolves without treatment.

By two to three years of life, the opposite problem often occurs, and the child can look knock-kneed (called *valgus deformity*). This peaks at about age three and can last until age seven or eight. All of this is entirely normal. It happens because of differential growth around the knees, where the bones on one side of each knee grow faster than the other.

What can I do?
Nothing needs to be done for bowlegs.

When does my doctor need to be involved?
Only if your baby's legs look different from each other, with one significantly more bowed, should you bring bowlegs to your doctor's attention. Also, as your child grows older and begins to walk, you should point out abnormalities with walking or balance. If bowing of the legs seems to be getting progressively worse rather than better, then your doctor should be informed. Continual bowing is called *Blount's disease*. It is caused when part of the growth plate in the leg grows too fast, so that the leg bone (the tibia) bows itself.

Later, if the bowing is so severe that your child is unable to stand or walk, then talk to your doctor. Once a child is three years old, the bowing should have largely corrected itself. If it hasn't, then you may need to consult a specialist. Severe bowing can be associated with other bony problems.

What tests need to be done, and what do the results mean?
Tests do not need to be done in the case of normal bowing. Only if the bowing is significant past two years of age, or if the two legs are unevenly bowed, will an X ray be done.

What are the treatments?
Bowed legs used to be braced or casted. Today they are treated much less aggressively. For a child with severe or persistent bowing, all that is typically needed is to watch his development closely, with visits to an orthopedist about every six months. If the bowlegs are so severe that they cause difficulty walking (which is extremely rare), or if a child has Blount's disease, then surgery may be needed.

What are the possible complications?
There are no complications of normal bowing. However, if the bowing does not resolve on its own or becomes rapidly and progressively worse, then Blount's disease or rickets should be considered. As described previously, with Blount's disease the tibia bows progressively, and unlike normal bowing that resolves on its own, this bowing worsens. *Rickets* is a disease of the bones caused by vitamin D deficiency. It can result in severe leg bowing and other changes in bones throughout the body.

Additional Resources
http://www.orthoseek.com/articles/bowlegs-kk.html
http://www.nlm.nih.gov/medlineplus/encyclopedia.html (Click on "Bl–Bz," then scroll down to "bowlegs.")
http://www.nlm.nih.gov/medlineplus/encyclopedia.html (Click on "Bl–Bz," then scroll down to "Blount's disease.")

CLUBFOOT AND FOOT DEFORMITIES
(Birth)

What is happening inside my baby's body?
One in 1,000 babies is born with a *clubfoot* — a foot pointing downward and twisted inward. Boys are affected more often than girls, and there is an increased likelihood of occurrence when other family members have a clubfoot.

True clubfoot begins early in development and may (or may not) have something to do with the way the foot is positioned while the child is growing inside his mother's womb. The ligaments and tendons on the back and inside of the foot develop more slowly than the rest, resulting in the typical shape. If the clubfoot is severe, then the developing bones may be affected as well.

Sometimes clubfoot is caused exclusively by the position of the fetus in the womb. This is often not true clubfoot but rather a variation called *postural clubfoot.* Unlike true clubfoot, postural clubfoot can be corrected simply by the pediatrician's moving of the baby's foot because the ligaments and tendons are normal. There is actually a group of problems like this called *positional deformities.* Among them are *metatarsus adductus* and other correctable foot deformities, as well as *torticollis* (see chapter 17). In these cases, the more cramped the womb, the more likely a child will have a mild problem with growth of some part of the body. Because twins and triplets are crammed into tight quarters, positional deformities are slightly more common in these babies.

Most clubfeet are identified right at birth. A pediatrician will attempt to gently turn the foot upward and outward, testing the flexibility of the shortened ligaments and tendons. A foot that appears to be clubfoot but is "fully correctable" — i.e., that can be moved into a normal position with gentle rotation — is a postural clubfoot. A foot that cannot be moved into normal position is a true clubfoot.

What can I do?

With true clubfoot, you should seek help from an orthopedist (a doctor specializing in bones). This should be done as soon as possible after birth. In the case of positional foot deformities such as postural clubfoot, you can learn about exercises that will gently stretch the ligaments and tendons so that the foot will move into a more proper position.

When does my doctor need to be involved?

An orthopedist needs to be involved anytime a clubfoot cannot be easily moved into a normal position.

What tests need to be done, and what do the results mean?

Usually no tests need to be done to diagnose clubfoot. Often it is seen on prenatal ultrasound. However, an X ray may be obtained soon after birth to look at how well the bones of the ankles and feet have formed.

What are the treatments?

A true clubfoot will be placed in a cast in order to gradually stretch shortened tendons and ligaments. Casts are removed and replaced every week until the shortened ligaments have lengthened and the foot can be held in proper position on its own. This is known as *serial casting*. X rays may be taken once casting begins to make sure that the foot has been cast into an appropriate position.

About half of all clubfeet are corrected with serial casting. The other half, however, require surgery. This decision is typically made between 3 and 6 months of life. Depending on how severe the clubfoot is, a surgeon may operate shortly after the determination that serial casting has failed. In less severe cases, the surgeon may wait to perform the surgery until the child is 8 to 12 months old. The surgery involves cutting the shortened ligaments and lengthening tendons. Following the surgery, the leg will be casted for 6 to 12 weeks. Once the cast is removed, a plastic brace may be used for the next several weeks or months.

The child may receive physical therapy in conjunction with casting. This is because casting limits the range of movement of the muscles and ligaments, and over time they can shrink and become tight.

What are the possible complications?

When clubfoot is not casted early, or if a child has severe clubfoot, surgery is likely. Walking on an untreated clubfoot can cause erosion of the skin along the side of the foot and long-term damage to the bones.

Additional Resources
http://www.vh.org/Providers/Textbooks/Clubfoot/Clubfoot.html
http://www.shrinershq.org/patientedu/legfoot.html
http://www.nlm.nih.gov/medlineplus/encyclopedia.html (Click on "Ch–Co," then scroll down to "clubfoot.")

27

Nervous System

The nervous system includes the brain, the spinal cord, and all of the nerves that travel to muscles and organs. This intricate network sends signals that tell the body what to do at a millisecond's notice.

The hardwiring of the nervous system is in place by the time a baby is born. But many of the nerves are naked, missing the insulation required to send information efficiently and quickly. This is why a newborn seems so sensitive to certain stimuli. A surprised child may gasp or scream, but a surprised infant will extend his arms and legs, jerk them in again, and then begin to wail. It is as if every nerve in his body is firing at once.

Over the first few months of your baby's life, the nerves insulate themselves with a covering called *myelin*. As this happens, you will notice that your baby becomes more coordinated, can control his body better, and begins to remember faces and places.

JERKING MOVEMENTS AND SEIZURES
(Birth–12 Months)

What is happening inside my baby's body?
When a baby is born, the nerves in her brain and throughout her body are not well insulated. Rather, they are like a bundle of

naked wires. So when one nerve is stimulated — by anything from a loud sound to a tickle — often many neighboring nerves are stimulated as well. Sometimes the result is a jumble of different reactions (kicks, stretches, cries); other times it is a coordinated series of muscle movements called a *reflex*. Either way, the lack of nerve insulation through the first few weeks and months of life explains why a perfectly content baby can suddenly flail her arms and legs and start crying. A baby will often display these movements when transitioning between being asleep and awake.

A reflex is an involuntary response to some sort of stimulus. Infants are born with a set of reflexes and then lose them in the first few months of life. These include the suck, moro, grasp, tonic neck, step, root, crawl, and parachute reflexes (see page 244). All of these represent specific responses to a touch or a sound or a motion. They are almost all present at birth, except the crawl and parachute reflexes that appear when the baby is a few weeks old. All of these reflexes disappear as a baby matures. If the reflexes are entirely absent, or if they persist significantly longer than anticipated, then it may be a sign of nervous system abnormalities.

Sometimes parents confuse normal infant reflexes with abnormal firing of nerves in the brain called seizures. This is especially true of the moro reflex. True seizures can appear in many different forms, but in babies, there are often easily identifiable seizure movements. These include rigid muscle contractions followed by *clonic movements,* which are alternating rhythmic contractions and relaxations of certain muscle groups such as the arms or legs. The jerking movements of a seizure usually last only a minute or two, and rarely longer than five minutes.

During the seizure, your baby can have difficulty breathing or may actually stop breathing. As soon as the seizure has stopped, she should begin breathing normally and will almost certainly be extremely sleepy.

The most common cause of seizures in children ages six months to six years is a high fever or a rapidly rising temperature. These are called *febrile seizures.* Between 2 to 5 percent of all children up to age six have at least one febrile seizure.

What can I do?

You need not do anything about normal infant reflexes.

In the case of a first-time seizure, call 911. If your child has had multiple seizures, you will learn quickly how to manage them and how to determine when to call a doctor or 911.

Do not attempt to put anything into the mouth of a child who is having a seizure. Though it may look like your baby could bite her tongue while seizing, putting an object in the mouth to prevent this can cause many other complications. If your baby is having a seizure, then sharp or blunt objects should be removed from her hands. Clear the area around her and make sure she is in a safe place (such as the floor or a crib) while someone else is calling 911.

If the seizure is caused by a fever, then a fever-reducing medicine should be given as soon as the seizure has stopped. Acetaminophen (Tylenol) or, in children over six months, ibuprofen (Motrin or Advil) can be used. Aspirin should never be given to infants or children.

When does my doctor need to be involved?

You should call your doctor if you notice that the normal newborn reflexes persist well beyond the time they are supposed to go away, or if they never appear at all. Doctors usually look for these reflexes during routine checkups.

The first time a child has a seizure, call 911 for an ambulance. Your doctor will be involved, but this usually happens once you are already in an emergency room. You should not call your child's doctor in lieu of 911 if the child appears to be having a seizure.

What tests need to be done, and what do the results mean?

If the reflexes are abnormal — if they persist well beyond the time they are supposed to go away or if they never appear at all — then a thorough developmental exam should be done. The exam evaluates a baby's neurological development in order to determine whether it is normal or abnormal.

If your baby has had a seizure, then your doctor will first try to determine the cause. Some general tests can be done to look for

NEWBORN REFLEXES

◆

Suck reflex: baby automatically sucks when something is touching the area around her mouth

Moro reflex: baby is held in someone's arms and then, while being safely cradled, is released in order to simulate falling against gravity; baby's arms and legs extend out and then bend in toward the chest, accompanied by a cry

Grasp reflex: baby will grasp an object placed in her palm with her fingers or along the sole of her foot with her toes

Tonic neck reflex: baby lying on her back turns her head one direction; the arm on the side to which the head is looking straightens while the other arm bends; this is also called the fencer response because the baby assumes the position resembling a sword fighter. When the head turns in the opposite direction, the arms switch positions.

Step reflex: baby is held vertically above a flat surface; her foot will lift up as if stepping when it touches the surface

Root reflex: stroke of the cheek causes the baby to turn in that direction and try to suck

Crawl reflex: baby appears as if she is trying to crawl when she is placed on her stomach

Parachute reflex: when baby is held securely and moved quickly to simulate a falling motion, her arms extend like a parachute as if to break the fall.

the most common causes. These tests include a complete blood count and a blood culture; an electrolyte panel; a urinalysis and urine culture; and a lumbar puncture (spinal tap). For details about these tests, see chapter 29.

A baby who has had a seizure may need a CT scan or MRI of the brain to look for abnormalities that may have caused the seizure. An *electroencephalogram (EEG),* a test that looks at brain waves, may also be performed. Wires painlessly attached to stickers on the scalp record the brain's electrical activity. Sometimes an EEG reveals where in the brain the seizure is occurring, providing clues to its cause.

Because high fever is the most common cause of seizures in children ages six months to six years, a rectal temperature should be checked. A child's temperature should be monitored closely so that a febrile seizure does not occur again once the fever-reducing medicines have worn off.

What are the treatments?

There is no treatment for normal newborn reflexes (because they are normal).

The treatment for seizures depends on the underlying cause. If your baby has a bacterial infection, then the infection will be treated with antibiotics. If the seizure is the result of a fever, then getting the temperature down is the first priority. If there is an abnormality on a CT scan, MRI, or EEG, then treatment will depend on the specific problem identified.

What are the possible complications?

If the normal newborn reflexes are absent or if they persist significantly longer than expected, then some central nervous system damage may exist and the baby should be evaluated.

The main complication of a seizure is not breathing. Because multiple nerves fire during a seizure, many muscle groups are stimulated at once and many normal functions — such as breathing — can be compromised. A baby may appear to turn blue during the seizure, but CPR and mouth-to-mouth resuscitation often cannot be performed until the seizure has stopped. The breathing will usually resume immediately after the seizure ends.

A baby who vomits during a seizure can swallow or choke on the vomit. If vomiting occurs, then the head can be turned gently to one side to help reduce the chance of swallowing or inhaling the vomit. Remember, do not put anything in the mouth during the seizure.

Additional Resources

http://www.packardchildrenshospital.org (Go to "search" in upper right-hand corner and type in "newborn reflexes.")

http://www.nlm.nih.gov/medlineplus/encyclopedia.html (Click on "S–Sh," then scroll down to "seizures.")

http://www.nlm.nih.gov/medlineplus/encyclopedia.html (Click on "F," then scroll down to "febrile seizure [children].")

http://www.cincinnatichildrens.org (Go to "search" in upper right-hand corner and type in "fever-related seizure.")

The Whole Body

While most infant health questions focus on one particular part of the body, there are a few that involve the entire body. These are issues that come up in almost every family at some point in the first year of life. Among the most common worries of new parents are fever, inconsolable crying, dehydration, sleep issues, and concern that their child looks blue.

These issues are more difficult to address because there is not necessarily one thing going on in the body or one symptom you can follow. To make matters more complicated, every baby is different, and some of these issues have to do with temperament as well as possible medical problems.

There are simple, logical ways to approach these topics. Fevers can be measured and treated. The source of inconsolability can often be found. Dehydration can be prevented or at least identified. Sleep patterns change with time, but they do have some normal variation. And blueness — the most frightening to most parents — is less scary if you know CPR.

FEVER
(Birth–12 Months)

What is happening inside my baby's body?
It is normal for the body's temperature to change during the
day — warm clothing, hot weather, and exercise can all cause a
slight increase in body temperature. *Fever* means a rise in body
temperature above the normal daily swings. The average body
temperature is 98.6°F (37°C). Fever is generally considered to be
any temperature above 100.5°F (38°C).

A young baby is like a snake: when it is cold outside, he gets
cold, and when he is bundled in several blankets and has a hat
on his head, he gets hot. Over the first few weeks of life, a baby
becomes more capable of regulating his own body temperature.
Until then, a warm environment can cause a child to feel warm
and can generate a "fever." Therefore, if a baby who seems to
have a fever was wrapped in warm blankets prior to his temperature being taken, then he should be unwrapped for about 10 minutes and the temperature rechecked. If he is still hot, then the
fever is genuine.

From infancy through adulthood, the body experiences fever
in a fairly consistent way: the heart beats faster and blood vessels
dilate, causing the skin to flush and warm. This process brings
blood close to the skin so that it can be efficiently cooled, eventually reducing the body temperature. Most of the time fever is not
harmful; rather, it is the body's natural way of fighting an illness.

When the temperature lingers between 99-100.5°F, the body may
feel warm but the temperature is not worrisome. A high fever, on
the other hand, is one above 104 or 105°F. Some children get
high fevers often, but for most a fever this high is unusual. The
complications of a high fever are covered later in this section.

Pediatricians are very aggressive when a baby younger than
4 to 6 weeks of age has a fever above 100.5°F. This is because a
baby this age has a very unsophisticated immune system — he is
barely making any antibodies and has very poor barriers to protect one part of the body from another. A baby infected with a

virus or bacteria can get very sick very fast and won't be able to communicate to his parents that he feels rotten. Therefore fever in a child younger than 4 to 6 weeks old is approached quite differently from fever in a child older than six weeks. This is covered in the section on tests and results that follows.

Infections can come from a number of places. Newborns can get them from the placenta or amniotic fluid right before delivery or from the mom's vaginal canal during delivery. Sometimes it can take up to six weeks for one of these infections to cause problems. Babies and older children pass infections back and forth through the air via coughs and sputters. Saliva carries many infections, so kissing, sharing foods, and mouthing toys can all contribute to the spread of infection.

What can I do?

The most important thing to do when it seems like your child has a fever is to take his temperature. There are many ways to do this. Mercury thermometers used to be very common but have recently been taken off the market; most thermometers are now digital.

A *rectal temperature* is the most accurate method. This is typically done using a digital thermometer inserted about one-half inch into the rectum. Though this is an odd sensation for the baby, it should not hurt. A thermometer can be used under the arm, with the tip placed securely in the armpit and the child's arm held close to his side so that air cannot get in or out. This will give a fairly accurate measurement, although it is generally agreed that this temperature is probably 0.5°F below the actual body temperature.

Temperatures taken in the ear, in the mouth, or on the forehead are even less accurate, measuring temperatures 1.0°F or more below the true temperature. An ear thermometer must read the temperature off the eardrum, and in babies this can be difficult because the ear canals are small and windy. Therefore ear thermometers are more accurate when children are older. Oral temperatures are also not very reliable in young babies because infants cannot necessarily keep the thermometer under the tongue with the mouth closed as needed. Paper-strip thermometers laid

HOW TO TAKE A BABY'S TEMPERATURE RECTALLY

◆

Rectal temperatures can be stressful for parents because of the fear that the thermometer will be placed too far inside and cause the baby pain. However, it is important to take rectal temperatures accurately. If the thermometer is not placed far enough inside, then the reading will be falsely low. The probe is the pointed side of the thermometer with the silver cap on the end. Clean it off with soap or alcohol and then rinse it with cool water before using (hot water can break the thermometer or can affect the result). You can use the thermometer with a probe cover (these come with the thermometer) or without; either way, grease the end with some Vaseline or other lubricant. Place the baby facedown on your lap, the bed, or the floor. Gently slide the probe in about half an inch. Never force it — if it is difficult to insert, then stop. Hold the thermometer while you are taking the temperature. Digital thermometers will beep when the temperature is done. The older mercury thermometers need to be kept in place two to three minutes for an accurate reading. Once you are done, wash the thermometer again before putting it away.

across the forehead are even less accurate and should probably never be used.

If your baby has a fever and is older than six weeks, then give him a fever-reducing medicine. It takes 15 to 20 minutes for the medicine to work. Don't wait to see or talk to your doctor before giving the medicine. However, if your baby is younger than six weeks, then call your doctor anytime the fever is above 100.5°F. In this case, fever-reducing medicines should not be given unless directed by a doctor. The medicines that reduce fever are described in more detail below.

When does my doctor need to be involved?
If your baby is younger than six weeks and has a fever higher than 100.5°F, then call your doctor immediately. In a baby over six weeks, your doctor should be called when the fever goes above 104°F.

If the baby is having other symptoms at the same time — such as extreme sleepiness (lethargy), repeated vomiting, spreading rash, or seizures — then medical attention is needed regardless of the baby's age.

What tests need to be done, and what do the results mean?
When a baby is under 4 to 6 weeks old and has a fever but no other symptoms — no runny nose, cough, diarrhea, etc. — then a broad range of tests must be done to look for the source of the fever. These tests include a complete blood count and blood culture, a urinalysis and urine culture, and a spinal tap (lumbar puncture). A chest X ray may also be done. All of these tests are described in chapter 29. In addition, the baby must be admitted to the hospital and started on intravenous antibiotics in order to treat any potential bacterial infection that may be the source of the fever. The antibiotics are given for at least 48 hours, until all of the results of the tests are available. Though this approach may seem overly aggressive, an infant under 4 to 6 weeks of age has an underdeveloped immune system, and an infection can quickly become overwhelming. This approach is the best way to ensure that an isolated infection does not spread to other parts of the body.

If your baby is older than 4 to 6 weeks, then your doctor will be a bit more relaxed. If the baby is eating and sleeping well, and has periods of playfulness, then it is likely that he has only a mild illness. If the fever is high or has persisted for several days, then your doctor will check for signs indicating the source of the fever, such as a runny nose, cough, ear pain, diarrhea, and so on. If the throat looks red and infected, then the pediatrician will often take a throat culture to check for strep throat. If it is flu season and the child has symptoms consistent with *influenza* or *respiratory syncytial virus (RSV),* then tests can be performed

COMMON INFECTION NAMES YOU MIGHT HEAR

◆

Candida. This is the cause of oral thrush. It can also cause diaper rashes and vaginal yeast infections. There are many types of candida, but the most common is Candida albicans.

Coxsackie virus. This virus is the cause of hand, foot and mouth disease, a blistering rash seen on the hands, feet, and mouth. Coxsackie is more common among toddlers but can occur in infants, especially when they have older siblings who bring the infection home.

E. coli. This bacteria is commonly found in the intestine. It typically does not cause intestinal problems, but when it is passed out through the stool and gets into the penis or vagina and then into the urinary tract, it can cause urinary tract infections.

Pneumococcus. This bacteria (a type of streptococcus) is one of the most common causes of pneumonia in the elderly. In young children, it can cause ear infections, pneumonia, blood infection, or meningitis. There is now a vaccine available to prevent this infection.

Rotavirus. This virus is the most common cause of gastroenteritis — vomiting and diarrhea — among children in the United States. It causes profuse watery diarrhea with a very pungent smell.

Respiratory Syncytial Virus (RSV). This virus is one of the causes of bronchiolitis, an infection of the lungs. Infants with bronchiolitis have very thick mucus, leading to a wet cough and often some difficulty breathing. Premature babies are at highest risk for infection with RSV, especially in their first winter. Once children are older than a year, RSV infection tends to be less severe — it causes runny nose and cough but involves the lungs much less frequently.

Staphylococcus. *Also known as staph, this bacteria is one of the two that commonly lives on the skin. It causes no problems when it is on the surface, but when it gets underneath the skin and into the body, it can create problems. There are several types of staphylococcus, some of which are more dangerous than others. One of the most common types is* Staphylococcus aureus.

Streptococcus. *This is the other bacteria commonly found on the skin. It is often called strep and usually causes no problems. Issues emerge only when it gets under the skin or penetrates into the body tissues. Group A streptococcus is the cause of strep throat. In very rare cases, a specific type of Group A strep can cause flesh-eating strep infection (also called necrotizing fasciitis). Group B streptococcus (also called GBS) often resides inside the vagina. A baby who acquires GBS during delivery can become quite ill in the first few weeks of life. Many mothers with GBS receive antibiotics prior to or during delivery in order to minimize the risk to the baby.*

Varicella. *This is the virus that causes chicken pox and, later, shingles. There is now a vaccine to prevent chicken-pox infection.*

using mucus from the nose to check for the presence of these infections. But if no source of fever is apparent and the fever is high or persistent (or both), then a CBC, blood culture, urinalysis, and urine culture will be done. When a child more than 4 to 6 weeks is extremely ill, a spinal tap and hospitalization may be required.

What are the treatments?

The two fever-reducing medicines available over the counter are *acetaminophen* (Tylenol) and *ibuprofen* (Motrin and Advil). These are sold as infant drops and children's liquid. Acetaminophen is also available in a rectal suppository.

Acetaminophen can be given at any age. It is dosed by weight, 10 to 15 mg/kg of body weight. It is important to dose acetaminophen appropriately, as overdoses may be toxic. Make sure to read labels of over-the-counter cough-and-cold remedies, as many of these contain acetaminophen. Never give more than one acetaminophen-containing medicine at a time. And note that over-the-counter cough-and-cold remedies are generally not recommended for babies under six months.

Ibuprofen can only be given *after* six months of age. It too is dosed by weight, 10 mg/kg of body weight. The dosing of these medicines is usually listed on the back of the bottle. This can be confusing, so if you have any questions, call your doctor.

For high fevers, acetaminophen and ibuprofen can be used together or can be alternated. Call your doctor for information about how to combine these medicines.

Baby aspirin is for teens and adults, not for babies. It should never be given to infants. Aspirin has been associated with *Reye's syndrome* in children, so it should not be used unless under the supervision of a doctor.

Once the source of the fever is identified, there may be medicines to treat that too. Bacterial infections are often treated with antibiotics — the specific antibiotic used depends on the exact type of bacteria. Viruses are most often allowed to run their course without specific medications, apart from fever reducers and pain relievers. The main exceptions are viruses in the herpes family — such as herpes simplex virus (HSV) and varicella zoster (chicken pox), for which there are effective antiviral medications.

What are the possible complications?

The main complication of a fever is a *febrile seizure*. This is a convulsion that occurs when the temperature is very high or when it rises quickly. Febrile seizures are covered in chapter 27.

Other complications of fever are generally related to the underlying cause. Bacterial infections can spread into remote parts of the body, causing secondary problems. This is why fevers are often approached aggressively, especially in babies younger than 4 to 6 weeks, as they are at increased risk of spread of infection.

Additional Resources

http://www.nlm.nih.gov/medlineplus/encyclopedia.html (Click on "G," then scroll down to "Group B streptococcal septicemia of the newborn.")

http://www.medem.com (Go to "search medical library" at upper right-hand corner and type in "fever.")

http://www.packardchildrenshospital.org (Go to "search" in upper right-hand corner and type in "sepsis.")

http://www.cincinnatichildrens.org (Go to search box at upper right-hand corner and type in "temperature taking.")

http://www.mayoclinic.com/invoke.cfm?id=HO00002

http://www.ninds.nih.gov/health_and_medical/disorders/reyes_syndrome.htm

◆   ◆   ◆

INCONSOLABLE BABY
(Birth–12 Months)

What is happening inside my baby's body?
An inconsolable baby is a baby who will not stop crying. Whether the baby is picked up or laid down, rocked or held still, fed or given a pacifier, the crying does not stop. An inconsolable baby almost always ends up being seen in the emergency room. However, there are a few things that can be checked prior to calling the doctor or running to the hospital.

One cause of inconsolability is a *hair tourniquet* — a piece of hair wrapped around a finger or toe. In boys, the tourniquet might also be found wrapped around the penis. After several minutes, the hair will block normal circulation to the area. The lack of circulation will eventually cause severe pain. Therefore look at each of the fingers and toes (and the penis) of an inconsolable baby.

Another cause for sustained crying is a *corneal abrasion.* This is a scratch across the outer covering of the eyeball that causes tearing and pain. Though a baby with a corneal abrasion still needs to be seen by a doctor, if you can identify this problem ahead of time, then at least you will know why your baby is howling. Corneal abrasions are covered in chapter 13.

An inconsolable baby may also have a *fever.* If the temperature is above 100.5°F (38°C), then a genuine fever is present, suggesting

an infection as the possible cause of the crying. Fever is covered
in the previous section of this chapter.

Abdominal pain is another source of inconsolability. A baby
may have vomiting, diarrhea, constipation, reflux, or excessive
gas. Each of these is covered in chapter 20. *Colic* — which is different from abdominal pain — may also cause inconsolability.
There are many theories on what causes colic. In general, it is
thought to be an inability to calm down once crying has begun.
Colicky babies many times become fussy in the late afternoon or
early evening and will often cry for several hours unless they are
continuously held, rocked, and soothed. Even then they may
continue to cry.

What can I do?

You can check for the common causes of inconsolability — hair
tourniquet, fever, and corneal abrasion. Hair tourniquets can be
removed by gently clipping the hair. If the skin is so swollen that
the hair cannot be removed without cutting the skin, then contact
your doctor.

Fever can be treated with fever reducers, as described in the
previous section. If your baby is under six weeks of age or a fever
does not respond to fever-reducing medicines, then she should
be evaluated by a doctor.

In the case of a corneal abrasion, although you may be able to
identify it, your doctor should see the baby.

Abdominal pain is treated based on its cause. Vomiting and
diarrhea can cause cramping pain. Gas may be caused by food
sensitivity, such as something in the breast milk or formula, or by
sucking in extra air during feeding or crying. Burping will often
help to minimize gas and massage can help to pass it. If a food is
upsetting the baby's stomach, then that type of food should be
stopped. Gas drops such as Mylicon or chamomile drops help in
some instances. All of these gastrointestinal topics are covered in
chapter 20.

There are many approaches to dealing with colic. Often, loud
vibratory noises soothe colicky babies. Taking a drive in the car,
turning on the hair dryer or the vacuum, or running the dish-

washer may help. These often need to be done in conjunction with swaddling the baby while rocking or bouncing him.

When does my doctor need to be involved?
If you cannot figure out why your baby is inconsolable, then call your doctor. Even when the source is obvious — such as a hair tourniquet — if you cannot fix the problem and the baby will not calm down, then your doctor should be called.

Corneal abrasion requires a call or visit to the doctor.

If a fever is the cause of the inconsolability and your baby is under six weeks of age, then you must contact your doctor.

Abdominal pain involving continual vomiting or diarrhea, especially with inconsolability, also requires a call or visit.

If an identifiable and reversible problem cannot be found, then call your doctor.

What tests need to be done, and what do the results mean?
The choice of tests will depend on the cause of the inconsolability. Hair tourniquets do not require any tests.

A corneal abrasion may be confirmed using a special eyedrop *(fluorescein)* that helps illuminate the location of the tear within the eye. This test is painless.

Fever may require a range of tests, including tests of the cerebrospinal fluid, blood, and urine. These are covered in the previous section.

Abdominal pain with excessive vomiting or diarrhea may require further testing. An exam of the abdomen is the first step. Sometimes an X ray will be done to look at the gastrointestinal system. An ultrasound may also be done, especially if *appendicitis* is suspected. (Appendicitis is extremely rare in young babies.) A CT scan may be used in cases where the X ray or ultrasound is equivocal. The stool can be examined for evidence of infection. All of these tests are described in chapters 20 and 29.

What are the treatments?
The treatment for inconsolability depends on its cause. A corneal abrasion is often treated with an eye patch and antibiotic ointment. This is described in chapter 13.

A hair tourniquet must be removed. This can be done using small scissors or even a cream depilatory (hair remover such as Nair).

The treatment of fever depends on its cause. Antibiotics can be used when the fever is a result of a bacterial infection, but they are ineffective for most viral infections. Fever reducers such as acetaminophen and ibuprofen are helpful when fevers are high. This is covered in the section on fevers in this chapter.

Abdominal pain is treated specifically based on its cause. The various causes of abdominal pain and their treatments are covered in chapter 20.

What are the possible complications?

The most worrisome complication of inconsolability is a parent's or caretaker's frustration. This can lead to shaking a baby. Shaking a baby can cause bleeding in the brain and damage to the neurons in the brain, which can result in severe mental impairment or even death. Anytime you feel close to this kind of frustration, you should put the baby in a safe place or in the care of another responsible adult and take a break. Cooling down for just a few minutes is usually all that is needed.

Additional Resources
http://www.medem.com (Go to "search medical library" in upper right-hand corner and type in "crying.")

◆　　◆　　◆

DEHYDRATION
(Birth–12 Months)

What is happening inside my baby's body?

Water makes up approximately 60 percent of the human body by weight. We keep our fluid level high enough largely by drinking liquids. We lose it through sweat, tears, saliva, urine, stool, and vomit. A small amount of fluid is also lost through breathing, as the air breathed out of the lungs carries water in vapor. *Dehydration* literally means too little fluid.

Blood travels throughout the body in arteries and veins. When there is a healthy fluid level in the body, the blood flows at a steady pace and there is enough extra water available to make tears, saliva, urine, and stool. In the case of dehydration, however, when the fluid level in the body drops, water becomes scarce. Tears dry up. The inside of the mouth becomes dry and the tongue sandpaper-like. The urine looks dark because it is concentrated with less water than usual, and total urine output decreases. The heart can beat rapidly and the blood pressure can change.

The most common causes of dehydration in children are **gastroenteritis** (stomach flu) and a low intake of liquids. Gastroenteritis causes dehydration because fluid is lost during vomiting and diarrhea. The stomach and intestines can be so irritated that every attempt to drink something results in one of the two. Therefore fluid is lost but cannot be replaced completely until the vomiting or diarrhea stops. Other causes of vomiting that may lead to dehydration include intestinal malfunction, food allergies, and severe reflux (see chapter 20).

The other common cause of dehydration is a low intake of fluids. This can result from unusual anatomy — such as a cleft palate that makes feeding difficult — or from pain in the mouth or throat. **Thrush** (yeast infection in the mouth), viruses (such as **hand, foot and mouth disease**), and bacteria (such as **strep throat**) can cause exquisite pain with swallowing. Infants and children will refuse liquids rather than experience the pain, eventually leading to dehydration. Occasionally dehydration can result from incorrect mixing of formula powder and water — when too little water is used, a child can become dehydrated. Therefore it is very important to mix powdered formula according to the directions on the label. Finally, in breast-feeding infants, a dehydrated mother can produce less breast milk, and this can contribute to infant dehydration.

Dehydration is often categorized as mild, moderate, or severe. Because water is such a large component of body weight, weight loss can be used as a crude measure of dehydration. The following is a rough way to assess the severity of dehydration:

Category of dehydration	Body weight loss
Mild	3–5%
Moderate	6–10%
Severe	>10%

Another way to classify the degree of dehydration is based on symptoms. A child with *mild dehydration* may have dry lips but the inside of his mouth will still be moist. He will urinate with relatively normal frequency and still cry with tears. His fontanel (see chapter 12) will be soft and flat. A child with *moderate dehydration* will have dry lips and less saliva than usual. He may urinate less frequently than normal but will still typically pee three or more times in a 24-hour period. He will make tears with crying. His fontanel is usually still soft but a little bit sunken. A *severely dehydrated* child looks quite ill. The lips and inside of the mouth are dry. There are no tears with crying. Urine output is significantly decreased, sometimes only once in 24 hours (or none at all). The eyes often look sunken and the child's energy level is quite low. The skin can lose its normal elasticity so that when it is pinched, it holds the shape of a tent. This is called tenting. His fontanel will be sunken.

What can I do?
Recognize dehydration early. Anytime you suspect moderate or severe dehydration, call your doctor right away. If a child cannot tolerate fluids by mouth, then intravenous fluids must be given instead.

With mild dehydration, a baby can be given liquids in an attempt to replace fluids. There are rehydration drinks available in supermarkets and drugstores. These have electrolytes to replace what is lost during ongoing vomiting or diarrhea. Unfortunately these drinks are not safe if they are the only liquid consumed for more than 24 hours. They also typically taste awful. Older children will tolerate clear fluids, diluted juices, flat sodas, and starchy waters such as rice water (see chapter 20). Infants, however, cannot necessarily tolerate these fluids. Breast milk and formula should be used, and your doctor should always be involved.

The key to replacing fluids is to do it slowly. A mildly dehydrated baby who has been vomiting will become quite thirsty. If he drinks a large volume of liquid, then chances are high that he will vomit again. Small sips stay down longer. Sometimes the easiest way to regulate how much a baby gets is to soak a washcloth and let him suck the liquid out. Popsicles work well with children more than a year old.

A baby with profuse watery diarrhea will be able to keep liquids down, but the fluids may go straight through him. This is more common when milk or dairy products are given. For infants, this can pose a dilemma because formula and breast milk are the safest liquids for rehydration, yet they may prolong diarrhea. Breast-feeding mothers should avoid dairy products to minimize the passage of irritating proteins through the breast milk.

When pain (from a severe mouth or throat infection, for instance) is the cause of dehydration, pain relievers may help promote fluid intake. The most common among these are acetaminophen (Tylenol) and — for babies older than six months — ibuprofen (Advil or Motrin). Both are effective pain relievers, but ibuprofen may cause stomach upset, especially in a child who is having stomach irritation already. Infections in the mouth must be treated appropriately with antifungals or antibiotics in order to reduce the pain and treat the underlying problem.

When does my doctor need to be involved?

If your baby has a significantly depressed energy level, then call your doctor. If the baby is not arousable, then call 911.

Anytime you suspect that your baby is moderately or severely dehydrated, call your doctor immediately. Look for a dry mouth with little or no saliva, no tears with crying, or poor urine output. These may appear with excessive vomiting or diarrhea, or with unwillingness or inability to take liquids by mouth.

If diarrhea is ongoing for several days but the baby is happy, eating and drinking well, and not dehydrated, then you do not need to worry. However, if the baby has had diarrhea for two weeks, then notify your doctor.

SIGNS OF DEHYDRATION

◆

Dehydration is categorized as mild, moderate, or severe.
This checklist helps to distinguish between the types.

	Mild	Moderate	Severe
Percent body weight lost	3–5%	6–10%	>10%
Lips	dry	dry	dry
Inside of mouth	moist	moist but less saliva	dry
Making tears?	yes	yes	no
Fontanel	soft and flat	soft, slightly sunken	sunken
Skin	supple	supple	tenting
Urination frequency	normal	decreased, but 3 or more times in 24 hrs	<3 times in 24 hrs

What tests need to be done, and what do the results mean?
First the baby will be weighed. This can help to determine the
degree of dehydration, but only if another weight has been done
fairly recently. Otherwise the weight can be used as a baseline to
follow whether the baby is becoming more or less dehydrated as
the illness progresses from this point on.

Depending on the cause of dehydration, other tests may be
done. If a gastrointestinal infection is suspected, then your doctor
will likely examine the stool and send a stool culture. A complete
blood count and blood culture may indicate whether the infection
has spread to the bloodstream. Assessment of electrolytes may be
necessary as excessive vomiting or diarrhea can alter the normal

balance in the blood. A chest X ray may be helpful to look for pneumonia, which can also cause vomiting. Urine tests — such as urinalysis and urine culture — may also be done, because vomiting can be seen with some urinary tract infections. For further details about many of these tests, see chapter 29.

What are the treatments?

The best treatment for dehydration is hydration. This can be accomplished in different ways. Oral hydration — giving a baby small amounts to drink and watching that he can keep it down — is best. Sometimes a medicine (such as *promethazine*) can be given in the form of a rectal suppository to help stop vomiting. With or without the medicine, if a baby can drink small amounts of liquid without vomiting, then rehydration has begun. You may be surprised by how small the volume of liquid can be — sometimes a baby will take only 5 ml (one teaspoon) every 5 to 10 minutes, but this is enough to begin to turn things around.

When a baby cannot tolerate oral hydration and is moderately or severely dehydrated, *intravenous fluids* must be started. An intravenous catheter (IV) is placed and fluid is given directly into the vein. The IV fluids often make a child feel better with remarkable speed. Once the baby feels well enough to drink liquids and can keep fluids down without vomiting, the IV can be discontinued; it is used only as long as necessary. A baby with moderate dehydration may only need an IV for several hours whereas a severely dehydrated child may need one for several days.

If your baby has an infection, then it must be appropriately treated, often with antibiotics. If the intestine is not working properly, and especially if it is blocked, then a procedure may need to be done to fix it. In some cases, this requires surgery.

What are the possible complications?

Untreated severe dehydration can have life-threatening complications. The body can go into shock as a result of too little blood volume. Seizures can result from reduced blood flow to the brain or from electrolyte imbalances. In the most extreme cases, dehydration can lead to death.

Additional Resources
http://www.nlm.nih.gov/medlineplus/encyclopedia.html (Click on "D–Di,"
then scroll down to "dehydration.")
http://www.clevelandclinic.org/health (Go to "Search by Topic" in upper
right-hand corner and type in "dehydration.")
http://www.quickcare.org/gast/dehydrate.html

◆   ◆   ◆

SLEEP
(Birth–12 Months)

What is happening inside my baby's body?
There are many techniques designed to help get your baby to
sleep through the night. Different strategies work for different
families. The point of this section is neither to discuss sleep training nor to dismiss it. Rather, it is to explain the workings of your
baby's internal clock and to help set your expectations for sleep
at various ages. Of course, there is a wide range of sleep habits.
Some babies will sleep longer from the get-go than others. But it
is important to understand the factors that affect sleep so that you
can maximize your own sleeping while at the same time providing
for your new baby. This section describes general sleep patterns
for full-term babies.

Infants sleep much of the day and night, even though it may not
feel that way. A newborn will sleep an average of 16 to 18 hours
in a 24-hour period, but he will wake every two to three hours for
feeding. This pattern makes adults feel sleep deprived but helps
babies get the sleep they need.

Some newborns are big sleepers. They will snooze for two or
more hours at a time, wake up and feed, and then go back to bed.
Others are catnappers. They sleep for 15 to 20 minutes at a time,
then open their eyes and look around, sometimes crying for food
but sometimes just hanging out, wide awake. These babies *do* get
the sleep they need, but they do it unpredictably.

By the third week of life, a baby can stretch out the time
between his feedings. Instead of eating every two hours, he will

occasionally be able to go three or even four. This is a function of being a better eater — if a baby can take more milk at a time, then the milk will satisfy him for a longer period. Babies under two months of age feed between 7 to 12 times a day, but some of those feeds are closer together, allowing for longer sleep in between.

Feeding and sleeping go hand in hand. A baby who drinks more at a time will generally be able to wait longer for the next feeding. A baby's intake is limited by several factors, such as the capacity of his stomach, the amount of milk he is offered (or that a breast-feeding mom produces), and his ability to feed vigorously rather than fall asleep in the middle. Therefore, once a baby can take more milk at a time, he can generally begin to stretch out his feedings and sleep for longer periods.

While duration of sleep is one issue, the timing of sleep is another. By the time they are about 4 to 6 weeks old, most babies have their longest stretch of sleep in the early part of the night. Many will fall asleep somewhere around 7:00 or 8:00 P.M. and wake around midnight. The feeding frenzy seems to begin in the hours that parents most need to get their rest. A baby's internal clock is probably related to life in the womb. When a pregnant woman lies down at the end of a long day, she will notice that the baby inside her becomes more active. Most moms report that the deep hours of the night tend to be the hours that babies kick and move the most. So as a baby is adjusting to life outside the womb, it takes some time before his clock resets. For most babies in the first 6 weeks of life, the middle of the night remains the most active time.

Compounding this is the availability of milk. While bottle-fed babies take fairly consistent amounts of milk with each feed, breast-fed babies vary their intake throughout the day. For most (but not all) mothers, by the end of the first month of their baby's life, milk production is quite high in the early morning and stays that way through the early afternoon. Then the production begins to taper off. By evening there is usually less milk available at each feed, so at night a breast-fed baby may become hungry after shorter intervals of time. Again, this gets back to the general point that feeding and sleeping go hand in hand.

WHAT IS "LETHARGY"?

◆

Use this word carefully. Parents often use the word "lethargic" to describe their child who has decreased energy. Lethargy is more serious than that. It means that a child is so sleepy that he is difficult to arouse or is floppy like a rag doll. Lethargic babies will not drink, and all they want to do is sleep. Even when you do something irritating, such as flicking the bottom of the feet, a lethargic child will not be very bothered. When you are describing your child's energy level to your pediatrician, choose your words carefully and try not to rely on the word "lethargic" unless appropriate.

And then, of course, there are the babies who never sleep for long periods. They will eventually be good sleepers, but for the first two to three months (or more!) they wake every couple of hours like clockwork.

What can I do?

In the first couple of weeks of your baby's life, you will have to be flexible. As you are getting to know your child, you will discover his feeding and sleep patterns. All newborns should be fed at least eight times a day. Many feed 10 or even 12 times.

Even though a newborn may look happy to be sleeping for long stretches, you will need to wake him up if he has gone more than four to five hours between feeds. By the time your baby is 4 to 6 weeks old, he can tolerate the stretches better. However, if he sleeps for longer than five-hour stretches in the first month of life, he will likely not feed enough during the rest of the day and therefore not gain weight as well as he should. Some babies must be woken even more frequently. Your doctor will tell you if you need to wake your baby more often for feedings.

Where you choose to have your baby sleep — whether in a crib in his own room, a bassinet or co-sleeper next to your bed, or in bed with you — is your choice. But become familiar with the safety issues. A baby should be put down to sleep on his back, alternating the position of his head from one side to the middle and then to the other side. Stomach sleeping is thought to be a risk for SIDS (sudden infant death syndrome). If you prop your baby on his side during sleep, use a wedge or a rolled blanket and be sure the prop is below the baby's shoulders. Even though babies are not supposed to roll over, they can flip and squirm, and nothing should be near the nose or mouth. Again, this is a risk factor for SIDS. Soft bedding, loose blankets, pillows, and stuffed toys should not be in the crib or bed.

When does my doctor need to be involved?

Talk to your doctor if your child is too sleepy to feed well or if he goes longer than 4 to 5 hours between feeds. You may want to seek your doctor's advice if your baby feeds too frequently — with intervals of less than two hours around the clock. If you have questions about sleep safety or risks for SIDS, your doctor will be able to review this information with you.

What tests need to be done, and what do the results mean?

If your baby is too sleepy and is not feeding frequently enough, then his weight will need to be checked more frequently. When a baby looks otherwise healthy and is simply not getting enough calories to satisfy himself, the feeding schedule should be modified, but other tests do not need to be done.

Very occasionally, dramatically increased sleepiness can be a sign of infection. If your doctor suspects this, then blood and urine tests may be done. These tests range from complete blood count and blood culture, to urinalysis and urine culture, to tests that check for diseases of metabolism. If a child looks ill and is feeding poorly, then a spinal tap may be necessary.

What are the treatments?

Sleep patterns evolve over time. If your baby is waking too frequently because he is hungry, then your doctor will assist in changing the feeding schedule. This should help increase sleep. However, if your baby is feeding and growing well and just happens to be one of those feisty children who does not sleep a whole lot, then there is no medicine or treatment to fix this — only time. There are many books available that provide strategies for helping your child to sleep.

What are the possible complications?
The only complication of too much sleep is poor weight gain. And the only complication of frequent short stretches of sleep with lots of nighttime wakings is a cranky parent and eventually a cranky child.

> *Additional Resources*
> http://www.uuhsc.utah.edu/healthinfo/pediatric/newborn/index.htm (Go to "Normal Newborn Behaviors and Activities" and then to "Newborn — Sleep Patterns.")
> http://www.cincinnatichildrens.org (Go to search box in upper right-hand corner and type in "sleep patterns.")

◇   ◇   ◇

BLUENESS
(Birth–12 Months)

What is happening inside my baby's body?
Red blood cells are the cells in the blood that carry oxygen, giving most skin a pinkish tinge. When red blood cells are exposed to oxygen, the blood looks red. When there is not enough oxygen, the blood looks blue. So a baby will look blue if there is not enough oxygen in her blood. This is called **cyanosis.** There are lots of reasons why this can happen in the first few weeks of a baby's life — some are normal and some are cause for concern.

A baby can look blue on certain parts of the body without being in medical danger. In fact, directly after birth, almost all babies have blue hands and feet. The hands and feet are parts of the **peripheral circulation** — they mark the end of the circulatory system and the turnaround point for blood (it has nowhere to go, so it must head back to the lungs for more oxygen). The peripheral circulation serves a good purpose: when your baby is cold, the blood vessels in her hands and feet will shrink down so that heat can be conserved around the center of her body. Sometimes the blue color is so dramatic that your baby can appear to be wearing gloves and socks! The area directly around the mouth is also part of the peripheral circulation, so your baby's outer lips can look blue as well. Blueness from this normal conservation mechanism is usually not cause for concern.

Whatever the color of the parents' skin, most babies look white at birth — darker pigment usually does not appear for several hours, sometimes even days. Given the pale color of most newborn skin, blueness on the body is usually easy to see. But over several hours, as a child of color becomes darker skinned, parents can find it difficult to tell when their child is blue. The best places to look are the palms, soles, and inside of the mouth. Remember, it can be normal to have bluish discoloration of the hands and feet. But it is not normal if the gums and the inside of the mouth look blue.

If the baby looks blue all over, has decreased energy, or cannot eat or even cry well, then the blueness is abnormal. The main causes of this discoloration are problems with the heart or lungs. In order to understand why this occurs, first you must have knowledge of how blood flows throughout the body. As blood travels around the body, oxygen is removed from the passing red blood cells, and as this happens, the cells change from bright red to bluish. This oxygen serves as the fuel for the organs (such as the brain), muscles, and tissues. The blood cells then return to the lungs so that they can be restocked with oxygen. The cycle begins again as the blood moves out of the lungs and through the body, where oxygen is removed. The heart is the pump that drives the cycling of blood through the body and lungs.

The human heart is divided into two halves: one side pumps "blue" blood (depleted of oxygen) from the body to the lungs while the other side pumps "red" blood (replenished with oxygen) from the lungs back out to the body. If the two sides of the heart have any abnormal connections — for instance, if there is a hole through the tissue that separates the two halves — then red and blue blood can mix. When this mixed blood flows through a baby's body, it can make her skin look blue. Detailed information about how the heart pumps blood is covered in some of the Internet references at the end of this section.

The lungs can also cause the skin to look bluish. If the baby's lungs are not working correctly — if they are infected, collapsed, or abnormally formed; if the *trachea* (windpipe down to the lungs) is blocked; or if the baby is not breathing at all — then they cannot fill properly with oxygen. In these cases, even though blood travels along the proper route, it does not pick up enough oxygen as it passes through the lungs. Therefore, when the baby's blood is pumped back through her heart and out to her body, the blood is still blue, causing the skin to look blue too.

There are many other potential causes of blueness. Some babies will hold their breath, and within seconds the skin can look blue. These are called *breath-holding spells.* A baby who is having a seizure may look blue because she is not breathing effectively during the seizure. If a baby ingests a toxic substance, then the toxin can cause blueness either directly by attaching to the red blood cells and disfiguring them or indirectly by slowing the baby's breathing. The list of possible causes is long and is covered in some of the Web links at the end of this section.

What can I do?

First, make sure the baby is breathing. A baby who is not breathing has no chest or belly movement. The nostrils do not flare and the child is quiet. Very shortly after she stops breathing — seconds later — she will look blue. If a baby is not breathing, start CPR immediately and call 911.

An infant younger than two months breathes predominantly through her nose — the mouth feeds and the nose breathes. Your baby will pull her belly in and out when she draws in air, and when she is the tiniest bit congested in her nose, she can be a very noisy breather!

When the vessels in the peripheral circulation are constricted — and especially when the area around the mouth looks blue — it can be hard to tell whether or not your baby is having difficulty getting oxygen. If your child has blue lips, then the best way to check that her oxygen level is safe is to open her mouth. If her gums are pink, then you can usually be reassured that the blood has plenty of oxygen. If there is *any* doubt, call 911.

What are the possible complications?

The most serious complication of low oxygen level is too little oxygen to the body's vital organs. The brain is the organ responsible for keeping many of the other organs functioning; if it is starved of oxygen, then it cannot perform its job, and basic functions such as breathing may be impaired. This is why the human body is designed to spare blood flow to the brain. The brain receives blood — and therefore oxygen — preferentially above all other organs in the body. Therefore, even though the blood oxygen level may be low, the level in the brain is typically higher. In the most extreme cases, low oxygen can cause organ failure and even death.

Additional Resources

http://www.packardchildrenshospital.org (go to "Health Library," then "Children's Health from A–Z," and then look under "Cardiovascular Disorders.")

http://www.cincinnatichildrens.org (Go to search box in upper right-hand corner and type in "heart.")

http://info.med.yale.edu/intmed/cardio/chd/

http://www.nlm.nih.gov/medlineplus/encyclopedia.html (Click on "Cp–Cz," then scroll down to "CPR.")

http://www.nlm.nih.gov/medlineplus/encyclopedia.html (Click on "Si–Sp," then scroll down to "skin discoloration — bluish.")

SIDS

◆

SIDS stands for "sudden infant death syndrome." It refers to the sudden death of an apparently healthy child under a year of age. Even after a postmortem exam, the cause of the death remains unknown. The most common scenario is for parents to find that their sleeping child has actually died. Many people confuse known causes of death — such as suffocation, contagious illness, or child abuse — with SIDS. Remember, in order for a death to be classified as SIDS, the cause must remain unknown.

While SIDS technically occurs up to one year of age, most SIDS deaths actually happen in children under 6 months, with the majority of cases at 2 to 4 months of age. Between 3,000 and 6,000 babies die from SIDS each year. The number has decreased significantly since pediatricians started recommending that babies sleep on their backs. There are some known risk factors for SIDS. These maternal risk factors are associated with a higher chance of SIDS: smoking during pregnancy, poor prenatal care, low weight gain, anemia, illegal drug use, and a history of sexually transmitted diseases. There are no known risk factors in babies associated with an increase in SIDS.

Additional Resources
http://www.sidscenter.org

When does my doctor need to be involved?

If you are ever worried about your baby's color, call 911. If you think your baby is not breathing, call 911 and start CPR. Call for help whenever you are in doubt.

What tests need to be done, and what do the results mean?

When a blue baby arrives at the hospital, the first step is to check the oxygen level in the blood. This is done using a **pulse oximeter** (also called a saturation monitor), an infrared light attached to the baby's skin by a sticker. The light detects blood flow and can estimate blood oxygen levels. The light will also measure the pulse (speed at which the heart is beating), which helps to determine if the baby's body is working hard to try to get more oxygen to the body.

Blood tests can detect the precise level of oxygen in the body. While blood tests are considered a more exact measure of oxygen than pulse oximeters, it takes time to get the results back, so a pulse oximeter is typically used first. Both pulse oximetry and blood oxygen are covered in more detail in chapter 29.

If the baby has a low oxygen level, then oxygen can be blown through a mask that is strapped to the baby's face and covers the nose and mouth *(face mask)* or through a small tube wrapped under the nose *(nasal cannula).* In some cases, a breathing tube called an *endotracheal tube,* or *ETT,* needs to be placed through the mouth, past the vocal cords, and directly into the lungs. The mouthpiece is attached via tubing to a breathing machine (called a *ventilator*) and "breaths" of oxygen are pumped directly into the lungs. The ventilator performs the work normally done by the lungs. These forms of oxygen supplementation are described in more detail in chapter 18. When the baby receives extra oxygen, the oxygen level in the blood is always remeasured. Based on whether the level goes up, down, or stays the same with the additional oxygen, the underlying source of the baby's problem can be more accurately identified.

Depending on the cause of the blueness, different tests will be done. If the heart is the cause, then a series of tests will look at the size, shape, and function of the heart. If the trachea or lungs are the cause, then an X ray can determine if the lungs are shaped properly, if they are blocked by a foreign body, or if they are infected. Blood tests can also help determine the type of infection. These blood tests, including blood counts and blood cultures, are described in detail in chapter 29.

What are the treatments?
When the oxygen level is low, a baby can be given oxygen directly. Sometimes oxygen needs to be blown only across the

child's face. This can be done using a face mask or nasal cannula. Other times oxygen needs to be pumped directly into the lungs by an ETT.

The treatment of low oxygen and blueness depends on the cause. If the lungs are infected *(pneumonia),* then antibiotics will often be needed. In older babies (more than 4 to 6 weeks old), these medicines can sometimes be given by mouth; in young babies (especially newborns), they almost always require administration directly into the veins. In order to determine the exact type of infection, blood tests and cultures can be obtained. When a child is first diagnosed with pneumonia, a very strong and broad antibiotic will be started; once the precise cause of the infection is identified, the medication can be changed to a more specific one. Lung infections caused by bacteria can be treated with antibiotics, but infections caused by viruses rarely have medications available — traditional antibiotics treat only bacteria and not viruses. Therefore, when a virus is the cause of pneumonia, the medical treatments usually include only oxygen and close observation. The virus must run its course.

There are other causes of lung malfunction requiring specific treatments. Collapsed lungs must be reinflated. Anatomical variations causing poor lung function have a variety of treatments, including surgery. If the airway down to the lungs is obstructed, then the cause of the obstruction will guide the therapy. Sometimes there is a foreign body, such as a toy or a piece of food, lodged in the airway. This will need to be removed by a specialist. Other times the airway is swollen because of an infection or an allergy. This can often be treated with medicines. Blocked airways are covered in much more detail in chapters 17 and 18. Other lung abnormalities are covered in the Web links at the end of this section.

If the heart is not pumping properly and this is the cause of blueness, then a cardiologist (heart doctor) will often be called in. Again, oxygen may be given through a cannula, mask, or breathing tube. In some cases, a medication can change the direction of blood flow through the heart, solving the problem. In other cases, surgery is required. Information about many different heart abnormalities can be found in the Web links at the end of this section.

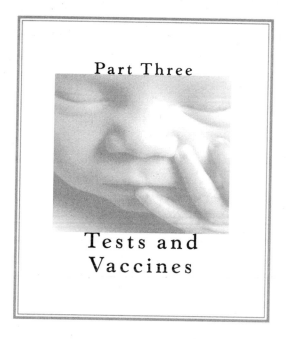

Part Three

Tests and
Vaccines

29

Lab Tests and
Radiology Studies

◇

BILIRUBIN

As described in the section on jaundice (chapter 11), about half of all babies have yellow skin discoloration in the first week of life. The cause of this discoloration is a high level of bilirubin. When there is too much bilirubin in the blood, the skin looks yellow. This is called *jaundice*. Chapter 11 describes in detail where bilirubin comes from and why the level can be elevated in a newborn.

Bilirubin is a normal waste product, a yellow pigment produced by the body. It is generally elevated when either the red blood cells are breaking down more quickly than usual or the liver or biliary tract is not functioning properly.

In order to check a bilirubin level, blood is usually drawn from a vein. The puncture site is cleaned with alcohol or another antiseptic, and a tourniquet is placed just above the area where the blood is to be drawn. This pressure restricts blood flow through the vein, causing the vein to fill with blood. Once the needle is inserted into the vein, blood is collected in a syringe or vial. When the blood has been collected, the tourniquet and needle are removed, and the puncture site is covered with a piece of gauze or a bandage to stop any bleeding.

In some cases, a bilirubin level may be drawn using a prick of the heel — collecting drops of blood from the broken skin. When this method is used, the heel is cleaned with alcohol or another antiseptic and a small nick is made in the skin of the heel. The skin will bleed slowly, and the blood will drip out. Applying squeezing pressure to the heel will speed the blood-collection process, but sometimes this bruises the heel a little bit. Whatever approach is taken — vein or heel — the blood must be sent to the laboratory soon after it is drawn.

The bilirubin level and the age of the child together determine the need for treatment. Jaundice is treated with *phototherapy*, which is described in chapter 11. The current recommendations for when to start phototherapy are as follows:

Age of baby	Consider phototherapy (bilirubin level)	Start phototherapy (bilirubin level)
<24 hours	any visible jaundice*	
25–48 hours	≥12 mg/dL	≥15 mg/dL
49–72 hours	≥15 mg/dL	≥18 mg/dL
>72 hours	≥17 mg/dL	≥20 mg/dL

At less than 24 hours of life, jaundice is always abnormal regardless of the bilirubin level.

When the bilirubin level is high enough to consider phototherapy or when phototherapy has been started, the level must be rechecked every 24 to 48 hours. The reasons for rechecking the levels include making sure that the bilirubin level is decreasing and deciding when treatment for jaundice is no longer necessary. Blood must be redrawn and sent to the lab each time the bilirubin level is rechecked.

Additional Resources
http://www.aap.org/policy/hyperb.htm
http://www.nlm.nih.gov/medlineplus/encyclopedia.html (Click on "B–Bk," then scroll down to "bilirubin.")

http://www.labtestsonline.org/understanding/analytes/bilirubin/glance.
html
http://yalenewhavenhealth.org/Library/HealthGuide/MedicalTests/topic.
asp?hwid=hw3474

◆   ◆   ◆

BLOOD CULTURE

A blood culture looks for infection in the blood. Unlike most other blood tests, a blood culture requires the skin to be carefully cleaned in order to avoid contamination by the bacteria that normally live on the skin. A tourniquet is placed just above the area where the blood is to be drawn. This pressure restricts blood flow through the vein, causing the vein to engorge with blood. Once the needle is inserted into the vein, blood is collected in a syringe or vial. Then the tourniquet and needle are removed, and the puncture site is covered with a piece of gauze or a bandage.

The blood samples are then placed in different environments — some with oxygen, some without — inside a warm incubator for 48 to 72 hours, sometimes longer. Bacteria or other organisms are identified by their growth patterns and appearance. Bacteria, viruses, or yeast can be cultured; antibiotics can be put into growing colonies to determine to which specific antibiotics the organism will be susceptible.

Often more than one blood culture will be performed. This is because there is a higher likelihood that the infection will be found if more than one test is done. These tests must be performed at different times; this means that the blood must be redrawn with a new puncture.

Though the blood-drawing procedure for a blood culture is very specific in order to maintain the sterility of the sample, other blood tests that don't require such stringent sterility can be drawn at the same time. Therefore, if a complete blood count is also required, then both tests can be done with one puncture. However, the reverse is not true. If a nonsterile sample is required and at the last minute a blood culture is desired, then unless the skin is prepared using appropriate measures, a separate blood draw will be required for the culture.

Additional Resources
http://www.labtestsonline.org/understanding/analytes/blood_culture/
glance.html
http://www.nlm.nih.gov/medlineplus/encyclopedia.html (Click on "Bl–Bz,"
then scroll down to "blood culture.")

◆   ◆   ◆

BLOOD OXYGEN LEVEL (BLOOD GAS)

A blood gas measures the amount of oxygen and carbon dioxide in the blood, as well as the acidity of the blood.

A blood gas is often drawn from an artery. This type of blood vessel is sometimes difficult to access — it is deeper and therefore less visible than a typical vein. In newborn babies, the umbilical cord has two arteries and a vein. When the cord is cut, the arteries and vein are easily visualized. The cord is clamped to prevent bleeding. If a blood gas is necessary, however, it can be drawn directly from one of these umbilical vessels.

The normal blood oxygen level is typically above 85 mmHg and may be much higher when supplemental oxygen is given. When there are problems with the heart or lungs, the level may fall quite low, with the body still continuing to perform normally. If the oxygen level falls below 55 to 60 mmHg, however, oxygen may be necessary in the form of a nasal cannula, mask, tent, or endotracheal tube. When the oxygen level is too low, the heart and lungs begin to work increasingly hard to try to get more oxygen into and around the body. The consequences of low oxygen and many of the techniques used to measure oxygen are covered in the section on blueness in chapter 28.

A blood gas will often need to be rechecked, especially if the first test showed abnormal results or if an intervention such as giving oxygen was made.

Sometimes a *pulse oximeter* can be used instead of a blood gas. Because a pulse oximeter measures only the saturation of red blood cells with oxygen, it provides less information than that derived from a blood gas. For more information, see the section on pulse oximeters later in this chapter.

Additional Resources
http://www.labtestsonline.org/understanding/analytes/blood_gases/
sample.html

◆   ◆   ◆

COMPLETE BLOOD COUNT (CBC)

A complete blood count is a test that looks at the basic components of blood: *red blood cells* that carry oxygen (denoted by
hematocrit, or *HCT*), *white blood cells* that fight infection
(WBC), and the *platelets* that help blood to clot *(PLT).* The CBC
is an excellent screening test to look for a variety of medical
issues, including anemia, infection, bleeding problems, and blood
cancers.

The CBC must be drawn from an artery or vein; it cannot
be done using a heel prick. The puncture site is cleaned with
alcohol or another antiseptic, and a tourniquet is placed just
above the area where the blood is to be drawn. This pressure
restricts blood flow through the vein, causing the vein to fill with
blood. Once the needle is inserted into the vein, blood is collected in a syringe or vial. Then the tourniquet and needle are
removed, and the puncture site is covered with a piece of gauze
or a bandage.

The blood must be sent to the laboratory shortly after it is
drawn or it may clot, making the test unreliable. A clotted CBC
must be redrawn. In a baby, because such small amounts of
blood are drawn, a clotted CBC is not uncommon.

The HCT measures the proportion of whole blood that is made
of red blood cells. In other words, it estimates how many red
blood cells are circulating in the blood. Another measure for red
blood cells is the hemoglobin (HGB). The HCT is simply a multiple of HGB — both measure circulating blood levels. For sim-
plicity, this section refers only to HCT.

Anemia is the medical term for a low HCT. The normal range
for HCT depends on age, and in general full-term newborns have
very high levels. By the eighth week of life, however, the number
of red blood cells falls sharply and the HCT is quite low. By 4 to

6 months of life, a baby's HCT is similar to an adult's. The normal HCT is listed below by age:

Age	HCT (%)
Birth	45–65
2 months	27–33
6 months	33–42

WBCs are part of the body's immune system. When there is infection or inflammation in the body, the WBC will usually be elevated. This can also happen in times of stress, such as right after delivery. There are also cases during which the WBC number is actually lower than normal. Viral infections may lower the WBC, as may certain medicines, problems with the bone marrow, cancers, or diseases of the immune system. The normal range of WBC is 5,000 to 11,000 cells/ml.

Different types of WBCs serve different purposes. The different forms of WBCs include the following:

Neutrophils (also known as polymorphonuclear leukocytes, or "polys") tend to be elevated when there is a bacterial infection, though they can be elevated for a number of different reasons.

Bands are the most immature form of WBC. When they are significantly elevated, there is almost always a bacterial infection.

Lymphocytes are the type of WBC that fights viral infections. Therefore, they tend to be present in higher numbers during viral infections.

Monocytes are elevated in the presence of a variety of infections.

Eosinophils are often numerous when there is inflammation or allergy.

Basophils may appear in the CBC with some specific diseases.

PLTs help the blood to clot. The normal range of PLT is 150,000 to 450,000 per ml of blood. When the number is low, the skin may become bruised or there may be bleeding from the nose, in the stool, or internally. When the number is high, blood clots can form easily.

In addition to the HCT, WBC, and PLT count, many other characteristics of the blood are measured in the CBC. These are covered in the Web links that follow.

Additional Resources
http://www.labtestsonline.org/understanding/analytes/cbc/glance.html
http://www.nlm.nih.gov/medlineplus/encyclopedia.html (Click on "C–Cg," then scroll down to "CBC.")

COMPUTED TOMOGRAPHY (CT) SCAN

A *computed tomography scan* — also called *CAT scan* or *CT scan* — is done using a circular machine lined with cameras. The scanner rotates around the baby so that X rays can be taken from all angles, and then a computer integrates the images to make a cross-sectional picture. Therefore a CT scan can show "slices" of the body. It uses the same basic technology as an X-ray machine, just with an added dimension.

CT can be used anytime a detailed picture of the body is required. It can image the brain, especially after a child has fallen and hit her head. It is also used to look at abdominal organs such as the appendix, liver, and spleen when certain illnesses are suspected. A baby of any age can have a CT scan.

The scanner is a machine shaped like a giant narrow donut. (It is not elongated like the MRI scanner.) The patient lies on a narrow table that slides into and out of the circle. This machine is not claustrophobic because it is not an enclosed space. Rather, only the part of the patient's body being imaged is "inside" the machine.

The older CT scanners took time to shoot the various X rays. The newer generation scanners, however, take only seconds. This is important because infants and young children once had to be sedated in order to have certain CT scans. Now, with the fast machines widely available, children can often lie still or suck on a bottle for 30 to 120 seconds while the machine takes pictures.

Occasionally a baby will need to have an IV placed in her arm. Then, before the pictures are taken, a liquid that will show up on the CT scan is injected into the vein. This liquid is called *contrast material* because it helps to show contrast between certain internal structures. Some babies also require oral contrast material, which they drink before the CT is performed. Sometimes the CT is done immediately after the contrast is given; other times 2 to 4 hours must pass before the picture is taken. A radiologist — a doctor who specializes in medical imaging — will decide whether or not to use contrast and what type to use, as well as how long to wait between giving the contrast and completing the CT scan.

Some babies may have an allergic reaction to the contrast material. Reactions can range from hives to respiratory failure *(anaphylaxis)*. Children with iodine allergy or shellfish allergy will be at increased risk for a reaction to contrast.

Just about any part of the body can have a CT image. It is a painless procedure, but there are small risks of radiation exposure. One way to think about this is in terms of normal daily radiation exposure. A single chest X ray is equivalent to the amount of radiation a person is exposed to over a two-and-a-half-day period just walking around and living on Earth. A CT scan, which uses multiple X-ray images, can be compared to 240 to 1,200 days of radiation exposure, depending on what part of the body is imaged. An airplane ride also exposes passengers to higher-than-normal levels of radiation. Five round-trips from Los Angeles to New York involve about as much radiation exposure as a single chest X ray.

Additional Resources
http://brighamrad.harvard.edu/patients/education/ct/ctguide.html
http://www.nlm.nih.gov/medlineplus/encyclopedia.html (Click on "Cp–Cz," then scroll down to "CT scan.")
http://www.umich.edu/~radinfo/introduction/risk.html

◆   ◆   ◆

COOMBS' TEST

The Coombs' test measures antibodies on the surface of red blood cells. Antibodies may occasionally form when a mother's blood type is different from her fetus's, or when more subtle differences between the mother's blood and the fetus's blood exist. When a mother forms antibodies to the fetus's blood — usually because the two blood types have come into contact during either the pregnancy or the delivery — the maternal antibodies attach to the baby's red blood cells, causing the baby's cells to die or break down. This, in turn, can cause short-term *anemia* or *jaundice* in the baby (see chapter 11).

The Coombs' test is generally performed soon after birth using blood saved from the umbilical cord. Because the test uses blood collected during delivery, it does not require a heel prick or a vein stick to collect the specimen. If a Coombs' test is done beyond the newborn period, then a blood draw from a vein is required.

A normal result is called a *negative Coombs'*. This means that the mother either did not make any antibodies against the baby's blood cells or did not make enough antibodies to cause any significant reaction. An abnormal result is called a *positive Coombs'*, where the mother made a significant number of antibodies. The result can be *microscopic,* meaning that there was a very mild reaction during the test; this indicates that the mother made at least some antibodies to the baby's blood.

Many hospitals perform the test automatically if the mother has a blood type that can cause the antibody formation. The babies of mothers with type O-positive, O-negative, A-negative, B-negative, or AB-negative will likely be tested. It is possible, however, to have a positive Coombs' test with any maternal blood type.

Additional Resources
http://www.nlm.nih.gov/medlineplus/encyclopedia.html (Click on "Ch–Co," then scroll down to "Coombs' test.")

◆   ◆   ◆

ELECTROLYTES

Electrolytes are the "salts" in the bloodstream and the minerals found in tissues. They are responsible for the general balance in the body, helping to eliminate waste products while balancing the body's acidity and water levels. The electrolytes measured in this test include sodium (Na), potassium (K), chloride (Cl), and bicarbonate (CO_2). Water balance is most influenced by sodium. Acidity is affected by bicarbonate.

The electrolytes must be drawn from an artery or vein; the test cannot be done using a heel prick. The puncture site is cleaned with alcohol or another antiseptic, and a tourniquet is placed just above the area where the blood is to be drawn. This pressure restricts blood flow through the vein, causing the vein to fill with blood. Once the needle is inserted into the vein, blood is collected in a syringe or vial. Then the tourniquet and needle are removed, and the puncture site is covered with a piece of gauze or a bandage.

The blood must be sent to the laboratory shortly after it is drawn or the results may be unreliable. Occasionally the blood is drawn through such a small needle that cells break apart, leading to inaccurate values. This is especially true for potassium. In this case, the blood must be redrawn.

Electrolyte levels are often checked when a person has major organ (such as heart or kidney) involvement or when the fluid balance in the body is in question. Dehydrated babies will often have electrolyte levels checked. The electrolytes are replaced through our diet and can also be regulated by various hormones in the body. If the levels are too low, then electrolytes can be replaced using oral or IV solutions in the hospital.

Additional Resources
http://www.labtestsonline.org/understanding/analytes/lytes/glance.html

◆   ◆   ◆

GLUCOSE (BLOOD SUGAR)

Glucose is sugar that serves as the body's primary fuel source. It circulates in the blood, rising with meals and dropping between them. *Hypoglycemia* means low blood glucose and *hyperglycemia* means high blood glucose.

In order to measure blood glucose, blood can be drawn from the artery or vein or from a heel (or finger) prick. When a vein is used, the puncture site is cleaned with alcohol or another antiseptic, and a tourniquet is placed just above the area where the blood is to be drawn. This pressure restricts blood flow through the vein, causing the vein to fill with blood. Once the needle is inserted into the vein, blood is collected in a syringe or vial. Then the tourniquet and needle are removed, and the puncture site is covered with a piece of gauze or a bandage to stop any subsequent bleeding.

When the heel (or finger) is used, the area is cleaned with alcohol or another antiseptic and a small nick is made in the skin. The skin will bleed slowly, and the blood will drip out. Applying squeezing pressure will speed the blood-collection process. Either way — vein or heel (or finger) — the blood must be sent to the laboratory or placed on a glucometer machine soon after it is drawn.

Normal blood glucose is 60 to 120 mg/dL. In newborn babies, however, a normal glucose can be lower — down to 40 mg/dL in a full-term baby. In older infants, children, and adults, hypoglycemia is generally defined as a blood glucose level less than 60 mg/dL. *Severe hypoglycemia* is less than 40 mg/dL (in some newborns, as low as 30 mg/dL). Hyperglycemia is generally considered to be greater than 120 mg/dL if the blood is not checked immediately following a meal. Hyperglycemia is pretty rare among newborns; when it occurs, it may be related to checking the blood-sugar level too soon after food intake. It should always be double-checked.

Severe or rapidly developing hypo- or hyperglycemia can be life threatening. Hypoglycemia in newborns is most often caused by maternal diabetes, although infants with feeding difficulties can also have hypoglycemia. Infections that have spread throughout the body can cause either hypo- or hyperglycemia. Very low or very high glucose in a baby can result in organ failure, brain damage, seizures, coma, or even death.

Additional Resources

http://www.labtestsonline.org/understanding/analytes/glucose/glance.
html

http://www.nlm.nih.gov/medlineplus/encyclopedia.html (Click on "G," then scroll down to "glucose test.")

◆   ◆   ◆

MAGNETIC RESONANCE IMAGING (MRI)

Magnetic resonance imaging (MRI) uses magnets and radio waves instead of X rays to take pictures of the human body. The images generated are similar to CT scan images in that they are cross sections (or slices) of parts of the body. However, these images usually have much better resolution than CT scans and therefore show greater detail.

The physics of this machine are complex. However, it should be said that this is a safe and effective way of imaging, and unlike CT scans, X rays, and other techniques, there is no radiation involved.

Unfortunately the MRI scanner can be claustrophobic for many people. It is a long, narrow tube surrounded by strong magnets. The patient must lie very still while a series of images are created, and an MRI can take an hour or more to perform. Because of the way the machine is constructed and because of the time it takes for an MRI to collect images, patients often need sedation during the scan. Infants and young children will many times need to be put to sleep; otherwise they will be unable to cooperate with the test. Newer "open-air" scanners may cause less claustrophobia.

As with the CT scan, the MRI can be enhanced with a dye injected into the vein. This contrast material helps to light up certain structures. A radiologist (doctor specializing in imaging) will determine whether contrast is needed. The contrast material used for MRI scans is different from that used for CT scans, reducing the risk of allergic reactions.

Additional Resources
http://www.nlm.nih.gov/medlineplus/encyclopedia.html (Click on "Mg–Mz," then scroll down to "MRI.")

◆   ◆   ◆

PULSE OXIMETER

A pulse oximeter is a noninvasive device used to monitor the percentage of *hemoglobin* — a component of red blood cells — that is saturated with oxygen. In short, it tells your doctor quickly and painlessly whether there is enough oxygen in your baby's body.

It consists of a probe that is attached to the patient's finger or earlobe (or in very small babies, the heel) and is connected by a long narrow wire to a small computer. The percent of hemoglobin that is saturated with oxygen is displayed, along with the heart rate and an audible signal for each pulse beat. Alarms ring when the oxygen level or pulse changes significantly.

The device uses a red light to illuminate the skin and measures how much of the light is absorbed. Therefore it is only effective if it is put on a part of the body where there is sufficient blood flow. Otherwise the pulse oximeter cannot accurately measure the oxygen level in the blood. Other factors, including certain medical conditions or the presence of specific toxins in the blood, may reduce the accuracy of the pulse oximeter.

A measurement of 100 percent means that the red blood cells are carrying 100 percent of the oxygen that they can possibly carry. The blood is fully saturated with oxygen. A level below 100 percent means that the blood is not carrying all of the oxygen it can possibly carry. An awake baby's normal oxygen saturation is 95 to 100 percent, but this percentage may be lower during sleep. In most cases, an oxygen saturation of less than 95 percent (while awake) is considered too low.

Additional Resources
http://www.nda.ox.ac.uk/wfsa/html/u05/u05_003.htm

◆　　◆　　◆

SPINAL TAP (LUMBAR PUNCTURE)

A spinal tap, also called a *lumbar puncture,* is a test of the fluid
surrounding the brain and spinal cord. This fluid is called *cerebrospinal fluid,* or *CSF.* A spinal tap will be done anytime a doctor suspects that there is infection in or around the brain. As
described in chapter 28, a spinal tap may be done on a baby who
has a high fever and no other symptoms in order to make sure
that meningitis is not the cause of the fever.

A spinal tap is done most often with the baby lying on one
side, knees curled up to the abdomen and chin tucked into the
chest — a "fetal" position. The baby is held in this position by
someone assisting the person performing the spinal tap. The skin
covering the lower spine is washed with antibacterial soap; sometimes a local anesthetic is injected. A needle is inserted between
two of the vertebrae. A sample of fluid is collected, the needle is
removed, and pressure is applied using gauze or a bandage.

Normal fluid is clear yellow. Cloudy fluid is likely infected. If
the needle punctures a vein during the procedure, then the fluid
may look bloody. It can also look bloody if there is actual blood
in the CSF.

Once the fluid is collected, it may be sent for several different
tests. It is checked for red blood cells (RBC) and white blood cells
(WBC), which can be indicators of infection. Normal CSF has no
RBCs and very few WBCs. The CSF is also checked for protein
and glucose. These are normal components of the CSF, but with
some illnesses the amount may be higher or lower than usual.
The fluid is often cultured using plates and techniques similar to
those used in blood and urine cultures. And, in some medical
centers, the fluid is sent for *PCR — polymerase chain reaction —*
a test that can identify very small numbers of viruses or other
infections.

A normal CSF contains the following:

RBC	0
WBC	0–5
Glucose	40–80 mg/dL
Protein	<45 mg/dL

Additional Resources
http://www.nlm.nih.gov/medlineplus/encyclopedia.html (Click on "Cp–Cz,"
then scroll down to "CSF collection.")

ULTRASOUND

An ultrasound, also called a *sonogram,* is a machine that uses
high-frequency sound waves to construct images of the inside of
the body. There is no radiation involved. You are probably familiar with ultrasound, as it is a technique used throughout pregnancy to look at the developing fetus.

The test is done with the patient lying down. A gel is applied to
the part of the body to be imaged. This gel conducts the sound
waves of the machine. Then a probe, ranging in size from that of
a golf ball to a paintbrush, is placed on top of the gel. As it is
moved over the area, a picture is generated on the screen. This
procedure does not hurt, but the gel may initially feel a bit cold
on the skin.

Some ultrasound machines have *Doppler,* a mode that can measure blood flow. These machines can determine whether there is
blood flowing to a specific area and the direction in which it is
moving.

Ultrasounds can also be done inside the body. In these cases,
the probe is inserted into the mouth, vagina, or rectum to look at
specific structures in the body. This is rarely necessary in children.
Before the procedure, a radiologist — a doctor specializing in
imaging — will review the type of ultrasound that will be done.

Additional Resources
http://www.nlm.nih.gov/medlineplus/encyclopedia.html (Click on "U," then
scroll down to "Ultrasound.")

◆   ◆   ◆

URINALYSIS

A urinalysis is a test of the urine. Waste products are normally eliminated from the body through the urine or stool. While some waste products are normal, urine can contain abnormal elements as well, and urinalysis helps identify these abnormal elements. Chapter 22 covers in detail the urinary tract and causes of abnormal urine.

Urine can be collected in one of two ways. The least invasive is a bag that is taped around the vagina or penis. The area is cleaned before the bag is taped on. When the infant urinates, the urine is collected. Alternately, a catheter — a narrow plastic tube — is inserted into the urethra and up into the bladder. Again, the area is cleaned before the urine is collected. Though the bag is a less-intrusive means of collecting the urine, the child can take a long time to urinate and the specimen can easily become contaminated. The catheter is more invasive but also faster, more sterile, and often more accurate.

The urine is checked for a number of byproducts. The acid level in the urine is measured using the pH scale. Normal urine has a pH of 4.5 to 8.0. The specific gravity is also measured. This number reflects how concentrated or diluted the urine is. A normal specific gravity is 1.005 to 1.025. Then the urine is checked for WBCs and RBCs, for glucose, and for other byproducts of normal bodily functions (such as protein, bile, and ketones). The presence of *any* of these helps determine whether there is a metabolic problem, kidney disorder, infection, or other problem. A normal urinalysis does not contain any of these byproducts.

Additional Resources
http://www.labtestsonline.org/understanding/analytes/urinalysis/glance.
html

◆   ◆   ◆

URINE CULTURE

A urine culture looks specifically for the bacteria that can cause infection in the urinary tract. Normally urine is sterile — it has no bacteria growing in it. The causes of *urinary tract infection* are covered at length in chapter 22.

Urine can be collected in one of two ways. The least invasive is a bag that is taped around the vagina or penis. The external genital area is cleaned with a sterilizing solution prior to bag placement. When your infant urinates, the urine is collected. Unfortunately, despite thorough cleaning, normal bacteria that grow on the skin can easily contaminate the bag specimen. Therefore, while a bag collection is often sufficient for a *urinalysis*, it is not the best method for a urine culture.

The more invasive — but also more accurate — approach to collecting urine for a culture is with a catheter. In this case, the external genital area is also cleaned with a sterilizing solution. Then a narrow plastic tube is inserted into the urethra and up into the bladder. This is a relatively sterile approach, because the urine is less likely to become contaminated with the bacteria that normally live on the skin.

A urine culture often requires only a few drops of urine. When both a urinalysis and a culture must be done, the specimen can be collected all at once, with part placed into a sterile cup (for the culture) and the rest collected in a nonsterile cup (for the urinalysis). Remember, though, that if the urine must be sterile for a culture, then the whole collection process must be sterile. Therefore, if a nonsterile approach is used for the collection — for instance, if the area is not cleaned with a sterilizing solution or if the primary collection container is not sterile — then a urine culture cannot be performed with that specimen.

The urine collected for culture is carefully put onto a culture plate, and the plate is then placed in a warm incubator. Over the next 24 to 48 hours, if there are bacteria in the urine, then they should grow on the plate. Antibiotics can then be added to the plate to determine which drug will be most effective in eliminating the infection.

A urinalysis can be a good early indicator of infection. If the urinalysis shows signs of infection (such as the presence of WBCs), then a urine culture is likely to grow bacteria.

Additional Resources
http://www.labtestsonline.org/understanding/analytes/urine_culture/glance.html
http://www.nlm.nih.gov/medlineplus/encyclopedia.html (Click on "U," then scroll down to "urine culture.")

◇   ◇   ◇

X RAY

An X ray is a form of radiation. The X-ray machine focuses on one specific part of your baby's body, and when a picture is taken, X rays travel through him onto special film behind his body. Depending on the density of different tissues and organs in the body, all, some, or none of the X rays will pass through. This generates a picture on the film. Dense structures — such as bone — look white on an X ray, while air looks black.

Only technicians and doctors (radiologists) perform X rays. The actual image takes only a second or two to film, but the patient must be perfectly still for the best image. Parents can stay with their children during an X ray but are often asked to wear lead coats to protect them from unnecessary radiation exposure.

Sometimes patients will be asked to drink a liquid called contrast that shows up as white in the film. This can further help to outline certain structures in the body.

Just about any part of the body can be X-rayed. It is a painless procedure, but there are small risks of radiation exposure. One X ray has very minimal radiation. In fact we are all exposed to radiation every day. A single chest X ray is equivalent to the amount of radiation a person is exposed to over a two-and-a-half-day period just going about daily life. A CT scan, which uses multiple X-ray images, can be compared to 240 to 1,200 days of radiation exposure. An airplane ride also exposes passengers to higher-than-normal levels of radiation. Five round-trips from Los Angeles to New York involve about as much radiation exposure as a single chest X ray.

Additional Resources

http://www.nlm.nih.gov/medlineplus/encyclopedia.html (Click on "X," then scroll down to "X-ray.")

http://www.fda.gov/cdrh/ct/risks.html

http://www.umich.edu/~radinfo/introduction/risk.html

30

Tests and Labs
Just After Birth

---◆---

MANDATORY TESTS

Each state has a set of required newborn blood tests. These tests screen for a variety of diseases. States have adopted these protocols because early diagnosis of some diseases can be lifesaving. In some cases, medicines can be prescribed before the illness affects a baby in any way. In other cases, a disease may not be entirely treatable, but certain lifestyle changes may prevent the disease from causing chronic devastating problems. The earlier in your baby's life these tests are done, the better your chance of having a healthy child.

Nurses or lab technicians perform the newborn tests using a few drops of blood taken from your baby's heel, usually while you are still in the hospital. Unlike many other blood tests, these do not require sticking the vein for blood. The drops of blood are placed onto a card that is mailed into a central state office. All of the tests are run off of this card. The blood should not be taken before a baby is 24 hours old; if it is, then the test results may not be valid. The results are usually available within one to two weeks.

Parents do have the right to refuse the newborn tests. However, because the results of these tests may be lifesaving, I always try to discourage parents from refusing to do them. Furthermore, different states require different tests based on the population and the regional incidence of particular diseases. Below is a summary of the most common tests done across the country. A normal result is called "negative." For a child with a "positive" (or abnormal) result, the test is typically repeated to confirm the result. If it is positive again, then there are many implications and treatments, all of which are described in the following text. If a test comes back as borderline, then it often needs to be repeated. While this is uncommon, an accurate result must be obtained as soon as possible, preferably within three weeks. The Web links at the end of this section provide information about state-specific mandatory tests.

PKU. "Phenylketonuria," also known as PKU, is an inability to break down phenylalanine, a chemical found in many foods. When phenylalanines build up in the body, they move into the brain and can cause mental retardation. PKU is found in about 1 in 10,000 babies. Once alerted to the condition, parents can avoid foods containing phenylalanine, and the consequences of the unchecked disease — such as mental retardation — can be prevented entirely. This means that these babies must be fed special formulas, and as they grow, their diets must be carefully regulated.

Sickle-cell anemia. This blood disorder is most common among African Americans (it occurs in about 1 in every 600 newborns in this population). Red blood cells carry oxygen to muscles and organs around the body. In most people, these cells are round. But with sickle-cell anemia, the cells are more rigid and not perfectly round. In times of stress — such as when a baby has an infection or is dehydrated — the abnormal cells can "sickle," taking the shape of minibananas. Sickled cells can get stuck all over the body and create problems with blood flow.

Because illness or stress causes the cells to sickle, babies who have been diagnosed with sickle-cell anemia are treated aggressively when they get sick. This approach helps to prevent sickling and its consequences. In extreme cases, children with sickle-cell anemia may get blood transfusions or even a bone marrow transplant, replacing the abnormal cells with healthy red blood cells that do not cause blood flow problems.

Galactosemia. This diagnosis means your child is unable to break down a type of sugar called galactose. Galactose is found in many foods, including breast milk and cow's milk. When galactose cannot be broken down, it accumulates in the blood and can result in severe consequences such as mental retardation, cataracts, and liver and kidney disease. However, if children with this disease avoid galactose-containing foods, then they can also avoid the consequences. Like those children diagnosed with PKU, these babies must be fed special formulas, and as they age, their diets must be carefully regulated. Galactosemia occurs in about 1 in 40,000 newborns.

Hypothyroidism. The thyroid gland is located in the neck and affects metabolism — the breakdown of food and the burning of calories. The hormone it produces is essential to the mental and physical growth of a child. When the gland malfunctions, calories are burned inefficiently. This affects energy levels, temperature regulation, weight gain, and the functioning of a large variety of organs, including the brain.

Thyroid hormone — the product of the thyroid gland — can be replaced or supplemented with an oral medicine. In the case of hypothyroidism, the sooner this medicine is started, the more likely a child is to maintain normal growth and development. Hypothyroidism is found in 1 in 40,000 newborns.

◆　　◆　　◆

OPTIONAL "EXPANDED" TESTS

As explained above, the tests required for newborns vary from state to state. There are only a few common tests done in almost all fifty states. With new technologies, however, many more diseases can be diagnosed at birth — diseases that can cause serious illness or death if not caught early. As diagnostic science has progressed, private companies have begun to offer "expanded" testing for a fee. These tests use the same few drops of blood gathered for the standard screening tests but check for up to 50 other diseases. While these diseases may be less common than those checked in the standard screening test, the same possibility of disease prevention or cure holds true for many of them. Among the tests offered in the optional screening programs are tests for biotinidase deficiency, congenital adrenal hyperplasia, cystic fibrosis, maple syrup urine disease, and homocystinuria.

In the past few years, a handful of states started programs offering these expanded tests for free. Parents are asked to sign a consent form giving permission to check the blood for the standard newborn screening as well as the expanded newborn screening. Each state offers a different number of tests in its expanded panel; some offer screening for up to 50 additional diseases. Like the standard tests for each state, the additional tests vary based on the local population. However, there is a movement to standardize all these tests nationwide. For now, in order to find out what tests are offered in a particular state, you should contact that state's department of health. You may not pick and choose among the optional tests. Should you decide to get them, you will get all of them.

Additional Resources
http://www.aboutnewbornscreening.com/default.htm
http://www.cdc.gov/nceh/dls/newborn_screening.htm

◈   ◈   ◈

HEARING TESTS

Your baby will not turn toward a sound until she is two or three months old. Often, in the first few days of life, she does not even jump when a loud sound is made near her ear. So how can you tell if your baby can hear well?

Many hospitals offer a newborn hearing screen and some require it prior to discharge from the hospital. Elsewhere it is up to the pediatrician to decide whether or not the test will be done. Check with your pediatrician to see if your baby will be given a hearing test prior to leaving the hospital. Some states now require tests before a baby can go home.

There are two tests that can be used — the BAERs (brainstem auditory evoked response) or OAE (otoacoustic emissions) — both of which must be done while your baby is sleeping. Neither will cause her any pain. *BAERs* uses wires taped to the baby's scalp. The baby's brain waves are recorded while a machine makes various clicks in the ear. If a baby shows no brain-wave activity in response to various sounds, then the test is abnormal. *OAE* uses a small earplug in the baby's ear. The device stimulates and detects sounds originating from the middle ear. An abnormal test records few or no sounds from the baby's ear.

If your child does not pass the test in one ear or both ears, then she must be retested. Sometimes the second test is performed a few hours later in the hospital, but other times the parents are asked to return to the hospital within a few weeks. Either way, the retesting should be free. If the tests again show abnormal results, then the baby is referred for a further set of tests. She might also be sent to an ear, nose, and throat doctor (called an otolaryngologist).

Early diagnosis of deafness is critical, because your child's speech and language development depend on hearing the world around her. Cognitive and psychosocial development can also be impaired if deafness remains undetected. The sooner hearing problems are caught, the sooner they may be treated using a hearing aid. Therefore all children should be screened for deafness before one month of age. Without this newborn screening, the average age at which deafness is diagnosed is between two and three years.

Some forms of hearing loss develop in the first few months of life. Anytime you think that your child cannot hear, you should contact your pediatrician right away. While it is a bit more difficult to test hearing in an older infant (because of cooperation issues), it is critical to pick up hearing loss as soon as possible.

Additional Resources
http://www.cdc.gov/ncbddd/ehdi/
http://www.infanthearing.org/
http://www.nlm.nih.gov/medlineplus/encyclopedia.html (Click on "B–Bk," then scroll down to "BAER—brainstem auditory evoked response.")

◆   ◆   ◆

VITAMIN K SHOT

Vitamins are not just nutritional supplements that you can buy from the drugstore. In fact, most are either present in the normal diet or manufactured by the body, and they are critical for routine body functions. Vitamin K is one of these. It is made in the GI tract and works with the liver to produce the material that helps blood to clot.

Babies are born with low levels of vitamin K. They get some — but not enough — from their mothers during pregnancy. And once they are born, babies do not produce as much as they need. Therefore, in the first few weeks of life, blood flows through a baby's body with little ability to clot. This can be a big problem if internal bleeding occurs: the baby may have no way to stop the process.

When uncontrollable bleeding occurs, it is called *hemorrhagic disease of the newborn (HDN)*. In extreme cases, some babies will bleed inside their brains. Without vitamin K, the bleeding will continue and can cause brain damage or even death.

Giving babies extra vitamin K just after birth can prevent HDN. The easiest method is by injection into the muscle of one thigh. This delivers a measurable dose that will last several weeks or until a baby begins manufacturing vitamin K on his own. Intramuscular vitamin K is safe. The main complication of receiving this medicine by injection is bleeding at the puncture site. However, bleeding is rare. There have been isolated reports of links between vitamin K administration and illnesses later in life. There is no data to support any of these claims. References to these reports are included in the Web sites listed at the end of this section.

Vitamin K can also be given orally (by mouth) if parents request it, but this is not the best course. The oral form of the vitamin must be given in several doses because it is difficult for the stomach to absorb it. The oral form may also cause vomiting, and when this occurs, it is unclear how much of the vitamin stayed down and how much was vomited up. If a child has diarrhea, then the oral form may pass through the intestines too quickly to be properly absorbed. Also, the oral dose does not last nearly as long as the intramuscular, so there are conflicting recommendations about how often to dose it. One commonly suggested schedule for oral vitamin K involves at least one dose at birth, one dose three to seven days later, and one dose at four weeks of life. If a dose is vomited within an hour of being given, then it needs to be repeated. Finally, oral vitamin K should absolutely not be given to premature babies, babies who are sick at birth, or babies born to mothers taking certain medications during pregnancy. For more information about oral vitamin K, you should speak with your doctor.

Anytime your baby has unexplained bruising or bleeding, or if a baby older than three weeks suddenly develops jaundice (yellow discoloration of the skin), a doctor should be consulted immediately. This is most critical if your baby has not received injectable vitamin K, as these may be signs of HDN.

Additional Resources
http://www.packardchildrenshospital.org (Go to "search" in upper right-hand corner and type in "vitamin K.")
http://www.racp.edu.au/hpu/paed/vitkinfo.htm
http://www.aap.org/ (Go to search box in upper left-hand corner and type in "vitamin K.")
http://www.mca.gov.uk/ourwork/monitorsafequalmed/currentproblems/cpvol24asec4.htm

◇ ◇ ◇

ANTIBIOTIC EYE OINTMENT

When a baby travels from the uterus to the outside world, she is exposed to all of the bacteria that live inside the vaginal canal. Although most bacteria cause no problems at all when they get into a baby's eyes, some — in particular, sexually transmitted diseases (STDs) such as *gonorrhea* and *chlamydia* — can. These infections can progress rapidly and in the worst cases result in vision loss.

Therefore babies are routinely given an antibiotic eye ointment to protect them from the complications of eye infection. In the past, *silver nitrate* was the preferred medicine. While this eliminated the bacteria, it often caused eye irritation. For this reason, *erythromycin* is now used. This antibiotic is generally well tolerated, creating little irritation while removing the bacteria effectively. Because the ointment goes directly into the eye, its absorption by the body is minimal. And because the antibiotic ointment is so well tolerated by the baby, there is almost no downside to using it. Therefore most doctors strongly recommend the ointment.

There is significant debate (mostly among parents) about the necessity of antibiotic eye ointment for all newborns. While the baby is exposed to many types of bacteria in the vaginal canal, and these may cause a bit of discharge in the eyes in the first week of life, if no STDs are present, then vision is not threatened. Likewise, if your baby is born by cesarean section, then she is not exposed to any of the bacteria in the vaginal canal in the first place. Therefore, if a mother had good prenatal care and has been screened for sexually transmitted diseases (and found to have none), then it may be reasonable to choose not to give the newborn the antibiotic.

I will stress, however, that the antibiotic eye ointment is benign. There is almost no absorption of the antibiotic by the baby, and the ointment itself will not irritate her eyes. Blindness, on the other hand, lasts forever. Consider this decision carefully.

Additional Resources
http://www.packardchildrenshospital.org (Go to "search" in upper right-hand corner and type in "eye prophylaxis.")
http://www.nei.nih.gov/neitrials/static/study19.htm

31

Vaccines

◆

Vaccines, also called immunizations, are designed to boost your baby's immune system against specific infectious agents, protecting him from serious and sometimes life-threatening diseases.

Vaccines come in many varieties. Some are lab-manufactured replicas of a piece of a bacteria or virus. These are called *recombinant vaccines*. Others are made by attaching proteins to parts of a bacteria. These are called *conjugated vaccines*. A few vaccines are produced by altering an entire bacteria or virus, using heat to denature its proteins, thereby rendering it an inactive and harmless infection. These are called *inactivated* (or *killed*) *vaccines*. Finally, some vaccines are made from a living virus. The virus is weakened so that when it is given in the form of a vaccine, it cannot cause a full-blown illness. These are called *live-attenuated vaccines*.

All of these kinds of vaccines work by tricking your baby's immune system into thinking the body has been exposed to a true bacterial or viral infection. The immune system then makes the appropriate antibodies to fight off that particular infection. Therefore, when the baby is exposed to the true virus or bacteria, the body has been primed and the immune system has its antibodies at the ready.

Over the past few decades, the number of vaccines recommended by the Centers for Disease Control (CDC) and the American Academy of Pediatrics (AAP) has increased significantly. The vaccines are listed on an immunization schedule that is revised regularly. Many schools require completion of the schedule prior to school entry. While these vaccines are strongly recommended, they are not required by law.

Many parents have raised concerns about the long-term effects of vaccines on their baby's health and development. Their concerns range from the use of a mercury compound *(thimerosal)* as a preservative to the administration of multiple vaccines at one time. For some, weighing the risks and benefits has complicated what has, in the past, been a simple rite of passage. This chapter is meant to summarize basic information about the vaccines given over the first few years of life. If you care to do additional research, a list of Web sites has been provided to help you navigate these waters. Although some of the vaccines described in the following text are not offered until after the first birthday — and therefore are not really relevant to newborn and infant health — they are included here because you will hear and read about them.

Given the attention that thimerosal has recently received, this preservative deserves an extra note. In 1999 the AAP voted to remove thimerosal from the routine childhood vaccines. As of 2001, each vaccine listed on the recommended schedule has been available thimerosal-free. Though there are still some vaccines produced using thimerosal as a preservative, almost all the vaccines stocked in pediatric offices are thimerosal-free. The vaccines that may still contain thimerosal are noted in the appropriate sections that follow.

DIPHTHERIA, TETANUS, AND ACELLULAR PERTUSSIS (DTaP)

DTaP combines vaccines against diphtheria, tetanus, and pertussis *(whooping cough)*. It is currently given as a series of five doses, recommended at 2 months, 4 months, 6 months, and 12 to 18 months, with a booster dose between 4 to 6 years.

Diphtheria generally causes a throat infection, though it can lead to problems in other parts of the body. The mucous membranes of the throat swell and then become thin and fragile. The infection can cause blockage of the airway, or it can spread into the bloodstream and then to the heart, nerves, or brain. Diphtheria is not common in the United States, but pockets of outbreak do occur. It is far more common in developing countries, so vaccination is considered important prior to international travel.

Tetanus is well known. If you step on a rusty nail or get a dirty cut, then the bacteria that carry tetanus toxin can enter the skin and multiply. The bacteria release a nerve toxin that causes muscle spasm, sometimes so severe that the muscles become completely rigid. Lockjaw (also called *trismus*) is a classic symptom of tetanus. The breathing muscles can become spastic as well, a potentially life-threatening complication.

Pertussis is more commonly known as whooping cough. In older children, teens, and adults, pertussis causes a persistent "staccato" cough that goes on for so long that the infected person must gasp and inhale deeply to catch his breath. This is the "whoop" of whooping cough. In infants — especially those under six months — pertussis can cause regular breathing to stop suddenly (called *apnea*) even before a cough is ever heard. If an infant with pertussis cannot get emergency medical care, then he can stop breathing entirely. In some studies, it is estimated that 60 percent of adults who have been coughing for more than three weeks carry pertussis. One reason why pertussis is so prevalent is that the immunity against the infection disappears 5 to 10 years after the last dose of the vaccine. Because teens and adults are not routinely vaccinated against pertussis (they get a diphtheria-tetanus vaccine without pertussis), anyone older than 10 or 12 years serves as a reservoir for this bacteria. While older children and adults can get very sick with pertussis, this is quite rare. Rather, it is infants who are at greatest risk when they are infected.

The DTaP formulation of the vaccine has been widely available since 1996. Before that, DPT was used instead. DPT had whole-cell pertussis, not acellular pertussis. The old DPT form was fraught with side effects. It often caused fevers up to 104 or 105°F that, in turn, led to febrile seizures in some children. It was also likely responsible for several infant deaths due to shock. When the formulation of pertussis was changed, the side effects of the vaccine became significantly less severe. DPT is no longer used in the United States.

The most common adverse reactions reported with DTaP include pain or soreness at the injection site (5 percent of children), low-grade fever (5 percent), fussiness (30 percent), and swelling at or around the injection site (8 percent). Only 1 in 3,000 children experiences high fever. Other adverse reactions include continuous screaming or crying for more than three hours (1 in 2,000), seizures (6 in 10,000), and allergy to one of the components.

Many people ask if the components of DTaP are available separately. While some countries do carry pertussis vaccine on its own, this vaccine is neither manufactured nor available in the United States. For now, the only way to be vaccinated against pertussis is to have the combined DTaP vaccine. Tetanus vaccine, on the other hand, is available either alone (T) or with diphtheria (TD). However, neither T nor TD are recommended for children under seven.

DTaP does not contain thimerosal as a preservative. However, both TD and T do still have mercury.

◇   ◇   ◇

HAEMOPHILUS INFLUENZAE TYPE B (HiB)

Haemophilus influenzae type B vaccine (HiB) is currently given as a series of three to four doses, recommended at 2 months, 4 months, 12 to 18 months, and depending on the manufacturer of the vaccine, a final booster dose between 4 to 6 years.

Haemophilus influenzae type B (also called *H flu*) accounted for 10,000 to 20,000 cases of **meningitis** each year until the vaccine was available about two decades ago. It caused at least 500 deaths annually. Although *H flu* is just one cause of meningitis, until the vaccine was available, it was the most common cause of bacterial meningitis in infants and young children. *H flu* doesn't cause just meningitis. *Epiglottitis* is an infection at the entrance to the airway. When *H flu* causes epiglottitis, the area swells and air cannot get down to the lungs easily. *H flu* can also cause infections in joints (called *septic arthritis*), skin *(cellulitis)*, lungs *(pneumonia)*, bones *(osteomyelitis)*, and the bloodstream *(bacteremia)*.

The vaccine became available in 1985, and today *H flu* is responsible for only about 100 cases of meningitis each year. Every single case of *H flu* meningitis occurs in children who are not vaccinated with HiB or who have not yet completed the HiB vaccine series.

In 25 percent of children, the HiB vaccine can cause redness, soreness, and swelling at the site of injection. Many fewer children — about 5 percent — will have fever and irritability in the 24 hours after the vaccine was given. All of these symptoms resolve in one to three days.

HiB is available on its own or in combination with other vaccines. Comvax combines HiB and Hep B vaccine. TriHiBit combines HiB and DTaP.

◆   ◆   ◆

HEPATITIS A (HEP A)

The hepatitis A vaccine is not given until a child is at least two years old. It is administered in a series of two injections that are 6 to 12 months apart. It can be given anytime after a child's second birthday (through adolescence and adulthood).

Hepatitis is an inflammation of the liver, often caused by viral infection. The viruses have been named alphabetically — hepatitis A, B, C, and so on all the way up through G, and more will certainly be identified. Hepatitis B and C are the most well known, largely because they can cause long-term liver damage. Hepatitis A, on the other hand, is far more common, much easier to catch, and usually less serious.

Infection with hepatitis A causes vomiting and diarrhea for up to six months. Many children who get the illness have no symptoms at all. In fact, adults are more often severely affected by this virus. Although uncommon, liver failure can occur. Hepatitis A is shed in the stool and passed hand-to-mouth, allowing rapid spread especially among day-care workers, who change diapers often, and restaurant workers, who wipe their noses while preparing food. Hepatitis A can also be spread through water; shellfish are a known reservoir for this virus.

The vaccine is now recommended for all children in the United States, with an emphasis in certain geographic areas known to have greater disease prevalence (namely the southwestern states). Because this virus is found throughout the world, the vaccine is considered important for travelers.

The side effects of Hep A vaccine are common but mild. They include soreness at the site of injection (20 percent of children), headache (5 percent), and decreased appetite (8 percent). These all resolve shortly after the vaccine is given. Rare cases of allergic reactions to the vaccine have been reported.

◇   ◇   ◇

HEPATITIS B (HEP B)

Hepatitis B vaccine is given in a series of three injections. It is the only vaccine known to be effective when given immediately after birth. The recommended schedule for Hep B is birth, 1 month, and 6 months. However, if the mother is known to be hepatitis B negative (i.e., she does not have evidence of current or past hepatitis B infection), then this schedule is flexible. Therefore, some doctors elect to give Hep B on the same schedule as the other infant vaccines, with doses at 2 months, 4 months, and 12 to 18 months.

Hepatitis B infection can cause lifelong disease. *Hepatitis* means inflammation of the liver. It is usually caused by a virus, and because there are so many viruses that can cause it, different types have been named alphabetically — hepatitis A, B, C, and so on all the way up through G. More will certainly be identified. Hepatitis B is transmitted through sex, needle sharing, and blood transfusions. It can also be passed from a pregnant woman to her child during labor and delivery.

Chronic hepatitis B infection is a worldwide problem. It is estimated that between 200 to 300 million people have the disease, with the majority of those cases in Africa and Asia. About 95 percent of people infected with hepatitis B eventually recover, but the remaining group can go on to develop liver cancer or cirrhosis (liver failure). Even those who recover may continue to infect others, as they often still have the virus in their blood.

Hep B vaccine has a few mild side effects including soreness at the site of injection (9 percent of children), fever (1 to 7 percent — statistics vary), and allergic reaction to one of the components. There have been reports that Hep B vaccine is associated with rheumatoid arthritis, diabetes, and multiple sclerosis, but none of these reports have been verified with studies.

Some manufacturers of Hep B vaccine use mercury as a preservative, but there are also mercury-free forms available. Ask your pediatrician which form your child will receive. Hep B is available on its own or in combination with other vaccines. Comvax is Hep B plus HiB vaccine. Pediarix is Hep B, DTaP, and IPV.

◆   ◆   ◆

INFLUENZA (FLU SHOT)

Influenza vaccine is an optional vaccine offered each year at the beginning of the flu season (usually between October and December). It is not part of the routine childhood immunization schedule and is not required by schools for admission. The vaccine cannot be given before a child is six months old. Children under nine years who are getting the flu shot for the first time need two doses at least four weeks apart. When the shot is given in subsequent years (or for the first time in children ten and over and adults), only one dose is necessary.

Influenza is the virus that causes the flu. This virus changes slightly each year, so every winter different strains are spread throughout the world.

Flu is marked by high fevers, upper respiratory symptoms (such as cough and runny nose), and muscle aches that can be so profound it may be difficult to stand or walk. Flu occurs more in older children and adults than it does in infants, but it is far more dangerous for the very young and the very old. In infants, influenza is one of the most common causes (if not *the* most common cause in some winters) of respiratory distress and hospitalization. Historically, flu epidemics have killed millions of people.

Children who are at higher risk for respiratory failure, hospitalization, or even death from influenza include those children with a history of prematurity, asthma, cystic fibrosis, chronic pulmonary or cardiac diseases, sickle-cell anemia, chronic renal diseases, and diseases of the immune system such as HIV (the virus that causes AIDS). Mothers in their second and third trimester of pregnancy are often encouraged to get flu shots at the beginning of the flu season.

Each year, as the strains of influenza evolve, the shot changes. Therefore the vaccine is only useful for one year at a time. Because its effectiveness depends on how well the scientists who design the vaccine can predict the upcoming winter flu strains, the flu vaccine is better some years than others.

Influenza is available in two forms: as an inactivated (killed) vaccine given as a shot or as a live-attenuated vaccine given in a nasal spray. The nasal spray form is new and is not yet approved for children under 5 years. The side effects of flu shot are something like a mild case of the actual flu and appear within 12 hours of receiving the shot. Many recipients report fevers and muscle aches. Redness and swelling can occur at the site of the injection. Because flu vaccine is prepared in embryonated eggs, it should not be given to anyone with severe egg allergy. If it is, then serious allergic reactions, including ***anaphylaxis,*** can occur. Most children with mild or moderate egg hypersensitivity can be safely immunized with flu vaccine. Very rarely, flu vaccine can cause inflammation and temporary paralysis of the nerves called ***Guillain-Barré syndrome.***

Many formulations of the flu vaccine have mercury preservative, but there are mercury-free forms available. You should ask your doctor which form your child will receive.

◆ ◆ ◆

MEASLES, MUMPS, RUBELLA (MMR)

MMR vaccine is given in two doses, the first at 12 to 18 months and the second at 4 to 6 years. It protects against three diseases: measles, mumps, and rubella (German measles). Viruses cause all three of these diseases. Each was once a common childhood illness with periodic major outbreaks in the United States — tens of thousands (up to millions) were infected at the same time. Epidemics of these serious diseases have been eliminated since the vaccine has been widely used.

Measles causes a bright red, splotchy rash that starts at the hairline and moves down the face and body. Children with measles often have a cough, runny nose, sores in their mouth, and eye infection *(conjunctivitis)*. The accompanying fever can make them fussy and sleepy. Though most get through measles with few problems, 1 in 1,000 children who have measles are hospitalized with severe complications, the most dangerous of which is brain infection *(encephalitis)* that can be fatal.

Mumps causes inflammation and swelling of the internal organs. It is the swelling of the salivary glands that gives a child the signature jowly look. The pancreas and ovaries, and the area around the brain (meninges), are also subject to swelling, as are one or both testicles (called *orchitis*) in up to 25 percent of boys. Rarely, orchitis leads to sterility. As with measles, the high fever seen with mumps can make children irritable.

Rubella is a milder illness. Often there are no symptoms at all. Some children will have common-cold symptoms, accompanied by swollen glands and a rash. However, if a pregnant woman gets rubella infection and passes it to her fetus, then the fetus can suffer from *congenital rubella syndrome*. If carried to term, these babies may be born with mental retardation, deafness, and blindness. Many of these pregnancies, however, end in miscarriage.

The MMR vaccine was originally three separate vaccinations. In 1979 it was combined into one, though for many years the vaccines were also available individually. Due to nationwide vaccine shortages, the MMR is now available in the United States only as a combination vaccine.

MMR is one of the three live-attenuated vaccines still on the immunization schedule. The other live virus vaccines are varicella and influenza.

The most common side effects of MMR are mild: fever (17 percent of children), rash (5 percent), and swollen glands in the neck (rare). The vaccine is also associated with seizure (1 in 3,000) and temporary low platelet count causing bruising or bleeding (1 in 30,000). A small number of patients report allergic reactions to one of the components. Because MMR is prepared in the fluid of chick embryos, it should not be given to anyone with severe egg allergy. If it is, then serious allergic reactions, including *anaphylaxis*, can occur. Most children with mild or moderate egg hypersensitivity can be safely immunized with MMR.

There is a great deal of controversy over the question of a causal association between the MMR vaccine and the rising incidence of autism. Recently there have been numerous studies showing no correlation between the MMR and autism, but the debate remains highly contentious.

◆   ◆   ◆

PNEUMOCOCCAL CONJUGATE (PREVNAR)

Pneumococcal conjugate vaccine (also known by its trade name Prevnar) is given in four doses: at 2 months, 4 months, 6 months, and 12 to 18 months. For children who did not get the vaccine as infants, there is a catch-up schedule, with two doses if it is given after 12 months of age and one dose if it is given after 24 months of age.

Pneumococcal conjugate vaccine protects against the bacterial infection known as *Streptococcus pneumoniae* (or by its short name, *pneumococcus*). It is a member of the same streptococcus family that causes other infections, such as strep throat. Approved by the FDA in 2000, the vaccine is the most recent addition to the childhood immunization schedule.

Pneumococcus causes lung infection (pneumonia), blood infection (bacteremia), infection of the fluid around the brain (meningitis), and millions of cases of ear infection annually. There are many strains of pneumococcus, but a small number account for the majority of illnesses. Therefore the vaccine only protects against the seven most common strains.

While pneumococcus infects people of all ages, it is most dangerous for children who are 6 to 18 months old. It is the leading cause of bacteremia and ear infections in this age group, and it is a common cause of bacterial meningitis.

The short-term side effects of pneumococcal vaccine are well studied. These include tenderness, redness, or swelling at the injection site (12 to 20 percent of children) and fever (30 percent). Long-term side effects are less well established, given that the vaccine is so new.

Pneumococcal conjugate vaccine has no mercury preservative. However, the form of pneumococcal vaccine given to older children, Pnu-Imune 23, does contain thimerosal. Pnu-Imune 23 is indicated only for certain children over the age of two. Ask your doctor if your child will receive the vaccine.

◇   ◇   ◇

POLIO (IPV)

Until recently the polio vaccine came in two forms: a live-attenuated form (called OPV) that was given as a drink and a killed form (IPV), given as an injection. Since 2000 only the injectable form has been available in the United States. It is given in a four-dose series: at 2 months, 4 months, 12 to 18 months, and a booster dose at 4 to 6 years.

Polio is a virus that can destroy nerve cells in the spinal cord and brain. Before the vaccine was available in 1955, it caused thousands of cases of paralysis. In some instances, it paralyzed the breathing muscles and led to suffocation and death. The last case of natural (wild) polio in the United States was documented in 1979. Between 1980 and 1994, there were 125 reported cases of polio caused by the oral form of the vaccine. The majority of these cases were in adults whose immune systems were in some way compromised (i.e., patients receiving chemotherapy or people with HIV infection). A few cases were in children with undiagnosed immune deficiencies. Because the oral polio vaccine caused some cases of polio, it is no longer used.

Worldwide, wild-type polio is still a problem. It is primarily found in Southeast Asia, Africa, and the Mediterranean, though there have been outbreaks outside these regions as well. Due to the persistence of the virus in parts of the world, the vaccine is always recommended for travelers. The World Health Organization has a goal for worldwide eradication of the virus. In order to attain this, the vast majority of the world's population must be vaccinated.

IPV has very few side effects. The only reported reactions include redness or soreness at the injection site (15 percent of children) and fever (30 percent). There have been no severe reactions reported.

◆   ◆   ◆

VARICELLA (VARIVAX)

The varicella (chicken pox) vaccine is given in a single dose anytime after a child is a year old. However, if the vaccine is given after a child is 11 years old, then two doses are required.

Chicken pox is among the most common childhood illnesses. Most children who get chicken pox naturally (also known as the wild-type or varicella zoster virus) have fever and an itchy, blistery rash lasting several days. But it is estimated that 1 in 2,000 children will experience more serious complications. Vigorous scratching of the pox can cause the skin to break and may lead to skin infection and scarring. The most serious type of skin infection is caused by a type of *streptococcus* bacteria called **flesh-eating strep**. The varicella virus can also circulate through the bloodstream, spreading to the lungs (pneumonia), liver (hepatitis), and brain (meningitis or encephalitis). The risk of these serious complications increases with age. It is estimated that 20 percent of adults with wild-type chicken pox get pneumonia, and an adult is twenty-five times more likely than a child to die from the disease.

Varicella vaccine is one of the few live-attenuated vaccines on the childhood-immunization schedule (the other two are MMR and influenza). The side effects include tenderness or swelling at the injection site (20 percent of children), fever (10 percent), and rash (5 percent). The rash looks similar to actual chicken pox, with small red bumps turning to blisters and then scabbing over. Unlike wild-type chicken pox — in which several hundred pox can appear all over the skin as well as in the mouth, esophagus, and even in the vagina — the varicella vaccine only causes a handful of non-itching pox. The rash typically appears seven to ten days after the shot but has been reported up to one month later.

It is estimated that 1 in 10 children who have received the varicella vaccine will get chicken pox when they are exposed to it months or years later. However, like the vaccine rash itself, the chicken pox in vaccinated children is extremely mild. There are only a handful of pox, they do not itch, there is rarely accompanying fever, and the pox are usually completely gone within a couple of days. Unvaccinated children, by contrast, can have hundreds of itchy pox and high fevers lasting seven to ten days or longer.

If a child has not received the varicella vaccine and is exposed to another child with the disease, then the unvaccinated child can get the vaccine within 72 hours of exposure to minimize the extent of his illness. However, receiving the vaccine after exposure does not help to the same degree that receiving it weeks or months (or years) earlier does. In addition, it is relatively rare that a parent is notified of her child's exposure. More likely, a child will be exposed in a public place where parents do not know each other and cannot forewarn one another when one child develops the illness.

Children under a year of age cannot receive the vaccine because it is not proven effective in this age group. Therefore, if a child under a year gets the chicken pox, then there is not much a parent can do other than to give fever-reducing medicine as needed, oatmeal baths for comfort, and often an oral antihistamine to help with the itching. The baby's nails should be cut short to minimize skin breakage with scratching.

While it was FDA approved in the United States only recently — in 1995 — varicella vaccine has been widely used in Japan and Korea since the 1980s.

Additional Resources
http://www.cdc.gov/nip
http://www.immunofacts.com
http://www.who.int/vaccines
http://www.nlm.nih.gov/medlineplus/childhoodimmunization.html
http://www.vaccinealliance.com
http://www.vaccine.org
http://www.immunizationinfo.org
http://www.vaccine.chop.edu

Bibliography

BOOKS

American Academy of Pediatrics. *2000 Red Book: Report of the Committee of Infectious Diseases,* 25th ed. Elk Grove Village, IL: American Academy of Pediatrics, 2000.

Antoon, Alia Y., and Denise M. Tompkins. *The Quick Reference Guide to Your Child's Health.* Los Angeles: Lowell House, 2000.

Behrman, R. E., R. M. Kliegman, and H. B. Jenson, eds. *Nelson's Textbook of Pediatrics.* Philadelphia: W. B. Saunders Company, 2000.

Shelov, Steven P. *Your Baby's First Year.* New York: Bantam Books, 1998.

Spock, Benjamin, and Steven J. Parker. *Dr. Spock's Baby and Child Care.* New York: Pocket Books, 1998.

WEB SITES

http://www.aap.org
http://www.aboutnewbornscreening.com
http://www.acog.org
http://www.caps.ca
http://www.cdc.gov
http://www.choc.com
http://www.cincinnatichildrens.org

http://www.clevelandclinic.org
http://www.fda.gov
http://www.immunofacts.com
http://www.infanthearing.org
http://info.med.yale.edu
http://www.labtestsonline.org
http://www.mca.gov.uk
http://www.medem.com
http://www.nei.nih.gov
http://www.nelsonpediatrics.com
http://www.nlm.nih.gov/medlineplus/encyclopedia.html
http://www.orthoseek.com
http://www.packardchildrenshospital.org
http://www.pedisurg.com
http://www.racp.edu.au
http://www.ucsf.edu
http://www.umich.edu
http://www.uuhsc.utah.edu
http://web1.tch.harvard.edu
http://www.who.int

Index

About the Author

Cara Familian Natterson, M.D., graduated from Harvard College and the Johns Hopkins School of Medicine. She completed her pediatrics training at the University of California at San Francisco. She is currently in practice at Tenth Street Pediatrics in Santa Monica, California. During the writing of this book, Cara and her husband, Paul, had their own newborn, Talia.